GREAT MOMENTS IN
WISCONSIN
SPORTS

TODD MISHLER

Chris —
We have enjoyed having you on our staff and appreciate everything you have done for us. It is true, we don't really know how we will get along without you. Good Luck & Best Wishes for your future life away from "Green Lake". We'll miss you & hope you'll think of at least some of us fondly!

GLEA

TRAILS BOOKS
Black Earth, Wisconsin

Library of Congress Control Number: 2004104305
ISBN: 1-931599-45-9

Editor: Stan Stoga
Designer: Colin Harrington

Cover Images: Courtesy of Russ Lake, the Northern Indiana Historical Society,
the Milwaukee Brewers, the University of Wisconsin, the University of Wisconsin-Platteville,
Vernon Biever, Western Golfing Association, the American Birkebeiner, the Favor family, Marquette
University, Clinton High School, the Pieper family, the Weber family and the Janesville Gazette

Printed in the United States of America by Sheridan Books.

09 08 07 06 05 04   6 5 4 3 2 1

Trails Books, a division of Trails Media Group, Inc.
P.O. Box 317 • Black Earth, WI 53515
(800) 236-8088 • e-mail: books@wistrails.com
www.trailsbooks.com

To family and friends who continue to support one guy's dream.
—T.M.

TABLE OF CONTENTS

INTRODUCTION

I hadn't yet signed on the dotted line to write my second book for Trails Media Group when my publisher asked me if I knew of somebody who would be a good author for a book that captured some of the glorious and memorable moments in Wisconsin sports history.

Excitedly, and perhaps foolishly, I immediately volunteered myself for consideration. Before I knew it, I was the author, and the volume you hold in your hand right now is the result. Yet it certainly wasn't easy.

One of my first thoughts after taking on the project was, how do I begin to research more than one hundred years of athletic performances in Wisconsin, a state that has had more than its share of memorable sports moments? Even more difficult, how do I determine what to include and what not to include?

About 15 to 20 memorable events were obvious, such as the Green Bay Packers' Super Bowl victories, the Milwaukee Braves winning the 1957 World Series, Eric Heiden claiming five gold medals in the Olympics, and so on.

However, the task of reaching a goal of 40 to 50 major feature stories about teams and individuals worthy of such a classification became exceedingly difficult, especially because the idea was to highlight a wide variety of sports at all levels—high school, college, and professional. Adding to the challenge was the need to recognize the many accomplishments of the state's female athletes, even though they hadn't shared the same opportunities as their male counterparts until the last 30 years or so, and therefore weren't featured nearly as often by the media.

I also was asked to gather an unlimited number of shorter items about record holders and winning streaks, while another component would be a series of anecdotes about off-beat moments, trivia, factoids, and other light-hearted material that would be sprinkled throughout the book. And, of course, there needed to be photos.

Well, I've never been a good swimmer, but this endeavor was never going to come together unless I threw myself in head first. That led to hundreds of e-mails and phone calls, and dozens of trips to libraries and historical societies. I found many dead ends, but I also discovered many unexpected twists and turns along a nostalgic and seemingly endless journey through time.

Included are exclusive interviews with such well-known athletes as Suzy Favor Hamilton, Mark Johnson, Darrell Bevell, and Anthony Pieper, and those with people who haven't been in the sports spotlight for some time, such as 1963 Badger Rose Bowl quarterback Ron Vander Kelen, 1950s major league pitcher Billy Hoeft, 1969 boys state basketball hero Lamont Weaver, 1971 high jump world record-setter Pat Matzdorf, and Sophie Kurys, who led the 1946 championship team in the All-American Girls Professional Baseball League.

I soon realized that all the stories, facts, and accounts that I uncovered along the way couldn't possibly be squeezed into this book. For every fascinating name, fact, or figure unearthed, three or four more tantalizing and interesting possibilities and/or questions presented themselves.

With time and space at a premium, I had to make some decisions about what to include and what to exclude. Others may not agree with all of the choices, but I hope the accounts will help readers relive some of the state's past glories. Maybe the book will rekindle a few forgotten memories and help people recall other remarkable or unusual moments captured in memorabilia tucked away inside people's closets, attics, or memory banks waiting to be rediscovered. I also hope that the book introduces younger readers to what older generations have known for a long time—that Wisconsin abounds with great athletic performances and performers at all levels.

My biggest wish is that these wonderful stories create discussion and rekindle memories of not just victories, but of losses, and not just of friends, but of foes. ★

ACKNOWLEDGMENTS

To my editor, Stan Stoga, for giving me the opportunity to tackle this project and for his guidance along the way. To the staff at Trails Media, many of whom also contributed to my 2002 book, *Cold Wars: 40 Years of the Packer-Viking Rivalry*, for their time and efforts. To Justin Doherty and the sports information crew at the University of Wisconsin for access to files and photos, and Trish DeAmicis of the National W Club for help in locating many former Badger athletes. To John Farina and Matt Blessing and their staffs at Marquette University. To Paul Erickson at UW–Platteville. To Robbin Barnes and Jason Parry of the Milwaukee Brewers. To Janet in the American Birkebeiner office. To the Northern Indiana Center for History. To the Wisconsin State Historical Society, other city and county historical societies and the library staff members across the state who answered questions and/or supplied information for dozens of the stories included here. To the schools, the athletes, their families and friends, and to anybody who helped throughout the process, especially those who provided photos or agreed to be interviewed. ★

AUTO RACING

Alan Kulwicki Wins 1992 Winston Cup

Known for its fiery crashes and competitors, bumper-to-bumper finishes and fender-bending excitement, seldom has NASCAR's Winston Cup series featured as much drama as it did during the weekend of November 15, 1992. And rarely has so little been known about one of its title contenders, this one being a college-educated engineer from Greenfield, Wisconsin, by the name of Alan Kulwicki.

So when the circuit arrived in Hampton, Georgia, for the season's last of 30 races, most fans and experts probably were focused on the other two leading contenders for the championship, local favorite Bill Elliott and Alabama phenom Davey Allison.

Allison won the week before in Phoenix to pass Elliott for the first time since July. So when the green flag waved for the Hooters 500, Allison led Kulwicki by 30 points and Elliott by 40. However, the closest points battle in series history featured three more drivers within striking distance should the leaders falter: Harry Gant was 97 points back, Kyle Petty trailed by 98, and defending race winner Mark Martin was 113 behind before the 328-lap finale at Atlanta Motor Speedway.

Kulwicki, the Winston Cup Rookie of the Year in 1986 and the owner/driver of his small team, was fortunate to have climbed back into the hunt. He had wrecked two cars at Dover, Delaware, in September, and fell to fourth place, 278 points off the pace. But Elliott struggled during the next month, suffering two engine failures, and allowed his pursuers back into the picture.

The top three would have to fight their way to the front from back in the pack. Elliott, the 1988 series champion, started 11th, Kulwicki 14th, and Allison 17th on the 1.5-mile oval where Rick Mast had set a qualifying record to grab the pole position. If Allison captured fifth place or better, the trophy was his. So, all three wanted to lead laps and earn bonus points in hopes of securing the championship that Sunday.

DRAWING BIG-TIME DRIVERS

Some of the most famous names in the history of auto racing have won events at Milwaukee's State Fair Park track. The notables included A.J. Foyt, Parnelli Jones, Rodger Ward, Gordon Johncock, Lloyd Ruby, Al Unser, Jim Clark, and Mario Andretti.

Allison's car sustained minor damage only 40 seconds into the race when Mast and Brett Bodine spun. However, he used a two-tire change during the second pit stop to grab the lead and collect the five bonus points that his two nearest rivals already had gained. Kulwicki encountered problems and slowly lost ground after first gear exploded during his first pit stop, meaning his crew had to push him out every time.

The race for the crown became a two-car affair after lap 253, when Ernie Irvan's vehicle shot sideways because of a flat tire. Irvan ran into the nose of Allison's Ford, sending him to the garage for repairs. Allison came back to finish 27th and was left to wonder what might have been.

Meanwhile, Kulwicki was leading at the time of Allison's misfortune. If he could maintain that spot until lap 311 he would be out front for more laps than Elliott and get an additional five points for leading the most laps. That meant a 67-lap run between stops for gas and a quick splash-and-go to get to the finish, so fuel strategy proved to be a vital factor.

Elliott regained the lead, but Kulwicki and crew chief Paul Andrews's goal was to hang onto second, which they did. So even though he finished almost eight seconds behind Elliott, Kulwicki earned the championship by 10 points. If Elliott could have won the battle for bonus points, it would have resulted in a two-way tie and Elliott would have been declared the winner because he had the tiebreaker of more victories during the season.

Kulwicki, who earned a cool $1 million for the Winston Cup championship, celebrated by cruising his No. 7 Ford around the track for his customary "Polish victory lap," which he started after his first win in 1988. "I'm just a little guy who moved down here from the Midwest," said Kulwicki, whose race team had only six cars and 13 members. "I wasn't a good old boy. I wasn't a millionaire. A lot of people said, 'You're crazy. You're nuts.' I just said, 'We'll see.'"

Consistency was a secret to Kulwicki's success. He had earned six poles and two wins heading to Atlanta, but more importantly, Kulwicki had finished 26 of the 29 events. He had grabbed 16 top 10s and had finished out of the top 20 only four times. As for Elliott, he had equaled Allison's victory total of five, including four in a row, but he had finished out of the top 25 in four of the previous five outings heading to Georgia.

The audience of 165,000, the largest ever for a NASCAR gathering up to that point, had witnessed a special weekend. They had watched "The King,"

Richard Petty, compete in his final event on the circuit and saw another relative unknown, Jeff Gordon, race in his first.

His counterparts praised Kulwicki's performance and 1992 efforts.

"It's almost impossible to win," Richard Petty said of Kulwicki's status as owner/driver. "He overcame the odds with determination, skill, and luck."

WISCONSIN—THE BIRTHPLACE OF AUTO RACING?

Some people consider the Badger State to have been the scene of the first auto race on record. It happened on July 17, 1878, and involved two machines, the "Oshkosh" and the "Green Bay," that chugged along 200 miles of country roads from Green Bay to Madison. In true auto racing fashion, one of the vehicles, the "Green Bay," ran into mechanical trouble and dropped out. The "Oshkosh" crossed the finish line after more than 34 hours and claimed the $10,000 prize.

Elliott found solace in his second-place finish in the standings. "I felt like I did everything I could do," Elliott said. "We ran good all day. To win here, in front of a hometown crowd, means a lot. But it's kind of bittersweet."

That's because the Polish Catholic from the Milwaukee suburbs grabbed the spotlight. Kulwicki had left Wisconsin in 1986, heading to Charlotte, North Carolina, to further his racing career. His home turf was the nearby Milwaukee Mile track at State Fair Park. Kulwicki's first win was at Phoenix, and he claimed trophies at Bristol in 1991 and 1992.

Alan Kulwicki, who clinched the 1992 NASCAR points championship in the final race of the season, works on a car with his father, Jerry, in the early 1980s. (Russ Lake photo)

"By all rights I probably should have failed," Kulwicki said while trying to soak up every precious minute of his ultimate victory. "I was swimming for my life. I just wanted to be one of the drivers. But obstacles are the things you see when you take your eyes off the road. The great Vince Lombardi said that, I believe."

Kulwicki never took his eyes off the target, and that's why he became a NASCAR champion that day.

"This being the Hooters race [his major sponsor], Richard Petty's last race, and my first championship, it all adds up to a very memorable day in my life, one I'll never forget," Kulwicki said. "This is a dream come true."

It proved to be a fitting ending to a typically grueling day behind the wheel. "I told the crew before the race, 'Don't even tell me anything until the last 50 miles, and then just tell me who I have to beat.' I could really go for a back rub and a bratwurst right now."

Tragically, Kulwicki didn't get to enjoy his Winston Cup title. On April 1, 1993, the 38-year-old Kulwicki and three other men died in a plane crash during approach to Tri-Cities Airport near Blountville, Tennessee. The private aircraft, traveling behind one carrying the late Dale Earnhardt Sr., was en route to that weekend's Food City 500 at Bristol, Kulwicki's favorite track.

Mark Martin, who had lived in Franklin, Wisconsin, and competed with Kulwicki in the American Speed Association series, said what everybody in NASCAR felt in their hearts after hearing the news. "I'm really sick because Alan didn't get a chance to enjoy the things he'd built, spent his whole life with a total focus to get to. And that's sad."

Ironically, Allison, whose younger brother Clifford had died in a crash August 13, 1992, in Michigan, also lost his life in 1993. In August, the helicopter he owned and was piloting lost control and crashed in the Talladega Superspeedway infield, and he died from head injuries.

Peter Jellen was Kulwicki's gasman and drove the team's transporter. He is with the Joe Gibbs Racing team and works with driver Bobby Labonte. Jellen recalled the emotions surrounding Kulwicki's death in an interview with the *Saint Louis Post-Dispatch* after he won the 2000 Winston Cup championship with Labonte.

"We never really got to enjoy that title," he said of Kulwicki's 1992 accomplishment. "That team was just clawing to survive every week, and when we lost Alan, we lost our friend, our driver and a lot of other things. It really felt like we got cheated, like we never got to defend what Alan and the rest of us had built."

Kulwicki competed in 207 races, winning five times and finishing in the top 10 on 75 occasions. ★

Matt Kenseth Claims Another Cup for Wisconsin

Matt Kenseth and his fans are glad that he doesn't finish the way he starts. The Cambridge, Wisconsin, native typically qualifies in the bottom half of the 43-car starting grid. However, the 32-year-old has mastered the uncanny ability of working his way toward the front.

Kenseth's strong showings have proved how much talent he has and enabled him to claim the NASCAR Winston Cup (now called the Nextel Cup) points championship in 2003, only his fourth year in stock car racing's best and most prestigious circuit. His fourth-place finish in the Pop Secret 400 at North Carolina Speedway in Rockingham on Sunday, November 9, gave him a 226-point cushion and clinched the coveted top spot in the season's second-to-last event. Kenseth led for a record 33 weeks and became only the second Wisconsin driver to accomplish the feat, adding to the late Alan Kulwicki's 1992 trophy and legacy.

The soft-spoken but tough-as-nails competitor had taken the points lead and held it since the fourth race of the year, eliminating much of the drama from a title chase that eventually caused the powers-that-be to change the points system for the 2004 campaign.

However, sitting on top and being the target week in and week out placed an unbelievable amount of pressure on Kenseth, as he noted after earning the crown—and the $5 million-plus prize that went with the distinction. "I feel like the world has been lifted off my shoulders today," he told an Associated Press reporter. "There's a feeling you get in your stomach when you're leading the race and you see somebody coming up behind you. . . . Like I've been leading a race for the last three months. I got all this stuff bottled up inside because I didn't want to get too excited the last few months. I don't know what I'm going to do now. It's an awesome feeling."

Kenseth drove his No. 17 Ford to first place just once, a triumph at Las Vegas in March that made him the first driver since Benny Parsons in 1973 to grab the title with only one visit to Victory Lane.

But Kenseth, like Kulwicki, was a model of consistency. He captured 11 top five efforts and 26 top 10s while settling for only three finishes of 30th or lower, including the season-ending, last-place outing at Homestead, Florida, when he blew an engine after 28 laps and took the rest of the day off. He still managed a final 90-point margin over Jimmie Johnson. That performance gave Jack Roush's team its first champion after Kenseth's protégé, Mark Martin, had finished second on four occasions.

Kenseth told the *Wisconsin State Journal* on the eve of the 2004 season-opening Daytona 500 that he expected nothing less from himself and his Robby Reiser-led team while defending his status.

"I don't think I have any more pressure on myself, but I don't know if there's any less pressure," Kenseth said. "You always want to do more; you always want to win again. You're never satisfied with what you have. If you're satisfied with what you did and what you've got, you might as well hang it up."

He sure didn't stand on his laurels, posting back-to-back victories at Rockingham and Vegas after a ninth-place showing at Daytona, and starting 2004 with nine Cup triumphs.

The Cambridge native earned rookie of the year honors, won his first event during 2000, and finished 14th in points. He also won a series-best five times while grabbing eighth place in the standings in 2002.

His quick rise to the top earned him more than $9 million in 2003 and pushed his career total to over $19 million, quite a run for somebody who became the youngest winner in ARTGO Challenge Series history with a triumph in La Crosse at age 18.

All of that short-track experience and success led him to the ultimate in '03 and his title-clinching performance, a race that he began in the 23rd spot. Kenseth needed to come in seventh or better at the site of his first Cup win to end the suspense that many of his fellow drivers knew in their hearts had probably been over for some time.

Most of his family—his father, Roy, was at the track with Matt—and friends watched the event at The Sports Page Bar and Grill in his hometown, a gathering that gained national television exposure on TNT's broadcast. And Kenseth left no doubt as he methodically moved his way through the field.

DEMON ON THE SHORT TRACKS

Dick Trickle was arguably the most successful short-track racer in America. The Rudolph native honed his skills in Wisconsin and around the Midwest, winning 41 races in 1971, a record 67 events in 1972, and 57 more first-place finishes in 1973.

Kenseth stayed out of harm's way during an afternoon that featured 10 cautions and the expected banging and bumping in traffic. "It felt like I was stepping through a minefield," Kenseth said. "We got run into one time, and there was just a lot of stuff going on and a lot of close calls."

Martin cut his teeth on many of the same Wisconsin ovals as Kulwicki did and said he knew that Kenseth had the talent to succeed in Winston Cup competition. "I've been wrong about a lot of things in my life, but I was right about Matt Kenseth," Martin said. "I'm real proud of that. I liked his style. I knew that he knew a lot about race cars because I knew where he came from and that he was winning races where he came from. I knew it was him and not his cars. I wanted Roush Racing to have him."

So, when the checkered flag waved that memorable November day, all of the Kenseth faithful at the Cambridge hangout erupted in celebration. The low-key driver also breathed a sigh of relief and finally started to enjoy his long, tough season.

"This is beyond my wildest dreams," Kenseth said. "I never thought I'd have the opportunity to sit in one of these cars, much less be the champion. I'm just thankful to be in good equipment with good people working on it." ★

MORE RECORDS, STREAKS, AND AMAZING MOMENTS

Winning in the Rain

Tim Flock won on the four-mile road course at Elkhart Lake's Road America to claim his fourth victory of the 1956 NASCAR season. The August 12 competition was the only Winston Cup race held on Wisconsin soil and proved to be the only series event in history ever contested during a rainstorm. Flock, the '55 series champ, competed on the circuit from 1949 to 1956.

The first auto race at Elkhart Lake was held in 1951. It took place over a 5.3-mile layout that wound through downtown streets and roads that surrounded the lake. Road America, site of the current track, didn't open until 1955. ★

Indy's Wisconsin Drivers

Milwaukee native William Jones became the initial Wisconsin driver to compete in the illustrious Indianapolis 500. He was 21 years old when he drove in the first Indy on May 30, 1911. Jones captured 28th place in the event, which also proved to be his final Indy.

On May 31, 1915, Whitewater native Eddie O'Donnell finished fifth in the competition. O'Donnell fractured his skull in a November 26, 1920, crash during a 250-mile race at Los Angeles Motor Speedway and died the next day. Gaston Chevrolet, who won the Indy 500 earlier that year, was the other driver in the wreck and died the day of the crash.

Paul Russo of Kenosha suited up for 13 of the 20 races from 1940 to 1959, finishing in the top 10 on six occasions. Russo's best effort was a fourth-place showing in 1957. Another Whitewater driver, Tom Bigelow, also made his mark at Indianapolis, taking sixth place in 1977 and eighth three years later, making nine trips from 1974 to 1982.

Janesville's Stan Fox carried on the tradition in 1987–95, grabbing seventh place in his first attempt and eighth in 1991. However, his last race there involved a horrendous, career-ending crash. ★

BASEBALL AND SOFTBALL

Sophie Kurys: In a League of Her Own

It was never a matter of if, but rather how soon, Sophie Kurys would come through for her teammates. Anytime she reached first base, her Racine Belles teammates, their opponent, and everybody in the stands knew that "The Flint Flash" wouldn't stay there for long.

Just because it was Game Six of the 1946 league play-off series made little difference. Kurys was an equal-opportunity thief; her next target waited 72 feet away. So when the five-foot-five-inch Kurys singled to lead off the bottom of the 14th inning in a scoreless duel, more than 6,500 people at Horlick Field in Racine stirred in anticipation.

She didn't disappoint them. Kurys stole second base, her fifth of the day. She barely took time to brush off before hightailing it toward third. And when Betty Trezza slapped that pitch into short right field for a single, there was only one more stop for the crafty and swift Kurys. She narrowly beat the throw to the plate, but it was enough to assure her place in history.

One of the four original members of the All-American Girls Professional Baseball League (along with the Rockford Peaches, Kenosha Comets, and South Bend Blue Sox), Racine had defeated defending champion Rockford four games to two to claim its second title in the league's first four years. They had won the inaugural crown in 1943.

For Kurys, the memory is as vivid as if it had happened yesterday. "Thoughts of that game are embedded in my mind," Kurys said in a phone interview from her home in Scottsdale, Arizona. "It was the best game we ever played. They hit the cover off the ball several times, but three or four of them were right at our pitcher [Joanne Winter] and we made some great plays behind her. I particularly remember the play Edie Perlick made in left field. She took off at the crack of the bat and made a leaping catch, the best I've ever seen.

"Rockford's pitcher, Carolyn Morris, had a no-hitter through nine innings," Kurys added. "It was a fantastic game. Max Carey, who was with the Pittsburgh Pirates and is in the Major League Hall of Fame, was in the stands. He said it was the best game he'd ever seen played."

Racine's manager Leo Murphy was wise in allowing Kurys to do her own thing on the base paths. Both of them were glad she packed so much talent and speed into her small frame when it came to the deciding final play.

Kurys said she knew it was going to be a close call, but she was positive she was safe. "I knew Rose Gachek was playing a shallow right field because Betty was a singles hitter," said Kurys, who is of Polish-Russian descent and was nicknamed "The Flint Flash" after her running prowess and hometown of Flint, Michigan. "It was a very close play at home, and I probably wouldn't have made it if I hadn't taken off to steal third and got those extra couple of steps. It was my best hook slide at the left corner of the plate. I got in by a toe."

It was the culmination of a magical season for Kurys and the Belles, who had finished 74–38 (.661) to outdistance Grand Rapids by three games and South Bend by four in a three-team chase for the regular-season crown. Kurys played in 113 games, had 112 hits, a league record 93 walks, and was hit by 10 pitches, which meant she reached base 215 times.

She attempted 203 steals and was successful a remarkable 201 times. She scored a league-best 117 runs and was second in batting (.286) to Dottie Kamenshek's .316. Kurys also established a league best .973 fielding percentage for second basemen. Needless to say, Kurys was named the league's Player of the Year, a season that she capped with one of the most exciting plays and endings in the league's 11-year existence.

Horlick Field "didn't have any fences in the outfield, but people had pulled their cars back there, like at a drive-in. They were standing on the roofs to get a better view," Kurys said in Lois Browne's 1992 book *Girls of Summer: In Their Own League*, which was the basis for the Hollywood movie *A League of Their Own*.

Racine had advanced to the championship round after beating South Bend, 3–1, including the series opener 3–2 in 17 innings behind the pitching of Anna May Hutchison. The Belles controlled games three (7–1) and four (10–2) to advance for a showdown with the Peaches. Rockford, which had finished fourth during the regular season, knocked off the second-seeded Grand Rapids Chicks, 3–2, in a rugged five-game series. The Peaches won 4–3 and 2–0 before falling 3–0 and 2–1. They advanced to the play-off series with a 2–0 victory in the finale.

Racine won the first two games of the championship series at home and grabbed one of three contests at Rockford for a 3–2 series lead. Rockford's Millie Deegan had gotten the better of a 1–0 contest versus Hutchison as the Peaches staved off elimination and headed back to Racine.

Sophie Kurys practices sliding into third base, where Racine Belles teammate Betty Trezza puts on the tag. (Photo courtesy of the Northern Indiana Historical Society)

Game Six became a pitching duel, at least on the scoreboard, between Rockford's Morris and Racine's Winter. The latter had fashioned a 33–10 mark highlighted by 63 consecutive scoreless innings at one stretch. Winter persevered in this contest to get her fourth win of the postseason and third in the championship series.

Although the underdog Peaches ripped Winter for 13 hits, they stranded 19 runners in the scoreless battle. Meanwhile, despite Morris's mastery through nine innings, Racine broke up the no-hitter in the 10th and Rockford brought in Deegan in the 12th.

That set the stage for the aggressive and memorable heroics of Kurys, who played all eight seasons of the Belles's existence, 1943–50, a stretch in which she stole a league record 1,114 bases.

Joyce Westerman of Kenosha played for four teams during her eight-year AAGPBL career, including two seasons with the Belles. However, as a catcher Westerman knew she'd be in for a long day behind the plate with Kurys aboard. "I was always like, 'Oh, oh, here's Sophie,'" Westerman said of her usually fruitless attempts to prevent Kurys from stealing. "Sophie was incredibly fast and always got such great leads on the pitchers, and she really knew how to slide. She was exciting to watch, but I hated to play against her."

Kurys notched 166 steals in 1944, including seven in one game, and 115 despite injuries in 1945. She briefly started in the outfield but moved to second base after the starter was injured, and Kurys remained a fixture at the position the rest of her career.

After the Racine franchise folded, she played professional softball for three years in Chicago and one in Arizona, retiring from the diamond at age 33. And through all of the plays and games, none stands out more than that Monday in 1946 at Horlick Field. "I'll never forget it," Kurys said. "The fans went crazy and lifted me up and carried me off the field. It was a wonderful feeling." ★

Billy Hoeft Pitches a Gem

Huge sheets of ice still piled up along the shores of Lake Winnebago like they often did in springtime. But that was nothing compared to how frigid Billy Hoeft made opposing batters feel on April 29, 1950. The lanky Oshkosh High School left-hander mowed down Hartford as the Indians earned a 4–0 nonconference victory at Menominee Park on the city's east side. However, a shutout wasn't good enough for the 17-year-old, who fashioned a no-hitter to boot.

And if that wasn't enough, it doesn't even begin to tell the story. Hoeft not only didn't allow a base hit, but he barely let his foes hit the ball: Hartford managed an estimated nine foul balls, and many of those occurred during the later innings while the visitors were trying to bunt their way aboard.

Hoeft struck out all 27 batters he faced in completing the unheard-of nine-inning gem, with catcher Don Biebel registering the first 26 putouts and firing a throw to first baseman Jack Retzloff for the final out after dropping Hoeft's 81st strike of the miraculous 108-pitch outing.

What made the six-foot-three-inch ace's performance even more astounding was that he had set down all 18 Menasha foes without a hit during his six-inning stint to open the season a week earlier.

Hartford coach Hal Beattie, whose squads had won five consecutive Little Ten league championships and weren't slouches in the batter's box, said his team was no match against the fireballing Hoeft. "We were in there cutting, all right," Beattie said in newspaper accounts. "Hoeft's control was so perfect my batters had nothing to be afraid of. He had three balls on only one batter and ran the count to two on five others. We tried to bunt on him the last three innings, but eight or nine fouls was the best we could do.

"We haven't a kick in the world about the umpiring or anything else," Beattie continued. "It was a cold day and our batters didn't have much to do in the field. . . . Perhaps if they had had a better chance to warm up they could have gripped their bats better and got around quicker on Hoeft's fastball. But as it was, we couldn't get a loud foul off him. On that one day, at least, he was just that good."

Hoeft's coach, E. J. "Snitz" Schneider, said his prize pupil knew early in the contest that something special was brewing. "After the first inning he came to the bench and said, 'Coach, I can put my fastball within an inch of where I want it today.' He could, too—and did."

The Indians, who collected only four hits of their own, gave Hoeft all of the support he needed in the second inning, scoring twice on successive singles from Clint Peters, Ralph Pausig, and Reigh Webster. Oshkosh added two insurance runs in the seventh. Webster tripled to lead off and scored on a passed ball, and Hoeft's battery mate, Biebel, walked, stole second, reached third on a wild pitch, and then stole home for the final tally.

Hoeft, who in June of that year signed a major league contract with Detroit, said family and friends periodically remind him of his sterling accomplishments on the mound, which included 16–7 and 20–14 records with the Tigers during a 15-year career.

However, nothing surpasses his effort of that cool spring day near his home on Otter Street, where he learned many of the tricks of the pitching trade from his late older brother Burt, who was a catcher on the American Legion team when Hoeft started out. "Some days you just can't do anything wrong, and that was one of them," a retired Hoeft said via phone from his home in Canadian Lakes, Michigan. "As I recall, they didn't hit a good foul ball off me that day, so I don't blame them [for trying to bunt]. It all boiled down to having good control. That's what 'Snitz' taught me the most. He said if you can't get the ball over the plate, you're no damn good. You have to let the seven guys behind you do the work."

They didn't have anything to do but try to stay warm like everybody else while Hoeft painted one of his masterpieces. Clarence Tesch learned first-hand, playing second base that day. "We just stood out there and watched him," the Oshkosh resident said via phone, adding a hearty chuckle. "Bill had a good fastball, good curve, and good drop ball. It was a phenomenal accomplishment, something that's never been done before or since."

Biebel, reached at his Sacramento, California-area home, got a bird's-eye view of his friend's almost pinpoint accuracy. "The greatest thing about Billy was his control, so he very seldom got behind the hitters," said Biebel, who played in Janesville in the Wisconsin State League after high school before embarking on a coaching and scouting career with the Chicago Cubs, for whom he also served as traveling secretary from 1959 to 1965. "We worked in the gym all winter long on that. He also had a curveball that would drop off the table, so I had to get way down to block those."

Biebel forgot about his offensive exploits that helped Oshkosh win that game, but he laughs to this day about what happened just before he threw the final runner out at first base to complete Hoeft's 27th strikeout. "To be honest, I don't recall what Billy threw on that last pitch," Biebel said, "but he had gotten two strikes on the batter and Bud Lowell, who was umpiring behind the plate, tapped me on the shoulder and said, 'Whatever you do, don't call for that damn curveball.' I don't think he wanted us to ruin Billy's chances at getting that last strikeout."

Hoeft said eliminating distractions is vital for any pitcher to be successful, especially while trying to handle a potentially pressure-filled situation like he found himself in that day. "You don't really think about what's happening around you," Hoeft said of inching toward a no-hitter as the innings wound down. "I don't recall ever thinking that it was the seventh or eighth or ninth inning and I better try harder, because that's when you usually screw things up. I just went out and did my job, tried to protect our lead, and let the chips fall. Winning was the number-one goal. Although, I guess, like any game of that nature, nobody on the bench said anything to me. They just got the hell outta the way because they didn't want to jeopardize things."

Hoeft's left arm did the talking anyway, as it did throughout his sparkling high school and American Legion careers. He combined for 49 victories, including four no-hitters, five one-hitters, six two-hitters and seven three-hitters, topped by 17 shutouts. His statistics show that in 461 innings, he struck out 819, walked only 70 and gave up 85 runs (1.66 ERA) and 188 hits.

He culminated his prep career with a 6–0 victory against Manitowoc, striking out 17 of the 29 Shipbuilders he faced, losing the no-hitter in the ninth inning on a bloop single to right field in front of a half-dozen big league scouts. "I didn't really start throwing the curveball until my first couple years of professional ball," Hoeft said. "I had a good fastball, but I've always said that pitching is all about getting it over the plate. When you do that, you can do a lot of things. I had a four-seamer that would rise and a two-seamer that would sink or I'd work a change off of that. But good control allows you to move it up and down and side to side."

As for the brightest of his many shining moments, Hoeft said it was definitely something he can be proud of. "Some people couldn't believe it," the southpaw said of his most perfect of perfect games. "They thought it was against the Sisters of St. Mary's or something like that, but Hartford was a pretty damn good team."

On that day, Billy Hoeft was much better. ★

"Bushville Wins": The 1957 Braves

Fred L. Tonne's photo in the *Milwaukee Journal* showed and said it all, at least when it came to everything that's right about America's pastime. Amid a citywide celebration, a gentleman's homemade sign read, "Bushville Wins."

Milwaukee may have deserved that label in the past, but not this time. In October 1957, the Braves were the feel-good story in baseball after knocking off the defending champion New York Yankees to win the franchise's first World Series championship since 1914.

It was the city's first and only Major League crown, and the euphoria was best described in the *Journal*'s story the day after the Braves had claimed a victory in Game Seven in the Big Apple: "A human sea flowed on Wisconsin Avenue. From the lakefront to the public museum, people were packed elbow to elbow. They shoved, drank, sang, kissed strangers and jitterbugged. They did things that they never normally would think of doing." An estimated 225,000 fans celebrated in the streets that night. But that's how this group of players had captured the imagination of their fans, the city, and the country.

Right-handed pitcher Lew Burdette was the biggest reason why such jubilation was possible. He notched his third victory and second consecutive shutout as Milwaukee popped the champagne after a 5–0 triumph at Yankee Stadium. The victory gave Burdette 24 consecutive scoreless innings, three short of Christy Mathewson's single-series mark and five from Babe Ruth's all-time fall classic standard.

Burdette became the 10th three-game Series winner—three of them did it during an eight-game series—and first since Harry Brecheen in 1946. He became the first hurler to throw three complete-game victories since Stan Coveleski of Cleveland in 1920. Burdette allowed 21 hits in his 27 innings, striking out 13 and walking four in posting a 0.67 ERA. "Let's face it," Burdette said, "I was trying my darnedest to beat 'em and I know they were trying like mad to get me out of there," he said afterward. "They kept yelling at me from the dugout all game. I couldn't hear what they were yelling about."

Yankees' catcher Yogi Berra didn't mince words when describing Burdette's unexpected and masterful performances. "We never figured on that man," Berra said. "The man we were worried about was [Warren] Spahn."

Spahn was 1–1 in the series but illness (influenza) meant Burdette got the call in Game Seven after only two days of rest.

Milwaukee catcher Del Crandall marveled at his battery mate's dominance over the powerful Yankees. "I don't think he was as fast as he was in the first two games he won," Crandall said after Game Seven. "But he never had better control. He was keeping that ball low all afternoon. Everything he threw—sliders, screwballs, sinkers—he had them all in there where he wanted them and where the batters didn't want them."

AN EARLY BREWER CHAMPIONSHIP

The Milwaukee Brewers clinched their first American Association pennant by beating Louisville, 3–1, in the first game of a doubleheader September 28, 1913. Cyril Slapnicka was the winning pitcher, while Milwaukee scored twice in the bottom of the ninth inning against the Colonels. An estimated 35,000 fans welcomed the Brewers at Milwaukee's Union Station after they returned home two days later.

Burdette didn't need much, but the Braves gave him the support anyway. Milwaukee native Tony Kubek's error opened the door for the Braves' four-run third inning. Third baseman Eddie Mathews doubled into the right-field corner to score Bob Hazle and Johnny Logan for the first runs against 1956 Series Most Valuable Player Don Larsen. Hank Aaron then greeted reliever Bobby Shantz with an RBI single for a 3-0 margin. Crandall belted a solo homer in the eighth to complete the scoring.

The Braves' defense also sparkled throughout the seven games, turning 10 double plays to five for New York, and the outfielders made several excellent catches. A prime example was in the ninth inning of Game Seven. The Yankees loaded the bases on three singles. Mathews gloved a smash down the left-field line off the bat of Bill Skowron and stepped on third base as the Braves started the victory celebration in the House that Ruth Built.

"I wasn't as sharp as in Milwaukee," Burdette said. "I couldn't reach back and get something extra in a pinch. But I did have good control and could get the ball where I wanted."

Burdette, whose hometown was Nitro, West Virginia, manager Fred Haney, and Aaron were interviewed the next morning on "The Today Show" with Dave Garroway. Back home, ardent supporters decorated Mathews's house and yard in Brookfield.

No one was happier than Braves owner Lou Perini, who had brought the team west from Boston after the 1952 season. "This is the biggest moment of my life," Perini said. "Anything that has happened to me in my business has been routine compared to this."

Milwaukee was the toast of the league, as National League president Warren Giles said, "This is the most popular victory in the history of baseball. Fans everywhere wanted Milwaukee to win."

New York skipper Casey Stengel gave credit where credit was due after his club fell to 6–2 in the World Series under his guidance. "You ran your team good all the way," he told Haney. "If we couldn't win it, there's no one I'd rather see do it than Milwaukee. That town deserves it."

"That's the kind of ball club we've been all year," shortstop Logan said. "We win the big ones."

And there was no bigger hitting star for Milwaukee in an otherwise pitching-dominated series than Aaron. He batted .393 (11-for-28) with three homers and seven RBIs as the Braves only hit .209 overall. But eight of the team's 47 hits left the ballpark. The Yankees batted .248 with seven long balls and outscored the Braves 25–23.

But that's how the seesaw series went as both teams grabbed one-game advantages. In Game One, ace Whitey Ford surrendered only five hits as the Yanks earned a 3–1 win over Spahn, who left in the sixth inning in front of 69,476. The Braves coaxed back-to-back walks to lead off the sixth, but Ford registered two strikeouts to squelch the threat. Braves' outfielder Wes Covington was a bright spot, going 3-for-4.

Game Two saw Burdette toss a seven-hitter and allow the only two earned runs in his three outings as Milwaukee evened things with a 4–2 triumph. Logan smacked a homer in the third after Covington's running catch on a drive by Shantz in the second prevented damage. Covington and Joe Adcock each had two hits. Milwaukee scored twice in the fourth to break a 2-all tie.

Kubek led the Yankees' barrage in Game Three with two homers and four RBIs during a 12–3 trouncing to put the Yankees up 2–1 in this postseason opener at County Stadium, a showdown that drew 45,804.

Kubek had three hits and scored three times as New York roughed up Milwaukee starter Bob Buhl and several relievers. Kubek hit a one-out homer to ignite a three-run first and capped a five-run seventh with his second round-tripper.

In Game Four, Mathews, who didn't have any base hits in the first three games, bounced back as his two-run homer on a 2–2 pitch lifted the Braves to a 7–5 victory in 10 innings after the hosts blew a 4–1 cushion in the ninth. New York scored three times to tie it and went ahead 5–4 in the 10th, but Logan tied it again with an RBI double to set the stage for Mathews. Aaron had crunched a three-run blast in the Braves' four-run fourth.

Adcock's single brought in Mathews in the sixth as Burdette was masterful again in Game Five, scattering seven singles, no more than one in any inning, as Milwaukee grabbed a 3–2 series lead with a 1–0 gem before the series shifted back to New York. Covington turned in another spectacular catch in the fourth against the left-field wall.

In Game Six, the Yankees knotted the series for a third time with a 3–2 victory. All of the runs were scored on homers, two by each team. The difference was Berra's two-run shot in the third off Buhl.

Milwaukee's thrilling championship run came after Aaron's late-September heroics. He lifted a 400-foot home run to center field to give the Braves their first National League pennant. ★

Warren Spahn Hurls 300th Victory

His slender six-foot, 175-pound build didn't tell the story when it came to Warren Spahn. He was an all-around athlete who just happened to be one of the best pitchers of all time, posting the most victories (363) of any left-hander in Major League baseball history.

His repertoire included a fastball, curve, and changeup, but in later years, as he lost some zip on the ball, he befuddled hitters with a screwball and slider. Spahn finished with a 363–245 record, including two no-hitters, in 21 big-league seasons. He reached the 20-victory plateau 13 times and led his league eight of those seasons and in complete games on nine occasions. He also won four World Series games.

So, what was his most memorable accomplishment among so many? At the time, the Buffalo, New York, native said it probably was the night of Friday, August 11, 1961. Milwaukee's ace became the 12th pitcher to win 300 games as the Braves beat the Chicago Cubs, 2–1, before a season-best crowd of 40,775, the largest attendance at County Stadium since a season-opening setback to the Saint Louis Cardinals.

The day before his big game, Spahn predicted it would be his biggest thrill in baseball as the Braves prepared to kick off an 11-game home stand. "A lot of wonderful things have happened to me in baseball, like pitching two no-hitters and being on a World Series winner, but this is the biggest," Spahn said. "I don't think I'm edgy, but, of course, I'm anxious to get it."

However, Spahn had to face a Cubs' squad that, although entrenched in seventh place, had produced a 2–1 mark against Spahn up to that point, and his lone win had come in a relief outing. Spahn had recorded 3–2 and 2–1 triumphs in his last two starts to improve to only 11–12, while the Cubs had lost seven of their last eight contests, including two against Milwaukee in Chicago.

FIRST TIME FOR EVERYTHING

The Milwaukee Brewers clinched their first postseason berth October 3, 1981, claiming a 2–1 victory over Detroit and winning the second-half title in the American League East to cap off the strike-marred campaign.

Milwaukee scored both runs in the eighth inning at County Stadium. Gorman Thomas's sacrifice fly with the bases loaded brought Robin Yount home with the deciding score. Rollie Fingers got the victory with one and a third shutout innings to give the Brewers a spot in the five-game playoffs against the New York Yankees, who went on to win the series 3–2.

But with the spotlight on him, Spahn responded in a fashion befitting his Hall of Fame career, outdueling a rookie junk-ball pitcher named Jack Curtis who had mastered the Braves to the tune of a 2–0 record so far. He gave up five unearned runs in his previous trip to the mound against Milwaukee, a game that was called after 11 innings due to darkness. Curtis, who was nine years old when Spahn won his first game, entered the battle with a 7–6 record after starting the campaign 6–2.

Both hurlers allowed six hits. Curtis, also a southpaw, struck out six and walked two, while Spahn's totals were five Ks and one base on balls. Spahn broke a scoreless tie with a sacrifice fly in the fifth inning. The visitors knotted things up again in the sixth when former Brave Andre Rodgers knocked in Ron Santo with a sacrifice fly. Don Zimmer contributed two of Chicago's hits against Spahn, who stranded eight runners.

Then Braves' center fielder Gino Cimoli broke the deadlock with an eighth-inning homer. It was Cimoli's third round-tripper of the season and 30th in six years in the majors, one more than Spahn's then NL record for pitchers. Cimoli also made a spectacular shoestring catch in the ninth inning after making only one start in the past five weeks.

"This was the toughest, most exciting game I ever pitched," said the 40-year-old Spahn, who had notched win number 299 by an identical score against San Francisco a week earlier. "The game was built up to a great degree. I couldn't help but feel it."

Spahn became the first 300-game winner since Lefty Grove registered his last big-league victory with the Boston Red Sox in 1941. Spahn joined Grove and Eddie Plank as the only lefties to reach the coveted plateau up to that point. Spahn, who owned a ranch in Oklahoma, received a telegram from his mother among the many accolades afterward.

Henry Aaron caught the last out in right field, and Spahn, the sixth pitcher in the modern era to reach the milestone, raced out to get the ball for his trophy case. The ball that started the game was given to the Hall of Fame in Cooperstown, New York.

In the tension-filled final inning, Spahn retired Rodgers looking at a third strike, and then Cimoli snared Jerry Kindall's line drive while sliding on his knees, for the second out. Pinch hitter Ernie Banks, who had been out of the Cubs' lineup with eye trouble, grounded one toward Milwaukee third baseman Eddie Mathews, whose throw sailed over first baseman Joe Adcock and bounced off the front of the box seats. Then pinch hitter Jim McAnany batted for Curtis and hit a 2–0 offering to Aaron to end the game.

George Altman's two-out single in the fourth broke up any possibility of Spahn tossing his third no-hitter, and the Cubs had runners on base in every inning after the second but couldn't take advantage against the crafty Spahn.

The Braves' fifth inning started when Cubs rookie Billy Williams committed a two-base error. Roy McMillan singled and Spahn's fly ball brought in the game's first run.

"I would have taken this any way I could get it, but I really wanted to win in a way so I could feel like I deserved it," Spahn said. "I threw a lot of fastballs. My control was spotty. I made some good pitches, but I was getting behind the hitters that inning they scored their run.

"The guys were breaking their neck for me out there," Spahn added. "Those plays at shortstop and center field really helped. [Catcher] Joe Torre was sweating on every pitch. You could see him think about what he was going to call for next."

Torre said Spahn turned in a masterful job. "He was the best he's been since I joined the club."

Spahn's remaining goals were to win 20 games again, which he did by winning nine of his last 10 decisions, to pass Plank's victory total of 325 and to finish with a career ERA below 3.00. "That [ERA mark] would be something for them to remember me by," Spahn said. "I think I'd like most to have that in the record books for them to judge what kind of pitcher I was."

A true workhorse, Spahn started 665 of his 750 games, surpassing 200 innings 17 times while recording 63 shutouts. He struck out 2,583 and walked only 1,434 and fashioned a 3.09 ERA. He wasn't a slouch at the plate or in the field, belting 35 home runs and starting 82 double plays.

Spahn spent three years in the Army during World War II, earning a Purple Heart and Bronze Star for heroic duty on the battlefield. Still, Spahn credited others while he had center stage that night. "That crowd [tonight] was the greatest tribute of all." ★

Brewers Take 1982 ALCS Crown

In the 1982 American League Championship Series against the California Angels, Cecil Cooper wasn't having a Cecil Cooper-like week. In the fifth and deciding game, he had struck out with two runners on base in the fifth inning and was 2-for-19 in the series up to that point. But the Brewers' first baseman, one of the best pure hitters in franchise history, made up for his slump in the biggest of ways.

With the bases loaded in the seventh, the left-handed-hitting Cooper laced a single to left field to score Charlie Moore and Jim Gantner for a 4–3 advantage. The Brewers made that cushion hold up as they won Game Five of the 1982 American League Championship Series en route to the team's first and only World Series appearance.

Fans erupt after the Milwaukee Brewers win the American League Championship Series against the California Angels in 1982. (Photo courtesy of the Milwaukee Brewers)

Milwaukee leadoff hitter Paul Molitor remembered afterward a conversation he had held with the soft-spoken Cooper who, if not for teammate Robin Yount's stupendous season at the plate, might have earned league Most Valuable Player laurels.

"After he struck out with men on first and third in the fifth, I mentioned to him, 'Cecil, your last at-bat is going to be the most important one. You're going to get one more chance. Whether it's leading off an inning or with men on base, you're going to get one more chance.' He made the most of it."

That he did. But despite his season and career success, Cooper said he had his doubts before coming through in the most clutch of situations. "When I was in the on-deck circle I looked up at my wife. She was motioning, 'You're going to get a hit, you're going to get a hit.' "

Cooper's error in the fourth inning helped give California its third run. On a bunt play, he tagged the runner with his glove instead of the ball. So he was seeking redemption in the crucial seventh inning. "I do know that I would have traded all 205 hits I got this year for that one," Cooper said. "That was, without a doubt, the greatest hit of all."

Moore's throw from right field to gun down Reggie Jackson at third base in the fifth inning was a pivotal play and made the Brewers' rally possible. Then Moore, a former catcher, blooped a single over the mound with one out in the seventh. The first- and third-base umpires said that California second baseman Bobby Grich had caught the ball for the second out, but the other two members of the crew said he had trapped it. A crowd of 54,968 agreed with the latter judgment, which won out.

Gantner then singled to center against Luis Sanchez. Molitor fouled out, but Yount walked on a 3–2 pitch to load the bases and set the stage for Cooper's memorable looping liner and reaction as he headed toward first base. Gantner slid in safely with the go-ahead run before celebrating with Moore. "We've got six more outs to go," Gantner said of his thought process despite the uproar throughout the stadium. "We haven't won this until we get six more outs. Let's get them and then go crazy."

WHAT A WAY TO END IT

En route to capturing the American League East crown in 1982, the Milwaukee Brewers pounded out a franchise record 216 homers. So it wasn't surprising that the long ball helped them clinch the championship in the last game of the season against the Baltimore Orioles.

In a four-game, season-ending series at Baltimore, the Brewers had dropped the first three, allowing the Orioles to force a tie for the division lead. However, eventual Most Valuable Player Robin Yount belted two of Milwaukee's four homers as the visitors pounded Baltimore ace Jim Palmer for a 10–2 victory to finish 95–67 and claim their first and only division crown.

Don Sutton pitched eight strong innings to get the win in helping the Brewers advance to the AL Championship Series against the California Angels, which they won, 3–2, to qualify for their only World Series appearance.

They did, and so did the rest of Milwaukee, which hadn't tasted a pennant since the 1958 Braves competed in their second consecutive World Series.

But the Brewers had accomplished the feat in the unlikeliest of ways, losing the first two contests in California before coming back by staving off elimination three consecutive times at home. Winning the ACLS didn't become reality, however, until California's Rod Carew hit a one-hop grounder to Yount at shortstop for the final out to send Bud Selig's franchise to the World Series, which it lost in seven games to the Saint Louis Cardinals.

Despite the series setback, the emotion of that ALCS wouldn't be forgotten for years to come. Having suffered through such a long dry spell, fans poured onto the field at County Stadium and into the streets, filling National Avenue, Blue Mound Road, and Wisconsin Avenue. The headline in the next day's *Milwaukee Journal* read, "Honks, high fives and high jinks," and there were plenty of all three to pass around.

Game Five's ending might not have been as cheerful without the work of left fielder Ben Oglivie and the Crew's pitching staff. Oglivie smacked a solo home run that cut the Brewers' deficit to 3–2 in the fourth inning. Winning pitcher Bob McClure got three outs in the eighth in relief of starter Pete

Vuckovich, including center fielder Marshall Edwards's leaping grab of Don Baylor's drive to the wall.

Ron Jackson singled off McClure, so Milwaukee skipper Harvey Kuenn brought in Pete Ladd. The Angels' Bob Boone then sacrificed pinch runner Rob Wilfong to second, but Molitor threw out Brian Downing for the second out. And then Ladd coaxed the future Hall of Famer and hitter extraordinaire Carew to ground out on a 1–2 pitch. Carew, a lifetime .332 hitter, batted just .188 in the series.

Ladd, a rookie, was so overjoyed he couldn't remember what happened once the hullabaloo erupted. "I don't have the slightest idea what my reaction was," Ladd said. "All I know was I was holding [catcher] Teddy [Simmons] and I wasn't going to let go of him."

Moore finished 6-for-13 in the series and Molitor was 6-for-19, but the Brewers only hit .218 compared to the Angels' .258. Fred Lynn was magnificent for California, going 11-for-18.

California had grabbed a 1–0 lead in the first inning, but Milwaukee tied the game in the bottom half on Simmons's sacrifice fly. The Angels then moved on top 2–1 when Lynn connected on his second RBI single in the third. They increased the margin to 3–1 on Boone's squeeze play after Cooper's gaffe in the fourth. Oglivie's blast then made it 3–2 in the Brewers' fourth.

The revelry wouldn't have been possible and the hops and grains wouldn't have flowed had it not been for Milwaukee's resolve after falling behind 2–0 on the West Coast.

In Game Four, reserve outfielder Mark Brouhard, subbing for an injured Oglivie in left, helped keep Milwaukee alive and was the major reason the hosts were able to even the series with a 9–5 triumph. The former Angels prospect went 3-for-4 with a single, double, homer, and three RBIs while setting an ALCS record with four runs scored. "When you haven't played in four weeks, there's not much you can do but look up and say a little prayer to the Lord and go out and do the best job you can do," Brouhard said afterward.

BADGER BASEBALL

Yes, the University of Wisconsin once had a baseball team. One of its most memorable seasons occurred in 1950, when Thornton Kipper's strong pitching performance carried Wisconsin to a 4–1 decision over Ohio State for the NCAA District 4 baseball tournament championship. The win gave the Badgers their first and only berth in the College World Series, where they won two games before being eliminated. Kipper won the district tourney opener with 4 1/3 innings of relief against Michigan State in UW's 13–6 win at East Lansing. In the title game, Bruce Elliott overcame an error to knock in the deciding run while finishing 2-for-4.

Brewers' starter Moose Haas overcame three rain delays to carry a no-hitter into the sixth inning. Lynn's RBI double down the right field line ruined the no-hit bid and shutout. Haas then gave up a grand slam homer to Baylor to cut California's deficit to 7–5, but Jim Slaton got the final five outs for the save. Brouhard's two-run round-tripper in the eighth sewed up the victory.

Don Sutton, picked up in an August trade with Houston to bolster the staff for the stretch run, got the Game Three victory as Milwaukee staved off elimination with a 5–3 win. Sutton took a four-hit shutout into the eighth inning, striking out nine, including Reggie Jackson three times. Milwaukee's offense featured three hits and three runs in the fourth and Molitor's two-run homer in the seventh.

In Game Two, right-hander Bruce Kison recorded a five-hit, eight-strikeout effort as the Angels moved ahead 2–0 with a 4–2 decision. Reggie Jackson's solo homer and Boone's two RBIs, including another one on a squeeze bunt in the second, handed Vuckovich the loss.

Baylor's five RBIs tied a playoff mark in Game One, and Tommy John was the winning pitcher as the Angels rallied for an 8–3 triumph. Milwaukee led 3–2 in the third when Baylor smashed a two-run triple off the wall in center against Mike Caldwell. Baylor also contributed a two-run single in the fourth and a sacrifice fly in the first. Gorman Thomas belted a two-run homer for Milwaukee's only big blow. ★

Paul Molitor's 1987 Hitting Streak

They didn't call him the Ignitor for nothing. When Paul Molitor stepped onto a diamond, something exciting almost always happened. And that's why he was a major reason for baseball's resurgence in Milwaukee during the late 1970s and early '80s. Besides the Brewers' American League pennant chases, perhaps nothing captured the imagination of fans across Wisconsin and the nation quite as did the Twin Cities native's accomplishment after the All-Star Game break in 1987.

It all started July 16, when Molitor reached California starting pitcher Kirk McCaskill for a double in the second inning. Molitor reached base via a hit for 38 more games after that, establishing the fifth-longest streak in Major League history with a single against Cleveland at County Stadium on the night of Tuesday, August 25. His string of success and luck ran out the next evening, thus ending another run at baseball's most cherished record, Joe DiMaggio's 56-game hitting streak.

However, nobody could take away from what Molitor had done, finishing one game short of Ty Cobb's 40-game run. Only six players recorded

Milwaukee's Paul Molitor swings for a hit during his 39-game streak in 1987. (Photo courtesy of the Milwaukee Brewers)

longer streaks than Molitor, and Pete Rose's 44-game string in 1978 was the only one that came after DiMaggio established his magical and probably unreachable standard in 1941.

During those 39 wonderful outings, Molitor finished 68-for-164 for a .415 average. Included in his batting display were seven homers and 33 RBIs.

Milwaukee won that August 25th game 10–9 behind five RBIs from Dale Sveum in front of a crowd of 15,580. It proved to be only the ninth time that Molitor went past three plate appearances to get a hit; this one came in his fourth at-bat. Molitor flied out to deep right field in the first inning, coaxed a walk his second time up, and grounded out to second base in the fourth.

He extended the hoopla for at least one more game when he stroked the first pitch from reliever Don Gordon in the sixth for a clean hit. "In the two or three times I've faced him, he's come in with a slider and I thought he might do it again," Molitor said of his approach heading to plate for that crucial at-bat. "It's when you're leaning over the plate looking for that when you tend to hit to the opposite field. He came in with a fastball and I hit a semi-line drive. I was semi-fighting it off. It was beginning to look like one of those nights when you swing the bat well and you come up empty."

That wouldn't happen for another 24 hours, but Molitor said his attempt for legendary status had been without dispute. "They've all been clean hits in the streak, but they haven't all been pretty," Molitor said. "At least it hasn't come down to a hit that was questionable or a defensive play that could have been an error. That keeps it away from any controversy."

All of the talk and what-ifs came to a disappointing end the next night as former Indian Rick Manning's pinch hit single with one out in the 10th inning brought home the winning run in Milwaukee's 1–0 victory against an Indians squad that would finish in the AL East cellar at 61–101.

Molitor was in the on-deck circle hoping for one last opportunity to extend his march. But when reality hit and the game was over, Molitor showed his customary class by being one of the first players to congratulate Manning for winning the game. "That was the first time I've been booed for getting a game-winning hit at home," Manning said about his unpopular single. "I thought I got traded back to Cleveland in the middle of the game."

JUAN'S NO-NO

In the same year that Paul Molitor achieved his remarkable hitting streak, left-hander Juan Nieves pitched the first and only no-hitter in Milwaukee Brewers history. On April 15, 1987, Nieves walked five Orioles in the 7–0 victory at Baltimore. Dale Sveum's solo homer in the fourth proved to be the game-winner and extended his hitting streak to nine games, and the contest ended on Robin Yount's memorable diving catch in right-center. The win was the ninth in the Brewers' string of 13 straight to open the season. It was quite a season.

Indians' rookie right-hander John Farrell, making his second career start, collared Molitor into an 0-for-4 performance. But that didn't prevent the crowd of 11,246 from calling Molitor out for an ovation after the game.

"It's an emotional night for me," Molitor said. "Being called out at the end of the game like that and glancing over and seeing my family. It reminds me of what I've been through, and it humbles you. I just thank God for the opportunity to do it. It's been a great experience."

Molitor was the first batter Farrell faced a week earlier in his big-league debut; Molitor had singled.

In this streak-ending game, Molitor struck out in his first at-bat and hit into a double play in the third, the first time he'd done that since April 15. In the sixth he grounded out to shortstop, and then he reached on the third baseman's throwing error in the eighth. Farrell, 25, allowed only three hits through nine innings.

The Brewers rallied against future Milwaukee reliever Doug Jones. Rob Deer was hit by a pitch, and pinch runner Mike Felder went to second on a grounder. Sveum was intentionally walked to put runners at first and second, bringing up Manning, who was batting for Juan Castillo. Manning singled to center on an 0–1 pitch. "I had a couple of chances to drive the ball, but I either fouled them off or missed them," Molitor said. "He had a better-than-average fastball and he kept our hitters off stride."

Farrell, who didn't last long in the majors, said he did his best to block out what was going on around him. "I knew what the situation was tonight, but the only times I was aware of it was when he was on deck or he came to the plate," Farrell said. "The crowd really helped him rise to the occasion then, but it helped me too. When I heard them, it pumped me up. He showed a lot of class after his last at-bat. He told me, 'Nice job.'"

That's why Molitor, who later won a World Series ring with Toronto and finished his career with Minnesota, received a first-ballot ticket to Cooperstown in January 2004. He finished with 3,319 hits, 605 doubles, 114 triples, 234 home runs, 1,782 runs, 1,307 runs batted in, 504 stolen bases, and a .306 average.

And he accomplished those gaudy statistics despite missing nearly 600 games because of injuries ranging from broken fingers to torn hamstrings and rib cage muscles to torn ligaments in his elbow. He underwent 12 operations during his career, ending the run with double hernia surgery. But nothing ailed Molitor during that magnificent stretch in the summer of 1987, when he joined the elite in baseball history.

Molitor obviously would have liked to see the streak continue, but he also was glad that the constant scrutiny, increased attention, and extra pressure were in his past.

"I've said all along that sooner or later it would come down to my last at-bat and I wouldn't get a hit," Molitor said. "This was the night." ★

Robin Yount Gets 3,000th Hit

He had long ago won the hearts of baseball fans in Milwaukee, but on the night of Tuesday, September 9, 1992, Robin Yount cemented his place in Major League Baseball's Hall of Fame. Yount became the 17th player and third youngest, after Ty Cobb and Henry Aaron, to reach the 3,000-hit plateau. He did it before 47,589 fans at County Stadium with a single against Cleveland's Jose Mesa.

As if preordained, Yount's momentous accomplishment had to happen against the Indians. After all, he had registered hits 1,000 and 2,000 against Cleveland hurlers.

But it might not have happened if he had not reached 2,999 the evening before. Unlike his eventual history-making trip to the plate that occurred in the seventh inning, Yount wasted little time to give the crowd of 40,000 what it paid to see. He singled to right field off Jack Armstrong in his first at-bat and finished 1-for-4 with a walk to help the Brewers beat the Indians, 7–3, and stay in the pennant race in what is still the team's last winning season.

So that left the Brewers' final home game before a seven-game road swing to Baltimore and Boston for the team's career leader in most offensive categories to reach the magical number, something the two-time American

League Most Valuable Player prayed would happen at home. "I'll do everything I can to make it happen," Yount said. "But if it doesn't I surely don't want to wait until we come home again. We're still in this pennant race. Winning this division is far more important than personal goals. I hope that's where the focus can stay."

Robin Yount waves to the crowd as teammates congratulate him on his 3,000th career hit, which he got in September 1992 at County Stadium. (Photo courtesy of the Milwaukee Brewers)

His teammates knew that's how Rockin' Robin was handling the situation, putting the team ahead of himself, which he had done since joining the club as an 18-year-old shortstop in 1974. "We're riding on Robin Yount's shoulders and the enthusiasm of the fans," said reliever Mike Fetters, thoroughly enjoying his first season in Milwaukee. "It's carrying over to us. This is the way it's supposed to be."

TWO ODDITIES IN SAME GAME

On August 16, 1976, Milwaukee Brewers' pitchers accomplished something that hadn't been done in the American League since 1910. They picked off three Oakland A's base runners.

That wasn't the only unusual occurrence during the Brewers' 4–3 victory. When Oakland's Billy Williams, a future Hall of Famer, was called out on strikes while refusing to step into the batter's box, he was thrown out of the game, the first time that had ever happened in Major League history.

Yount was only 1-for-10 against Mesa lifetime coming into the game, which had been delayed for 32 minutes by rain. He tapped out to first base on a check-swing, 3–2 pitch in the first inning. He then struck out on a 2–2 offering with two runners aboard in the third. Mesa got him on strikes again to end the fourth after Milwaukee had scored four runs and had one runner on base.

But then came the seventh and a place in baseball history for the consummate professional, who later became a rare first-ballot electee to Cooperstown with buddy George Brett and Nolan Ryan. And in classic Yount style, he went the opposite way with the pitch, lacing his single to right-center. "I hit the bag and turned around and Gumby [Jim Gantner] was there and Paul right behind him," Yount said afterward. "It's not like it happens every day." That's for sure.

The ovation after his milestone hit, which occurred at 9:48 p.m., lasted more than 10 minutes. First base was removed and a film retrospective of his illustrious career was played on the scoreboard. "You don't get feelings like that very often," Yount told the media. "I let it last as long as I could." He became the first player to reach the 3,000-hit mark since Rod Carew did it for the California Angels in 1985.

But even Yount, who took the game play by play and inning by inning in his all-out effort to be a winner, had lost his focus as the pressure of the moment began to wear on him while he walked to the plate for his fourth at-bat. "At that point, I finally got into the game instead of letting all the other stuff going on around me consume me," he said. "At that point, I was finally locked in."

For that moment, and perhaps for thousands of other ones before that during his career, his teammates mobbed Yount at first base and gave him a ride on their shoulders. Gantner and Molitor led the throng in a predetermined celebration, which was only fair because they had toiled alongside Yount for 15 years.

"We talked about what we would do if it would happen," Molitor said. "Jim and I said, 'When he gets it, we're going.'"

Molitor later joined the 3,000-hit fraternity, getting his as a member of the Minnesota Twins in 1996—and on Yount's birthday no less.

It was the second time that night that Yount uncharacteristically showed emotion on the field. The first had been his visible disgust after striking out the second time in the fourth. But nobody blamed him for either.

LIKE FATHER . . .

The headline in the April 23rd *Shawano Leader* read, "Rickert hurls perfect game." The strange thing is that the headline ran in 1982 and again in 2004, and two different Rickerts were involved, father and son; both accomplished their feats as seniors pitching for Bowler High School. Things got even weirder because the two no-hitters were against the same team, Iola, and both games were played on a Thursday.

Mike Rickert struck out 12 batters in the 2004 game, while his father, John, fanned 11 hitters 22 years earlier.

The players weren't the only ones who were proud to be part of the spectacle. Then club owner and President Bud Selig said it was one of the most special moments in franchise history. "It's a great moment for him, his family, and the franchise," Selig said. "You imagine something, but when it comes it's legendary. It was thrilling. It's something I'll remember the rest of my life."

Even his opponents couldn't help but contemplate what Yount had accomplished. "In the first inning I was going with fastball only and in the next two at-bats I was showing my fastball for a strike and then going with the slider," Mesa said. "He was swinging at my slider like he wasn't seeing the ball. Maybe he was blinded by the flash from the cameras."

Cleveland manager Mike Hargrove, who came up with the Indians in 1974, the same year that Yount started, said he couldn't help but marvel at the milestone. "I've known Robin a long time, and he's one of the few guys around you can say he deserves all the best he can get," Hargrove said. "He's a good man besides being a good player."

Yount lined out to shortstop to end the game, a 5–4 loss, a week before his 37th birthday. But Milwaukee skipper Phil Garner said that aspect of the evening played second fiddle to "the Kid." "I know Robin feels worse than anyone that we didn't win the ballgame," Garner said. "Hey, we'll win more ballgames. That shouldn't take away from his accomplishment."

It was the crowning achievement of a career that saw Yount finish with 1,632 runs scored, 3,142 base hits, 583 doubles, 126 triples, 251 home runs, and 1,406 RBIs.

Yount also reflected on what had transpired that night. "All along I said it wasn't any big deal, that it was just going to be another hit," Yount said. "Obviously, it turned out to be not just another hit. The way the fans came out and reacted, it turned out to be more than I thought it would be. It's something I'll never forget." ★

MORE RECORDS, STREAKS, AND AMAZING MOMENTS
PROFESSIONAL BASEBALL
Four Games and Then Some

On May 12 and 13, 1972, the Milwaukee Brewers and Minnesota Twins couldn't get enough of each other. That's when the teams played 21 innings before the 1 a.m. curfew halted action. Play resumed the next day, and Mike Ferraro singled in the winning run as the visiting Brewers claimed a 4–3 victory in 22 innings in a contest that lasted 5 hours, 47 minutes.

But that wasn't the end as the regularly scheduled meeting went 15 innings, establishing an American League record for most innings played in consecutive games, breaking the mark of 36. Ferraro homered to give Milwaukee a lead in the 15th, but Craig Nettles answered with a two-run blast off Jim Slaton to hand the Twins a 5–4 win, ending the two-day marathon in a time of 9:23. ★

Final Round-Tripper

Hank Aaron, in his 23rd and final Major League season, hammered his last home run as the Milwaukee Brewers defeated the California Angels, 6–2, on July 20, 1976. It was Aaron's 10th long ball of the season and 755th of his illustrious career.

On October 3 of that year, Aaron finished his Hall of Fame career with a base hit in front of a crowd of 6,858 at County Stadium, also registering his last RBI (2,297). ★

Saving the Best for Last

Milwaukee reliever Rollie Fingers tied the Yankees' Sparky Lyle with his 216th save in the Brewers' 6–4 win over New York on July 23, 1984.

He was shelved by injury the rest of that season, but Fingers bounced back to record number 217 on April 13, 1985, against Texas, to set the American League standard. Fingers notched his 233rd and final save to end an 11–10 win over Minnesota on September 4 of that year. ★

Easter Sunday Miracle

The Milwaukee Brewers had opened the 1987 season with 11 consecutive victories, tying Oakland's 1981 American League record. But the best was yet to come.

On April 19, Milwaukee trailed the Texas Rangers, 4–1, heading into the bottom of the ninth inning. However, slugger Rob Deer knotted the score with a three-run homer to left field with one out. And one out later, shortstop

The fans couldn't have been happier as homers by Rob Deer and Dale Sveum rallied the Brewers to their 12th of 13 straight victories to open the 1987 season. (Photo courtesy of the Milwaukee Brewers)

Dale Sveum smashed a two-run shot to right-center as the Brewers claimed a 6–4 victory for number 12. The Brewers won their next game over Chicago to tie a Major League record (held by the 1982 Atlanta Braves) with 13 straight wins to start a season.

Ironically, Milwaukee also set a team record for futility in May of that year, dropping 12 games in a row. ★

HIGH SCHOOL BASEBALL AND SOFTBALL
Back-to-Back Masterpieces

Less than a year after Cincinnati Reds hurler Johnny Vander Meer became the first and only Major League pitcher to toss back-to-back no-hitters, the feat was duplicated—in northwestern Wisconsin. It occurred in April 1939, when Eau Claire High School senior Doug Forster turned the trick against Whitehall and La Crosse Aquinas during a four-day span.

Eau Claire pounded out 17 hits against Whitehall, but Forster didn't need much help as he notched a perfect game while striking out 15. Only twice did Whitehall batters come close: Bill Thompson snared a drive to deep left field in the third inning, and in the seventh a Whitehall batter fouled off four pitches on a 3–1 count before grounding out. Forster contributed two hits and two runs to his cause.

In the second game, three Aquinas runners reached base, two on errors in the first and second innings and one on a walk in the sixth. Forster finished with 12 strikeouts.

Forster also was one of the top regulars that year in batting for the Old Abes, registering eight hits in 25 at-bats. He finished with a 9-0 pitching record, allowing only 16 hits in 47 and 1/3 innings. Coach Mark Almli's troops finished the season 13–0, including Forster's 14–0 and 8–0 masterpieces. He went on to pitch in the minor leagues but never made it to the big time. ★

Young and Talented

In 1985, the River Valley High School girls softball team featured a starting lineup of three freshmen, two sophomores, and four juniors. All that youth didn't faze the Blackhawks as they captured the Class B state championship with a 5–2 victory over Denmark. They duplicated that performance with a second consecutive unbeaten season to improve their winning streak to 42–0 with a 3–2 decision against Wilmot in the tourney final.

River Valley, located in Spring Green, extended its string to 47 straight games before a setback to Iowa-Grant in 1987. Jane (Liegel) Briehl was one of the freshmen starters on that first title team, and in 2002 she coached the Blackhawks to the Division 2 championship contest, which they lost 3–0 to Shawano. ★

Holy Terrors

People who follow Fox Valley Association baseball can't forget the name Matt Erickson. That's because the former Appleton West star is at or near the top in most seasonal and career offensive categories, mainly established in 1993–94.

The ex-Terrors' standout holds league career records for average (.552), hits (74), on-base percentage (.667), and at-bats to strikeout ratio (one strikeout per every 134 at-bats). He is tied for second with 14 doubles, third in RBIs with 49, second in runs scored with 62, and third in walks with 40. In 1994, he set an FVA season mark for average (.609), tied for third in doubles with eight, and bettered his own mark from the previous year (.650) with an on-base percentage of .727.

Needless to say, Erickson was a major cog for the Terrors as they won the loop championship seven consecutive seasons in 1989–95. Appleton West has won or shared the FVA baseball title 17 times since its inception in 1971. ★

Diamond Royalty

Marion High School, with an enrollment of about 300 located between Wausau and Green Bay, is the queen of Wisconsin girls softball. Its teams have won six championships in eight trips to the state tournament, all in Class C from 1985 to 1992, including three in a row to end that successful run. Kimberly and Denmark are next with five.

Ashwaubenon, which leads the way with 14 appearances at state, won three trophies consecutively in 1992–94, while Loyal was the first to win three straight in 1978–80 but has lost its last three finals tries.

Madison West won the initial tourney title in 1976, setting a record for runs scored that hasn't been matched since its 27–8 win over Elmwood in the single-class event. Seneca has the mark for most runs in an inning with 11 during its Division 3 pasting of Washburn (22–1) for the 1983 crown, a game in which it also established a standard for hits with 22.

Five pitchers have tossed no-hitters in the history of the tournament. Kelly Hoff of Westby was the first when she blanked Black River Falls in 1989. The feat wasn't repeated again until 2000, when Alexis Main of Stevens Point baffled Homestead and Katie Karbon of Appleton East handcuffed Fort Atkinson. Erin Lynum of Altoona joined the club with her mastery of East Troy in 2001, and Brooke Schliewe of Horicon became number five with her gem against Wausaukee in 2002. ★

BASKETBALL

Badgers Win NCAA Tournament

Coach Harold "Bud" Foster's philosophy for success focused on a tenacious defense and patient, structured offense. It proved to be a winning combination March 29, 1941, when his underdog Wisconsin squad claimed the university's only National Collegiate Athletic Association men's basketball championship.

The Badgers finished off a 20–3 campaign with a 39–34 triumph against Washington State, which was a six-point favorite in the title showdown at Municipal Auditorium in Kansas City, Missouri. Wisconsin's Big Ten champions didn't care about point spreads or that there were about 2,000 empty seats as they extended their season-ending winning streak to 15 games. University of Wisconsin team captain Gene Englund led the way with 13 points, while tourney Most Valuable Player and fellow all-American John Kotz added 12.

The Badgers overcame those odds, as well as the Cougars' distinct height advantage by the name of six-foot-seven, 230-pound center Paul Lindeman. The WSU star had averaged 20 points per game as the Cougars eliminated Creighton and undefeated Arkansas in the Western Regional of the eight-team tournament.

Those victories gave Washington State a 26–5 record as it prepared to face a Wisconsin club that wasn't exactly a slouch either, having won its first league crown since 1918 and recording its best conference mark since also going 11–1 in 1923. After all, the Badgers had shattered Indiana's year-old standard of 519 points with 536 in the 12 games.

Wisconsin grabbed a 6–0 lead, only to see Washington State bounce back. Jack Frial's Cougars grabbed 10–8 and 12–9 leads, but Kotz, a Rhinelander native, made two hoops to push the Badgers back out front. Wisconsin proved it could bounce back during the regular season, winning six of seven games in which it trailed at halftime, and it needed that kind of resiliency again in the back-and-forth finale.

Washington State scored eight straight points to grab an 8–6 margin. Then Wisconsin resumed control at 17–12 only to watch Cougars' guard Kirk Gebert make two field goals and a free throw to knot things at 17. Don Timmerman and Kotz then hit baskets to give the Badgers a 21–17 edge at the break.

Kotz and Ted Strain canned free throws and Englund and Charles Epperson drilled hoops as Wisconsin went on another run for a 30–24 advantage in the second half.

Washington State made its final bid, climbing to within 34–32. But Kotz made a short shot, Strain tossed in a free throw, and Bob Alwin made the final two-pointer to end the scoring. The Badgers also had won four games in which they were outscored from the field because of superior shooting from the free throw line.

UW sank better than 68 percent of its free throws during the campaign, with sophomore Fred Rehm of Brookfield tops at .825 (33-of-40), including 13 of his last 14 tries. Kotz was next at .746 and Englund third at .714. The Badgers, who had finished in ninth place in the conference and were 5–15 overall in 1940, needed every one in this showdown against the Cougars.

UW was successful on 7 of 9 free throws, while the Cougars, who made only 53 percent during the regular season, faltered a bit and barely bettered that average at 6-of-11 (55 percent). Gebert accounted for 10 of the Cougars' 14 baskets while finishing with a game-high 21 points. Wisconsin had seven players score, but neither squad fared well from the field: the Badgers made 16 of 67 shots for 24 percent, and the Cougars were 14-of-63 for 22 percent.

WHAT A WHITEWASH

Wisconsin recorded the only shutout in Big Ten men's basketball history when it posted Parsons College, 50–0, on January 6, 1914, at home. Coach Walter Meanwell's Badgers laid claim to the mythical national championship with a 12–0 conference mark and 15–0 overall record. Wisconsin limited three other league foes to single digits as it registered its first undisputed league title.

Those statistics pretty well matched the Badgers' offensive output during the season, as well as during their postseason run in which they connected on 43 of 163 attempts for 26 percent in the three games. However, they limited Dartmouth, Pittsburgh, and Washington State to 23 percent.

Wisconsin's postseason magic started in the East Regional at the UW Field House. Englund and Kotz scored 18 and 15 points, respectively, to carry the Badgers past Dartmouth, 51–50, on March 21 before 12,500 fans. Dartmouth held a 24–22 lead at the intermission, and The Big Green grabbed the upper hand again at 44–42 when Gus Broberg scored two of his game-high 20 points with about eight minutes left.

However, the Badgers tied it again on Epperson's hook shot and claimed their first lead since early in the game on Englund's inside basket. Kotz added two free throws to put Wisconsin up 51–46 with just more than a minute remaining. Dartmouth scored the game's final four points, including a desperation field goal from near half court as the final gun sounded.

UW also hosted the regional title showdown against Pittsburgh. Wisconsin avenged a 36–34 home setback to the Panthers with a 36–30 win, overcoming a 23–18 Pitt cushion early in the second half in front of 14,000 well-wishers the next day.

That's when the two Badger offensive stars took over. Kotz nailed two baskets and Englund one to push Wisconsin ahead 24–23. Englund tallied 11 points, while Kotz chipped in 10, and the Badgers never relinquished the lead after that. Kotz was only a sophomore that year but earned all-Big Ten Conference laurels and became a two-time all-American. Englund, who came from Kenosha, was the league's MVP in 1941 and was named the all-America center after scoring a then-record 162 points in conference tilts for the Badgers.

John Kotz of Rhinelander helps lead the Wisconsin Badgers to their first and only NCAA basketball championship in 1941. (Photo courtesy of the University of Wisconsin)

In a 2000 *Milwaukee Journal Sentinel* article coinciding with the Badgers' return to the Final Four for the first time since that Cinderella 1941 season, Rehm said that the secret to Wisconsin's success was pretty simple. "Bud was a strict coach, and if you didn't play his style, you'd get substituted," Rehm said. "We played strictly man-to-man defense and a very patterned offense. There might be 32 options off one play. If the first one didn't work, he went into the second and third as the situation arose, and so on down the line."

That system emphasized getting the ball to Kotz and Englund, who amazingly made only 26 percent and 29.5 percent of their field goal attempts, respectively, in the tourney.

Rehm, a Brookfield resident who played high school ball at Milwaukee Pulaski, said in a phone interview in 2003 that everyone had a role to play and did their jobs for the team's sake.

"I believe I scored the first couple buckets of the [championship] game, but my main priority was defense," said Rehm, the lone surviving starter from that UW squad. "I usually had to cover the other team's leading scorer, and I was one of the leading rebounders. I remember in that game that we put the clamps on their leading scorer [Lindeman]. Gene [Englund] was on him, but we all took swipes at the ball anytime we went by and he had it, and that really flustered him."

It was a different time and a different game for basketball fans, before the advent of the 65-team events that are part of today's television-hyped extravaganza.

ALL CUED UP

On the same weekend that the Badgers were winning the NCAA men's basketball title in March 1941, Manitowoc native Leslie Brennan was representing the University of Wisconsin in the first national intercollegiate billiards tournament, which was held in the UW's Memorial Union. The senior chemical engineering major had helped the Badgers finish third in the team competitions behind Florida and Michigan two weeks earlier. However, Brennan dropped the championship match to Kansas' Lloyd Greene, 75–39.

Here is how *Wisconsin State Journal* sports editor Henry J. McCormick described the outcome. "Wisconsin had the ability to win this game by a big margin, but the Badgers played it as they had played every other game all year when they figured they were the big pants. . . . And the Badgers definitely wore the big pants in this game."

Englund had presented WSU captain Ray Sundquist with a basketball made of cheese before the game, but the headline in the *State Journal* that Sunday read "Badgers Bring Home Bacon." And a throng of 12,000 ate up the team's success, greeting the train upon the Badgers' return after midnight Monday. Curfew for female students was moved back one hour to 1:30 a.m.

Now that's March Madness. ★

Reedsville Knocks Off the Giants

Carl Maertz has lived among Hoosiers since 1956. But ask him about the movie by the same name, and the Wisconsin native will tell you that it was made about the wrong town.

The 1987 film starring Gene Hackman is based on the story of Milan, a town in southern Indiana with a school of 161 students that upset every tournament challenger en route to winning the 1954 boys state basketball championship in a single-class system.

From his home in Valparaiso, Indiana, Maertz said the film's producers should have checked their hoops history and turned the pages back eight years, to when Reedsville proved it was the real giant killer.

He should know. Maertz was a junior starting guard on the Panthers' 1946 squad, representing a student body of 87, which ousted Goliaths such as Racine Park, Wisconsin Rapids, and Eau Claire to become the smallest school ever to win a one-class crown in the Badger state. "I'm not saying what Milan did wasn't great, but we were much smaller than they were," Maertz said. "They don't ever want to hear about [Reedsville] around here."

That's too bad, because it was something for the ages, as the Panthers earned the right to face the favored Eau Claire Old Abes in the title showdown in a field that also included Tomah, Ashland, Madison East, and Beaver Dam.

Eau Claire had won state championships in 1917 and '27 but didn't celebrate a third crown. John Gable, a Cuba City native, led his Panthers to a 48–39 decision in front of a record crowd of 13,800 at the Field House in Madison. The contest was tied at 39 in the fourth quarter, and the Panthers again made the plays down the stretch, whitewashing Eau Claire during the final four minutes.

Center Ed Shimon outplayed his Eau Claire counterpart, Warren "Trapper" Hoff, while scoring 24 points. Fellow senior Bernard Kubale complemented Shimon with 14 points, while Berval Thorson led the Old Abes with 13. Hoff added 10 points but managed only two in the second half. Free throw shooting was subpar in this seesaw affair, as Reedsville made only 14 of 33 and Eau Claire drilled just 7 of 19.

Reedsville washed away a 5–3 deficit with an 8–0 outburst and finished the first quarter on top, 13–8. The Panthers increased their margin to 19-8 on Shimon's hook shot, but the Old Abes responded, registering 11 of the final 14 points to climb to within 22–19 at halftime. The Panthers maintained control at 34–29 before Thorson and Jack Houman combined to score the Old Abes' next, and what proved to be last, 10 points to make it 39–all. Shimon's free throw started the game-ending 9–0 run for Reedsville.

Maertz, a University of Wisconsin–Madison graduate, said the Panthers rode the coattails of their tremendous fan support. "We had people in the community and the whole country rooting for us," Maertz said. "And I think the majority of the crowd was for us, partly because we were something of a novelty. We had created a great deal of excitement. I can remember fans in the hotel across Park Street chanting all night long."

The Panthers gave them good reason, knocking off Eau Claire, which at the time had a population of 46,000 and one high school with an enrollment of 1,600. The latter figure was more than twice the size of Reedsville.

However, the Panthers didn't save all the hoopla for the finale, as they downed the Racine and Rapids entrants in similar fashion in a tourney that saw every first-round game decided by nine points or less, including East's double overtime triumph.

Reedsville upset Park, 30–28, in its opener, shocking most fans in attendance. An estimated 16,300 fans watched the first round, which was 6,000 more than the standard set the year before. The Panthers connected on only 10 of 46 field goal attempts (22 percent), but they held Park to an even worse 9-of-57 showing for 16 percent.

BADGER STREAK BREAKERS

In perhaps the University of Wisconsin's most impressive regular-season victory in school history, sophomore guard Don Hearden of Kimberly scored 29 points as Wisconsin walloped top-rated Ohio State, 86–67, in a Big Ten basketball game at the UW Field House on March 3, 1962, the only time in 14 tries that the Badgers have knocked off the nation's number-one team. Ohio State had won a league record 27 straight games and 74 of its previous 77.

The upset was doubly sweet because the Buckeyes' lineup featured future Hall of Famers Jerry Lucas and John Havlicek, and future coaching curmudgeon Bob Knight was a key reserve.

Shimon and Kubale topped Reedsville's offense with 14 and 11 points, respectively, both contributing four field goals. Park, which had claimed the championship in 1943, couldn't find the basket in the final 10 minutes of the first contest of the 31st annual event. The biggest factor was the loss of six-foot, five-inch center Eddie Olson, who fouled out with 9:27 remaining and 11 points, and Racine leading 28-19. Shimon took advantage, accounting for nine of his team's final 11 points as the underdog Panthers grabbed the lead at 29-28 with 2:48 left.

Reedsville's standout missed a free throw with 1:29 remaining, but Park misfired on four charity tosses after that. Shimon was fouled and sank one free throw after the buzzer sounded for the final margin.

Park trailed 2–0, 6–5, and 7–6 and then held the upper hand until its final cold spell. Reedsville trailed 19–14 at the intermission and 28–23 after three quarters in a game that saw it miss 11 free throws and Park come up short on 12.

Then the Panthers improved to 21–2 with their 14th straight victory with a 47–43 overtime thriller against Wisconsin Rapids, while Eau Claire knocked off Madison East, 59–55, in the other semifinal game. Eau Claire center Warren Hoff tallied a then-tournament record 32 points, which bettered Rhinelander star John Kotz's mark of 28 that he had set in 1939.

Reedsville was ahead by one with 5:17 left when Shimon fouled out. Bob Mader scored a game-high 21 points for Rapids, but Kubale picked up the slack for Reedsville with 18.

Rapids raced to an 8–0 cushion, but the Panthers tied it at 8 and again at 12 after the first quarter. Rapids maintained control at halftime with a 26–19 lead and took a 34–29 margin into the final quarter.

Trailing 35–31, the Panthers made their decisive run, scoring the next eight points.

Sophomore Henry Behnke ignited the run with the first two baskets. Shimon added a free throw for a 36–35 advantage before fouling out, but Reedsville continued the spurt. Rapids evened the score again, but Kubale converted a three-point play. Then Mader knotted things one last time with a basket with three seconds remaining. Behnke and Roman Kugle converted field goals in the extra period to send the Panthers to the championship contest.

Although he might have agreed with the fact that his Panthers definitely played the role of David in this scenario, Gable said his team was confident it could play with the big boys. "It's really great, but it's just like we expected to do when we came down here," he said afterward. "I told the boys just before the district tournament at Brillion that we were going to the state tournament in Madison, and we've kept our word."

And nobody could have written a better script. ★

Beloit College Takes On the Big Guys

There was no better example of David versus Goliath than during the late 1940s and early 1950s, when little Beloit College felled some of basketball's giant programs while competing on main stages across the country.

Coach Dolph Stanley directed the Buccaneers for 12 years, compiling a 242–58 record from the 1945–46 season through the 1956–57 campaign for a .807 winning percentage. His teams claimed the Midwest Conference title from 1945 to '51 and won 40 consecutive league games during one stretch. The high-scoring Buccaneers, better known to their followers as "The Bucket Brigade," whipped foes by such scores as 122–43, 111–41, and 141–53.

Beloit played such opponents as Louisville, South Dakota State, Eastern Kentucky, Arizona, and Hawaii and made five appearances in the NAIB tourney in Kansas City. Stanley's squads defeated NCAA Division I programs such as Colorado State, Western Michigan, Southern Illinois, San Diego State, Valparaiso, Indiana State, Houston, Fresno State, Brigham Young, Washington State, Creighton, DePaul, Wichita State, Loyola of Chicago, and Florida State during their magnificent run. And they performed at such hoops meccas as Chicago Stadium, the Cow Palace in San Francisco, and Madison Square Garden in New York City.

The latter venue was the crowning moment. After the 1950–51 season, Beloit was asked to play in the National Invitation Tournament. At that time, 16 teams were invited to the NCAA tournament. Some schools also competed in the NIT, which was the more glamorous event during those days.

That year's NIT field included North Carolina State, Arizona, and Cincinnati. And even though the Buccaneers lost their opener to Seton Hall, 71–57, on March 10, the invitation itself cemented Stanley's and Beloit's lofty status in basketball circles.

Beloit started the 1951 season only 5–3, but it then ripped DePaul, 94–60, on the road (posting a stadium scoring mark in the process) and entered the postseason at 18–4. But in the end the Buccaneers couldn't match the muscle of their much taller, stronger Seton Hall foes. Seton Hall, which was led by six-foot-10-inch center and future National Basketball Association player Walter Dukes, led only 36–33 at the intermission.

Ron Bontemps, who played for Stanley in high school in Taylorville, Illinois, was the star for the talented Buccaneers. The six-foot-three-inch center scored 19 of his 24 points in the first half as Beloit raced to an 8–1 lead and stayed right with the Pirates.

Beloit had averaged 93.7 points per game in league play and featured three of the loop's top 10 scorers in Bontemps (21.2), Lou Proctor (17.3), and the late Fran Stahr (15.2). However, Beloit finished at 30 percent shooting from the floor (21-of-69) after converting 45 percent during the regular season. The Buccaneers also made only 15 of 28 attempts from the free throw line.

FIRST OF ITS KIND

On April 8, 1905, Fond du Lac won the Lawrence College Invitational, which was the first high school basketball tournament held in Wisconsin and in the United States.

The tournament winners were recognized as the undisputed boys state champions through 1915, when the Wisconsin Interscholastic Athletic Association took over. Fond du Lac claimed that first title in 1916, defeating Grand Rapids (now Wisconsin Rapids) by a 22–7 score.

A banner headline in the *Beloit Daily News* read: "Bucs in Tourists' Role After 71–57 Loss to Seton Hall." The team stayed at the Vanderbilt Hotel and was feted by Beloit College alumni while staying in the Big Apple for several days.

The fact that Stahr had graduated in February and wasn't eligible to play in the NIT hurt the Buccaneers. But Bontemps, who retired in 1989 after 38 years with Caterpillar, said Beloit simply ran out of steam. "They were really tough, and we stayed with them for most of the game," Bontemps, 77, said via telephone from his home in Morton, Illinois. "We weren't all that tall, so we played a 3-2 zone defense and relied on getting the ball out to one of our guards and they'd take off like jets. We used our speed and defensive pressure to beat opponents.

"But we just didn't have enough that night," added Bontemps, who during his first year at Beloit was a teammate of Johnny Orr, who became a legendary coach at Michigan and Iowa State. "Walter Dukes killed us. That brings back bad memories."

Proctor finished with 12 points, while Seton Hall's lineup featured Dukes with 20, Bob Hurt with 13, and Nick Bruckner with 11.

Despite the disappointing showing in the Garden, Bontemps and Beloit College had played big-time basketball while coming from a small-town setting. There were no divisions or classifications in the NCAA, but Beloit held its own against almost every program in the country.

Beloit set a collegiate scoring record, averaging 85.3 points per game. And Bontemps, who went on to help lead the United States' 1952 Olympic gold medal basketball team, was the major contributor.

He credited Stanley for the school's great string of success. "He was very smart, had a basketball mind and had all kinds of ideas," said Bontemps, who starred on Stanley's 45–0 Illinois state championship team in 1944 and joined the University of Illinois program before being drafted and serving in Japan and the Philippines during World War II.

"We used to hear talk about North Carolina, Dean Smith, and the four-corners offense. We were basically doing that when I was at Beloit, spreading people out and taking advantage of our passing and cutting to the basket. Coach was a shrewd basketball man, but I respected him extremely." ★

Underdog Dodgeville Claims the State Crown

The game wasn't going to be close. Milwaukee's North Division High School was favored by as much as 15 points in the 1964 boys state basketball championship game against Dodgeville. So, why should the Dodgers even show up at the University of Wisconsin's Field House in Madison? Well, after the game, more than 13,000 fans were glad they did.

Dodgeville did more than show up that March 21, becoming the last small school to earn a trophy in the single-class tournament with a convincing 59–45 triumph over the Blue Devils in a close contest they blew open in the second half.

Earlier, North had looked almost unstoppable in downing Waterloo by 13 points with a then-record-setting 94-point outburst behind Blanton Simmons's 36 points. Esthetial Ford had chipped in 21 points for the victors.

However, defense wins championships in most sports, and it did in the championship game as Dodgeville controlled the boards against North and throttled its high-powered offense.

Center Rick Brown tallied 20 points, Bob Rock added 14, and Carlos

"Corky" Evans contributed 12. But the biggest difference was that the Dodgers limited the high-flying Simmons to a paltry three points. Ford scored 17 points, but that wasn't enough to prevent Dodgeville from polishing off its 26–0 season, the ninth time a state champion had finished with an unblemished record.

Coach John "Weenie" Wilson, who had suffered a serious heart attack three years earlier and died after another one in 1968, was the architect of this cohesive and well-trained Dodgeville program that had been trounced, 74–52, by Manitowoc in the finals the year before. "I'm so happy I don't know what to do," Wilson said after the Dodgers' surprising upset.

It was the eighth time that a school had earned back-to-back appearances in the championship game, but it proved to be difficult, especially in the first half.

PERFECT POSTSEASONS

John Cantwell (15) shoots while teammates Mike Dodge (34) and Loren Wolf (21) watch underneath in Shawano's game against Waupaca en route to winning the 1956 boys state basketball championship. (Photo courtesy of John Cantwell)

The late John Kenney was perfect as a coach— in the postseason, that is. He led Shawano High School's varsity boys basketball team for two years, 1955–56 and 1956–57, and won state championships both times.

The Indians finished 14–6 the first year but rolled through the playoffs, winning the eight games by an average of 14.9 points. The closest they came to defeat was their 79–77 victory over West Allis Hale in the state tournament opener. Shawano then blasted Sauk City by 24 before winning it all with a 74–65 triumph over Appleton.

Shawano had an easier time the next winter, finishing 18–2. The only setbacks were to number two-ranked Two Rivers, which it avenged with an 82–75 state tourney semifinal win. The Indians won their eight postseason outings by an average of 22.5, including the three regional contests by 31-, 50-, and 40-point margins. They downed Madison West, 66–61, in the championship encounter.

Kenney then was offered teaching and coaching positions in Winona, Minnesota, where he stayed for 23 years until his retirement in 1980.

Milwaukee North led 23–19 at the intermission, but Dodgeville took control during a 17–6 third quarter and cemented its place in history with a 23–16 margin in the fourth. Brown, the team's senior big man, scored nine points during the crucial third quarter, and Dodgeville dominated the boards after the break by a 21–9 margin to win that battle 40–39.

"We knew they would press and we had our patterns picked out," Wilson said of the team's pregame strategy that also included the other starters, Pat Flynn and Bruce Harrison. "We figured [Blanton] Simmons had to come to the keyhole to shoot and we planned for that."

North attempted 71 shots and made only 19 (27 percent), while the Dodgers were good on 18 of 38 for 47 percent. Simmons made just one of his 16 field goal tries, while Dodgeville's Brown canned 8 of 11.

Blue Devils' coach Vic Anderson said later that Dodgeville simply outplayed his talented bunch. "I knew if we were going to lose a game, it would be one like this where the boys just got real cold," Anderson said. "Dodgeville deserved to win. Dodgeville was the best-disciplined team in the tournament."

Rock, who lives and works in Madison, said Dodgeville's task wasn't easy, especially to open the game, because the team had to overcome a serious case of the jitters. "One thing I remember is that Coach was a stickler about us keeping our minds on our business, and that included during warm-ups," Rock said in a phone interview. "He would bench us if he caught us looking at the other end of the court. But with [Milwaukee North], I know all of us were watching out of the corner of our eyes. I mean, the crowd started counting, 'one . . . two . . . three . . . ,' they had 15 guys who could stuff the ball. So we were a little intimidated."

Evans, a forward on the all-senior starting five, said from his New London home that the Dodgers prevailed because they stuck to what had gotten them that far. "We knew we couldn't play their kind of game. We had Rick Brown, and he was a tough, powerful center. We were down at halftime and didn't feel like we had played very well, so we knew we were still in it. Coach told us that we could win this thing. We definitely were the underdog, but we had learned patience from our experience the year before. So we trusted what he said and stayed with our game plan."

That meant leaning on each other and trusting their leader.

"As juniors we had another great class ahead of us, but we all played some and learned a great deal from that experience of having been in the tournament and the championship the year before," Evans said. "We knew each other so well because we played a lot during the summer, and Coach was a purist in that he stressed five guys playing as one. He was an unbelievably good coach who emphasized the fundamentals. We didn't care who got the points. It was a matter of making the extra pass and hitting the open man.

"He [Wilson] could be a tyrant who made practices much harder than the games. He tested your manhood, and not everybody could have played for him. But we were loyal to him and he was loyal to us. We knew we'd run into the Madisons and Monroes, so we took it one game at a time. We got on a hot streak as juniors, but as seniors we expected to win."

And that's what they did, entering the Platteville Sectional with a 20–0 record.

The Dodgers downed an 8–13 Bloomington squad by an 88–44 margin, whipped Soldier's Grove, 85–42, and then met Monroe in the finals. Dodgeville had eliminated the Cheesemakers, 64–50, the year before and came out on top again this time, 59–48, to make the final field of eight teams.

The Dodgers faced a 20–4 Merrill squad in the opening round of the 49th state tournament, a field that also featured Eau Claire Memorial, Waukesha, Frederic, Waterloo, and Manitowoc. Dodgeville downed Merrill, 48–43, before a crowd of 12,771. Flynn scored 14 points to lead the way, while Brown added 12 points. The Dodgers grabbed an 8–6 lead after the first quarter but trailed at halftime and through three quarters before pulling away behind an 18–12 margin in the fourth. Flynn tied the contest at 37 with a field goal, Brown added a basket, and Flynn made two free throws for a 41–37 margin. Wilson's reaction: "Wow, that's hard on a guy like me."

His team made it a little easier in the next round, dumping Waukesha comfortably, 60–40. Brown registered 15 points and 17 rebounds as Dodgeville's stingy defense limited its eighth postseason opponent to less than 50 points to increase that total to 18 of 25 for the season. Flynn, Rock, and Evans chipped in 13 points apiece to the cause, while the Dodgers limited Waukesha scoring star Mike Grainger to 12 points. The losers' lowest scoring output of the season up to that point had been 68 points.

And then came the unforgettable championship encounter that remains one of the most thrilling finals after all of these years. "It's amazing how so many people still talk about what we did, and they remember more about it than I do," said Rock, who took it all in as a crowd some 3,000 strong greeted the caravan upon its return to Iowa County that night.

"I feel fortunate to have been a part of something special like that, the dynasty we had for a short period of time," Rock added. "We were 23–2 as juniors and then went undefeated as seniors. Today, coaches couldn't pull some of the things he [Wilson] did, but he enforced things with the parents' support. We spent a lot of time together on and off the court, but we had to be off the streets by 6 p.m. We were a bunch of guys who walked and talked basketball. There were nights when we went home and cried, but we listened to what he said. He got us to where we wanted to go." ★

Lamont Weaver Hits Game-Tying 55-Footer

The horn sounded as the lanky left-hander fell to his knees near his team's bench and the scorer's table, the basketball still arcing high in the air. Pandemonium soon ensued, and it took officials several minutes to restore order. The reason for such hysteria on that Saturday night, March 22, 1969?

Lamont Weaver had just made a desperation 55-foot shot that banked off the backboard and through the net, tying Beloit Memorial High School's game against Neenah (70-all) to send the Wisconsin Interscholastic Athletic Association state basketball championship contest into overtime.

His prayer on the south side of the University of Wisconsin Field House was the highlight of an unforgettable showdown that went into double overtime, with the Purple Knights finally prevailing, 80–79, on Weaver's two free throws with 36 seconds left.

That shot still resonates as the ultimate moment in the history of the boys state tournament after hundreds of games since its inception in 1916. "Lamont Weaver's shot is pretty hard to duplicate here, or anyplace else," said Dave Wedeward in a 1997 *Madison Capital Times* story talking about the myriad memories that occurred before the final state tourney that year in the Barn, the nickname for the Field House.

If anybody should know, it would be Wedeward, longtime sports editor of the *Janesville Gazette* who has attended as many state tournament games as anybody in the past half-century. "With what can happen in two seconds today, that wouldn't be quite as remarkable," Wedeward added. "The way they milk the clock these days, two seconds can be an eternity. Back then, you would've figured it was over. It was a shock for everybody in the Field House, there's no doubt about that."

Newspaper stories around Wisconsin deemed everything else from the game anticlimactic, even the two extra periods. "Most people would remember

Lamont Weaver's 55-foot shot at the buzzer is arguably the most memorable moment in the history of the boys state basketball tournament. His effort tied the score and forced overtime as Beloit Memorial went on to defeat Neenah in two extra periods for the 1969 title. (Photo courtesy of the Janesville Gazette)

that that [shot] won the state championship, but it didn't," Wedeward said. "In fact, they were almost dead to rights a couple of times in those overtimes."

Somehow Bernie Barkin's squad, which entered the game 25–0 after losing to Manitowoc, 63–51, in the finals the year before, found a way to win.

Pat Hawley made two free throws with 10 seconds left for Neenah to force the 75–all tie ending the first overtime. Beloit center Bruce Brown's put back tied the game at 68 with 28 seconds left. Then Hawley's 10-footer in the lane gave the Rockets a 70–68 lead with three seconds remaining and seemingly had handed Neenah the upset victory.

But miracles do happen, and one did that evening in front of 12,923 stunned fans.

Beloit's Chuck Loft called a timeout and Dave Kilgore slammed the ball off the floor as the Purple Knights huddled with the late, legendary Barkin. Meanwhile, Rocket fans nearby overflowed onto the arena floor in anticipation.

Today, Dan Wohlfert, still a Beloit resident, can recall the circumstances exactly. After all, he was the person who in-bounded the ball to the six-foot-one Weaver. "I was saying again and again, 'We cannot lose,'" Wohlfert said via phone. "And Coach Barkin kept our heads in the game and was positive about the whole thing. Lamont and I were both lefties, so when they handed me the ball, I ran to my left. Neenah put a real big guy in to guard me, but he got there a little late so I got a jump on him. Lamont was cutting left and I hit him with the pass and he let it go. After Lamont made that shot, I thought Neenah would be deflated, but they had a good coach and didn't get down."

Ron Einerson's Rockets got off a shot at the end, but it didn't come close, and the Knights couldn't believe what they had just accomplished.

"We actually got the gold," Brown said in the victorious locker room. "At this moment I can't conceive what this really means to me."

"It's unbelievable," Loft said. "I thought I was dreaming. It's the greatest feeling in the world to be champs."

What about the man of the hour? "I had faith in the Knights and we socked it to 'em," Weaver said. "I was praying all the way, and we finally did our thing."

Perhaps reserve Mike Masterson summed it up best when he said, "How did 'Mont make that shot?" Nobody knows, but it helped Beloit improve to 42–17 in 18 state tourney appearances after a seesaw affair.

Neenah led 22–14 after the first quarter and 35–29 at the half. Loft then finished a three-point play to put Beloit up 41–40 in the third quarter. The Knights grabbed a 60–54 lead with 4:37 remaining, but Neenah registered seven straight points for a 61–60 advantage.

Brown scored 26 points and Weaver finished with 25. Brown set a mark by making 75 percent of his field goals (27 of 36) and added 28 of 33 free throws (.848) in the tourney. Kilgore and Wohlfert chipped in 11 and 10, respectively, for Beloit. Neenah's Tom Kopitzke scored a game-high 27 points. He made 10 field goals and seven of eight free throws, while Tom Koepke finished with 20 points and Hawley added 14.

There weren't nearly as many hair-raising moments along the way for Beloit, which defeated the Old Abes of Eau Claire, 73–65, in the tourney opener. Brown led the Big Eight champions with 26 points, drilling 11 of 12 field goals and four of five free throws. Loft canned six of seven shots from the floor, chipping in 14 points, as Beloit finished with four players in double figures. The Knights led the contest by 23 points midway through the final quarter. Beloit held the Old Abes to 33 percent shooting (25 of 75), while torching the nets at almost 66 percent (29 of 44), including 17 of 24 in the first half.

BUCKS GET THE BIG O

Not many basketball fans remember who Flynn Robinson and Charlie Paulk were. But on April 21, 1970, they were dealt to Cincinnati.

Not big news, you say? In exchange, the Milwaukee Bucks received Oscar Robertson, an all-star in each of his 10 seasons with the Royals with plenty left at age 31. Robertson was the NBA's first "big" point guard at 6-5, and he averaged 19.4 points, 5.7 rebounds, and 8.2 assists during his first season in Milwaukee, helping the young franchise to its first and only league championship. The Bucks won 66 games and advanced to the NBA Finals against Baltimore. For only the second time in NBA history, the Finals ended in a 4–0 sweep, and the Big O finally had the ring that had eluded him in Cincinnati. Robertson averaged 18.3 points in Milwaukee's 12–2 postseason run.

Robertson played three more seasons with the Bucks, who never won fewer than 59 games. In 1973–74, the last of his 14 campaigns, he helped Milwaukee reach the Finals. However, Boston won the memorable seven-game series.

"The only record we're interested in is winning," Barkin said after his team's first victory in the 54th annual event. "We had a defeat last March that is still burning." He was referring to the championship loss to Manitowoc in 1968, but in order to take that next step the Knights had to dispose of Kimberly, which it knocked out of the semis en route to that title appearance.

Beloit did its part with a big second half to pull away for a 70–56 verdict. The Knights trailed 13–8 after the first quarter and 25–20 at halftime. But Brown and his mates bounced back. Held to six points in the first half, he scored 12 in the third quarter on his way to a game-high 30. He nailed 8 of 10 shots and 14 of 17 from the line. "He was fantastic under there," Barkin said of Brown, whose three-point play gave Beloit a 43–42 lead early in the final quarter. "But you got to give credit to those feeders, too."

Weaver contributed 20 points on 8 of 16 from the floor and 4 of 4 free throws as Beloit outscored Kimberly by a 30–14 margin in the fourth period.

Neenah advanced by tripping Glendale Nicolet, 81–78, after blowing most of a 17-point advantage as the Rockets were outscored 33–19 in the fourth quarter. Neenah was making its fourth trip to the finals (but the first since 1939), and Beloit was making its eighth. "These kids have been looking forward to this since last March," Barkin said. "You have to give these kids credit."

They deserved it after their performance in what became only the second overtime final to that point. Beloit made 30 of 59 field goals and 20 of 27 free throws, while Neenah finished 30 of 62 and 19 of 24, respectively, after holding several nine-point leads in the first half. Beloit also won the rebounding battle, 41–32, in bouncing back to claim its first crown since 1947 while becoming the state's 12th unbeaten champion.

As for Einerson, the Rockets' first-year coach, he couldn't have asked for much more from his team. "When the kids gave what they gave, I can't say I was disappointed."

An estimated 3,000 vehicles made up the procession back home, where "Knights Are No. 1" signs and 15,000 supporters welcomed the team. *The Beloit Daily News* described what it was like: "Families came out of their homes, some in pajamas, pin curlers and housecoats. Sparklers and flares were lighted. The entire roadside was a mass of leaping, laughing, cheering humanity."

And the memories still flow today, says Brown, who's lived in the Peach State since September 1969 after becoming a scholarship player at Georgia Tech. "One thing I remember was the crowd, which was obviously large and probably a sellout for that place," Brown said in a phone interview. "When Neenah came down and scored with a few seconds left, all of the media and cameras focused on them. But when Lamont made that shot, it was like stone-cold silence, everybody with their mouths hanging open, for what seemed like forever.

"It was a hard-fought game," Brown added. "I just came away thinking it was so unbelievable. But I remember thinking all along that we weren't going to lose. Sometimes during the season we needed a little luck, like on the road against Racine Horlick, but we pulled them out. It was the state tournament, so I knew we had to figure out a way to win. And the other players felt the same way. We had the benefit of having been there the year before, so we weren't going to fall apart or panic. As slim as our chances were at that point, we gave ourselves that chance and capitalized on it."

Wohlfert said that game and Weaver's heroics are burned in his mind. "It's funny how long that shot has lived on," Wohlfert said.

Nobody knows that better than Weaver, a Beloit resident who has worked at the University of Wisconsin–Whitewater for 23 years. "I can still see that shot going through the air after almost 35 years," Weaver said. "I could tell it was headed in the right direction, but to bank it in like that I never could have imagined."

He, the school, and the city are glad it happened the way it did and not the way the team practiced. "We worked on that type of play in practice, and the idea was to lob it up as close as possible so that Bruce could try and tap it in," Weaver said. "I knew I had the right angle and the timing was right, but I threw it too far." Just far enough.

And amazingly, Weaver's accomplished the feat since then. "I did it when I went down to Kansas State on a recruiting trip," he recalled. "I was walking through and they asked if I was the guy from Wisconsin and how I had done it, so I twirled and made the shot again. Then I made it a couple more times for a TV station while in Madison for an anniversary of the game. I had to ice my arm because I must have taken 50 or 60 shots."

But it only took one attempt to make history. "It's interesting because most people don't remember that the free throws are what won the game," Weaver said. "The main thing was Coach calming us down in the huddle after I made the shot. He got us ready to play the overtimes. It was a great game." ★

Bucks Crowned NBA Champs

"This is the first champagne I've ever had, and it tastes pretty sweet." Veteran guard Oscar Robertson spoke those words Friday night, April 30, 1971. Like he did throughout most of his career, the future National Basketball Association Hall of Famer let his play do most of the talking.

However, he had just helped Milwaukee claim its first and only NBA championship, so the words meant more and the celebration was more deserved than most for an all-star performer who had toiled in relative obscurity with the Cincinnati Royals for 10 years before being traded to the Bucks in the preseason. This series showed the country what kind of player Robertson was and proved that he was the missing piece for an up-and-coming franchise.

Milwaukee whipped the Baltimore Bullets with a 118–106 victory in front of 11,842 fans, making it only the second sweep (4–0) in NBA Finals history; the Celtics were the first to accomplish the feat when they downed the Minneapolis Lakers in 1959.

Robertson finished a strong postseason run with 30 points while making 11 of 15 shots from the floor and drilling eight of nine from the line. He also dished out nine assists in his 38 minutes of work.

Lew Alcindor was named the series Most Valuable Player after adding 27 points. But Robertson, who had vetoed a trade to Baltimore before the campaign started and the deal was worked out with Milwaukee, ignited the Bucks' fourth straight comfortable triumph. He scored 21 points as Larry Costello's Bucks cruised to a 60–47 halftime cushion that was never seriously threatened.

Gene Shue's Bullets shaved the deficit to seven early in the third quarter, but Milwaukee responded after Costello called a timeout. The visitors ripped off the next 10 points as shooting guard Jon McGlocklin made two baskets and Robertson hit the final one as the Bucks regained control. Small forward Bob Dandridge chipped in 21 points and 12 rebounds in a contest that saw Baltimore break the 100-point barrier for the first time in the Finals after it had downed the Philadelphia 76ers and New York Knicks in rugged seven-game series.

Shue said his banged up and somewhat depleted squad—Baltimore guard Earl "the Pearl" Monroe was hampered from a groin injury he sustained in Game Three—probably wouldn't have been able to overcome a superior Milwaukee roster. "The Bucks had a great record, they had a great series and they beat us decisively," Shue said. "They couldn't be more deserving."

BUCKS NOT THE FIRST CHAMP

On February 10, 1913, the Fond du Lac Company E National Guard basketball team defeated the touring New York Nationals, 28–23, for the second time in three days to claim what the *New York Times* labeled the professional championship of the United States. Fond du Lac also claimed that honor the next year after compiling a 39–0 record and winning a series from the Oswego Indians of New York.

Twenty-seven years later, the Oshkosh All-Stars earned their first National Basketball League championship on March 12, 1941, whipping the Sheboygan Redskins, 54–36, to sweep the best-of-five playoff series. The All-Stars repeated that feat the following year. The NBL was the predecessor of today's National Basketball Association and featured teams such as the Fort Wayne Pistons and Minnesota Lakers, who eventually moved their operations to Detroit and Los Angeles, respectively.

Milwaukee shot .561 from the field in Game Four while limiting the Bullets to .411. Alcindor made 10 of his 16 field goal attempts and seven of 11 free throws, while the fifth starter, forward Greg Smith, added 14 points and McGlocklin contributed 12. Center Wes Unseld topped Baltimore with 23 rebounds and added 11 points, while guard Fred Carter tallied 28 points to spearhead the Bullets' attack.

Smith, McGlocklin and reserve center Dick Cunningham were the only players left from Milwaukee's original expansion team roster from two seasons earlier. "This is a long way from a small town in Kentucky [Princeton]," Smith said. "I started out just wanting to make the team. I figured if I could last a year, I'd be happy. This is too much for me to believe it's true."

For the champions, it was their 88th triumph of the season (including exhibition games).

And despite not putting together a crisp game in the series, Milwaukee still won three of the four contests by double-digit margins. "We didn't have a real good game and we still won four straight," said McGlocklin, who still covers Bucks games from the broadcast booth. "Oscar was the key for us. He comes to play, he runs the team. He's it. People expected it of us and we expected it of ourselves, so we reserved our emotions for the championship."

The Knicks were expected to be Milwaukee's competition and had owned the regular-season advantage 4–1. But Dandridge, who got involved in a punching match with Baltimore forward Jack Marin (both received technical fouls but neither was ejected), said that was old news as he rejoiced in the Milwaukee locker room afterward. "It doesn't make any difference who we beat," Dandridge said. "All that matters is that we won."

Bucks reserve Bob Boozer agreed wholeheartedly. "This is the ultimate," Boozer said. "I've had many a thrill in basketball, playing in the Olympics, making all-American, but this has to be the greatest. I broke in with Oscar at Cincinnati and I've seen him at his greatest. He really let it all out tonight."

Robertson deflected the praise, but his play and leadership couldn't be denied.

"I was just glad I was able to be there at the right time," Robertson said. "If I hadn't, somebody else would have been."

Maybe, maybe not. Regardless, Milwaukee had finished the regular season with a 66–16 record, while the Bullets logged a 42–40 mark, including four defeats in five outings against the Bucks that featured a 52-point setback. However, Baltimore, which lost key substitute Eddie Miles to an Achilles injury, advanced to the Finals, disposing of the defending champion Knicks after trailing the series 2–0.

The Bucks posted a league record shooting percentage of .509 and then handled the San Francisco Warriors and Los Angeles Lakers in five games apiece to win the West, which proved to be warm-ups for thousands of Bucks fans who greeted the team upon its return to Milwaukee that Saturday afternoon.

Despite its share of miscues, Milwaukee controlled the action from the get-go with a balanced offensive arsenal. In Game One, the Bucks, who had finished 24 games better than the Bullets during the regular season, took a 1–0 advantage with a 98–88 win at the Milwaukee Arena.

Alcindor missed most of the first half with foul trouble before 10,746 fans, but the Bucks still led 50–42 at the break. The Bucks' offensive centerpiece had scored 8 points and grabbed one rebound in nine minutes of action. But he dominated in the second half with 23 points and 16 rebounds, knocking down 10 of 13 shots. Robertson added 22 points and Dandridge 15, while Monroe led the Bullets with 26.

Game Two was the team's most dominating performance of the series, at least on the scoreboard. The Bucks pulled away from a 26–all tie after the first quarter to win 102–83 in Baltimore behind a 30–16 third quarter. Alcindor led the way with 27 points, but he had plenty of help as usual. Robertson chipped in 22 points and 10 assists, Dandridge scored 16 points, and McGlocklin connected on seven of eight field goals for 14 points. Marin topped the Bullets with 22 points as Baltimore made only 36 of 97 shots (.371) to Milwaukee's 44 of 87 (.506). Milwaukee drilled 14 of 16 free throws, while Baltimore finished 11-of-17.

The Bucks prevailed 107–99 in Game Three at home as Dandridge accounted for 29 points. Milwaukee led by 16 twice, including 68–52, only to let Baltimore climb to within 70-68. Backup guard Lucius Allen scored four as the Bucks ran off six consecutive points en route to the verdict. Alcindor scored 23 points and hauled down 21 boards in his battle against Unseld, whose totals were 20 and 23, respectively. All-star Gus Johnson missed his second game for Baltimore because of bad knees. Robertson added 20 points and Smith 15 as the Bucks shot 48 percent from the field while again putting the clamps on Baltimore (.387). ★

BUCKS SNAP L.A.'S RECORD RUN

Kareem Abdul-Jabbar scored 39 points to lead five players in double figures as the defending NBA champion Milwaukee Bucks stomped Los Angeles on January 9, 1972.

The hosts' 120-104 triumph at the Milwaukee Arena snapped the Lakers' league record 33-game winning streak. Almost 11,000 fans watched as Jerry West led six L.A. players in double digits with 20 points, but it wasn't enough.

The string had broken Milwaukee's previous NBA mark of 20 consecutive victories, which the Bucks set the year before en route to their first and only title.

Los Angeles' achievement remains the longest in the four major professional sports leagues, bettering the Major League standard of 26 wins in a row that the New York Giants established in 1916.

McGuire-Led Marquette Earns NCAA Title

Al McGuire had led his Marquette Warriors to a top-15 ranking in the national polls every season from 1969–77, the only school besides UCLA to have done so. However, the indomitable McGuire almost missed what proved to be the biggest game of his 13-year coaching career in Milwaukee: the 1977 NCAA Championship.

McGuire went for a ride on his beloved motorcycle before the contest at The Omni in Atlanta and had to haggle with security people because he didn't have any identification that proved who he was. He finally got in when longtime assistant Hank Raymonds vouched for him.

Once the game began, there was no mistaking who the real Al McGuire was. McGuire's "back-alley scrappers" played the game of their lives in claiming a 67–59 win on a rainy night in Georgia, an evening that later saw *Rocky* win the Academy Award for Best Picture.

North Carolina played without center Tom LaGarde, small forward Walter Davis participated with a broken finger, and star guard Phil Ford was affected by a bad elbow that limited his outside shooting. However, what the inspired Warriors accomplished that night couldn't be overlooked.

Mainly because senior forward Bo Ellis picked up two quick fouls early, Marquette threw several varieties of zones at the Tar Heels. Later in the first half it utilized its own version of Carolina's Four Corners or stall tactics on offense, which kept the ball in guard Butch Lee's hands in one-on-one situations as often as possible.

Behind Lee and Ellis, Marquette assumed control with a 39–27 cushion at the intermission. Michael O'Koren's shooting and pressure defense enabled the Tar Heels to climb back into the contest early in the second half as they pulled to within 41–39, a run that McGuire had warned against at halftime.

North Carolina continued the surge, which had reached 14–2 for a 41–all tie. But Jim Boylan's jumper put Marquette back on top. The Tar Heels responded with two hoops to take their first lead since early in the game.

Tied at 45, Carolina coach Dean Smith instructed his team to go into his famed Four Corners scheme. Two minutes elapsed without a Tar Heel shot. Marquette got the ball back, and Boylan put the Warriors ahead again.

FIVE-OVERTIME THRILLER

When Independence High School's boys basketball team beat Blair–Taylor on December 14, 1995, the game became one for the books. That's because the Indees outlasted the Wildcats by a 102–101 score in a Dairyland Conference showdown that took five overtimes.

Qunit Yap scored 47 points in the game for the winners, 24 in regulation and 23 in the extra sessions. He finished with 18 rebounds and made 19 of 22 tries from the free throw line, including two with six seconds left in the final overtime. A last-second shot by Blair–Taylor's Matt Dale bounced off the rim, giving Independence the victory.

Marquette improved its margin at 51–47. Warriors' center Jerome Whitehead made two free throws with 1:56 left for a 53–49 advantage. Bernard Toone missed two free throws for MU, but Davis connected on two after Toone was called for a technical on the play in which he threw an elbow after O'Koren poked him in the eye.

Boylan made two charity tosses to push the Warriors back up by four, 55–51, with 1:25 remaining. Ellis sandwiched four free throws around Davis's basket for a 59–53 margin, and then Gary Rosenberger's two free throws and Lee's layup put the game away at 63–55 with 26 seconds left. Lee finished with 19 points and was named the tournament's Most Valuable Player. Ellis and Boylan added 14 points each, while Whitehead contributed 11 rebounds.

After the buzzer, McGuire went into the locker room and shed tears alone before returning to the court to participate in the celebration. "Emotionally drained," McGuire said during his postgame press conference. "I'm pleased for the guys. It doesn't seem real. Ya know, you think about something like this, but I've always been an alley fighter. I don't usually get into the silk lace situations. It seems like it is preordained, but I don't like to use the words of the TV announcers, the clichés."

McGuire was definitely his own man, and Marquette fans couldn't have been happier. The revelry in Milwaukee, where it was also raining, saw fans climbing light poles, jumping on vehicles, riding on the top of city buses, and hanging from traffic signals and business shingles. The negative side to the partying cost the city $11,000 in damages.

Delirious and inebriated fans then jammed the concourse at Mitchell Field to greet the team upon its return home at 2:30 a.m. It was the end of a dreamlike weekend, something that seemed destined not to happen several times during the regular season and during March Madness.

The soon-to-be champions were well on their way to becoming McGuire's greatest collection of underachievers. Lloyd Walton and Earl Tatum were gone from a 27–2 squad but they still featured four future pros. MU faced seven nationally ranked foes and won only two of those regular-season tilts. Its 20–7 mark was the worst in 10 years, and a 4–5 record in February didn't look promising, but that didn't matter after the Warriors qualified for the tourney.

Marquette advanced to the championship game with a 51–49 win over Cedric "Cornbread" Maxwell and University of North Carolina-Charlotte on Whitehead's dunk just before the buzzer. Charlotte coach Lee Rose protested, but the basket counted. Whitehead, who finished with 22 points, grabbed a court-length pass from Lee. He went up to dunk it but Maxwell partially blocked it. The ball hit the backboard, bounced off the rim, and dropped through the net.

"In a situation like that, it's hard to concentrate on what's happening," Whitehead said. "It seemed as though Bo [Ellis] and Maxwell had their hands on it. But a lot of things go blank. The ball, it seemed to come over my head. I reached out for it, grabbed it and then I guess I put it in."

"When I made that shot, I hear the buzzer and then look at the clock," Whitehead added. "But the clock still shows the score 49–49. I was so excited about it going in that I don't remember too much of the end. I just wanted to make sure it counted."

McGuire pleaded his case with official Paul Galvan and anyone at the scorer's table who would listen because there had been no signal as to whether the basket counted or not. Finally, Galvan ended the suspense with a "the basket's good" motion, setting off celebrations in The Omni and among thousands of students on Wisconsin Avenue in Milwaukee.

The 49ers had led 47–44 with 1:44 left, but Lee made two baskets to push Marquette ahead 48–47 with 29 seconds remaining. Rosenberger added a free throw for a 49–47 margin with 13 ticks on the clock. Then Maxwell hit a 10-foot runner with four seconds left to set up the final theatrics.

It was a game that shouldn't have been that close, as Marquette raced to a 23–9 advantage only to see Charlotte take off on a 10-point run as it inched to within 25–22 at the half. Charlotte then forged out to a 35–30 lead with 14 minutes left after Ellis was whistled for his fourth foul. But Whitehead led Marquette back on top with a 14–4 spurt.

North Carolina had also pulled out a nail biter, scoring 14 consecutive points and hanging on for an 84–83 victory against the Running Rebels of Nevada-Las Vegas.

The Warriors were forced to rally several times before reaching the Final Four. That included the Midwest Regional at Omaha, Nebraska, where they defeated Cincinnati, 66–51, on March 12 behind Ellis's 17 points and 15 from Whitehead after trailing 31–28 at halftime. Toone came off the bench to score 18 points and led a 13–0 second-half surge.

Then Marquette downed Jack Hartman's Big Eight champion Kansas State Wildcats, 67–66, after rallying from a 10-point, second-half deficit in the semifinal in Oklahoma City. Lee scored a game-high 26 points and tied the game at 58 with 4:30 left. But reserve Jim Dudley's six points and spirited play combined with fellow sophomore Toone's efforts led the Warriors' 17–4 burst.

McGuire had been slapped with a technical, and his tirade in the postgame press conference became known as the St. Patrick's Day speech. "Kansas State should have beaten us," McGuire said. "They played better than we did, they were better prepared. We were fortunate there was not a lot of time left and we were able to come back."

The Warriors then trailed Wake Forest, 35–31, at the intermission but another strong second half gave them an 82–68 triumph. Ellis scored 20, Lee 19, and Toone chipped in 18, all in the second half, including nine during a 14–2 spurt that gave Marquette a 54–45 margin en route to a spot in the Final Four, its second in four years.

It was a magical ending to a sometimes tumultuous season on Lake

Michigan. McGuire had announced in December that it would be his final season, and the Warriors promptly lost back-to-back games against Louisville and Minnesota and were beaten three in a row in February—all five were at home—almost dooming their chances at an NCAA bid. Raymonds was named head man and athletic director January 28, while Rick Majerus was the other co-coach.

Marquette's seven defeats were the most by any team selected for the tournament up to that point, and the Warriors grabbed the final at-large bid for the 32-team field. It didn't matter because they had regrouped and advanced to Atlanta.

Marquette, which limited Tar Heels' star Phil Ford to 6 points, grabbed a 39–27 halftime lead en route to its first and only NCAA crown. But there were tense moments, as Smith's squad roared back to grab a 45–43 lead. O'Koren finished with 14 points and Davis scored 10 of Carolina's final 12 points to finish with a game-high 20. But it wasn't enough to prevent McGuire from registering his 404th coaching victory.

Lee said the team's resolve proved to be the difference when it trailed 45–43 with 13:48 remaining. "No way we were going to die at that point," Lee said. "We've been down too many times to start to panic." Marquette made 14 of 15 free throws to ice the win.

McGuire, who won 78 percent of his games at MU, was colorful as usual afterward. "Basketball is like a game of pick-up sticks," McGuire said. "You hold them, you drop them and you pick them up again. Every game forms a pattern, and then you pick up the pattern. That's why I never stress details before a game. We played a chess game for a while. I was a little emotional, but not a lot."

Smith said that McGuire and the Warriors deserved the accolades. "They prevented us from scoring inside," Smith said. "We gave it all we had, but it wasn't enough. They had a little something more. I thought Marquette played an inspired basketball game." ★

Final Score: Florence 2, Crandon 1

It's not often that someone can brag about scoring two points in a high school basketball game and be the toast of the town at the same time. However, that's the popular and unusual position Nick Baumgart found himself in after the Florence-Crandon game on January 21, 1977. And to top it off, the junior guard was the game's leading scorer.

That's because his Florence Bobcats defeated the Crandon Cardinals, 2–1, in a Northern Lakes Conference boys showdown which is believed to be the lowest-scoring game in U.S. high school history in which both teams scored points.

"I remember it was our next possession after they made the free throw," Baumgart said about his game-deciding basket only two or three minutes into the first quarter. "I was trying to create something, so I drove down the left side of the lane and hit about a five- to seven-footer."

Little did anybody in the Crandon gym know that it would prove to be the last points they'd see.

TOP DOG . . . FOR A WHILE

On December 15, 1949, Nate DeLong of River Falls State Teachers College (now University of Wisconsin–River Falls) registered 33 points in a game against St. John's University of Minnesota.

His outburst, which included 11 field goals and 11 free throws, meant DeLong had become college basketball's all-time leading scorer with 2,207 points. DeLong, a 6-6 center, scored 27 points in the first half to move him past Jim Lacy of Loyola of Baltimore, who had 2,199, as River Falls won the game, 77-54.

DeLong accomplished the milestone in 93 games for a 23.7 average.

To this day, the Crandon coach at the time, Harold Resch, steadfastly says that it wasn't his intention to have the game turn out the way it did. It just unfolded that way. Resch didn't think his Cardinals, 4–2 entering the contest, could keep up with the high-flying Bobcats, the league's top-scoring squad that was leading the standings at 5–1.

"Florence was picked to be the conference champ and had a talented team, while we were rebuilding and had lost two straight games," said Resch, who still lives in Crandon. "I suspected that Florence would play zone to take advantage of their height and experience. I told Ben and Rick Samz, our guards, that we would hold the ball on the top of the key to force them out of their zone if that's how they started the game."

Resch's scouting report was perfect, and the antsy Bobcats decided to force the issue. However, that's when the hosts scored their only point as Ben Samz made the second of two free throws after being fouled on a drive to the basket.

The Cardinals' stalling tactics had pulled Florence out of its zone, which allowed the much-quicker hosts to penetrate, something Bobcats' coach Stan Jesky feared would lead to a Crandon upset. Baumgart, who had transferred from Green Bay Preble, drilled his runner. Crandon resumed its slow-down offense, while Florence was happy to sit back in its 1-3-1 zone defense.

Then another crucial but sometimes forgotten play occurred. Baumgart intercepted a pass and went in for what he and Florence followers thought was a second hoop and 4–1 advantage, a basket that could have changed the complexion of the game entirely. But the official whistled Baumgart for an offensive charging call and waved off the score, leaving the contest at 2–1.

"I thought I was fouled on the play, but they didn't see it that way," said Baumgart, who has been a teacher at Florence for 15 years. "I was thinking that was a critical situation at the time because I think that would have made Crandon quit stalling. But I've been an official for 15 years, so I know how that goes."

The Cardinals proceeded to wind the clock until the final seconds of the first quarter and missed a shot at the buzzer. Florence won the second-quarter tip but failed in its only attempt at padding its cushion. "I figured that if they were not going to defend us, we would have the advantage because we could shoot at the end of the period and could get the lead at halftime," Resch said. But Crandon stayed in its deep-freeze attack, again missing an attempt as the first half ended.

Still, despite taking many more shots from increasingly frustrated Crandon fans than his players were taking at the basket, Resch was confident that his strategy would work if his team remained patient. "At halftime, I tried to convince our team that it was to our advantage to control the tempo," Resch said. "I told them if they would score and start getting a lead, we would have to attempt to score more."

Florence corralled the third-quarter tip, but its next field goal attempt came up short and it waited out the Cardinals' stall tactics and survived a third last-second try.

The same scenario unfolded in the final period as the tension-filled gym slowly got louder.

Resch called three timeouts in the final minute to set up plays and hopefully get Florence to make a mistake. The last one came with about 10 seconds remaining. "We had a wide open shot by Gino Lamond with about eight seconds left, but he missed," Resch recalled. "We got the rebound and took another shot that missed. The ball rolled on the floor and a jump ball resulted. Florence got the tip and time ran out."

Despite so little action, Baumgart said it's funny how time has affected what people remember about the game. "I remember they shot and missed and a scramble for the ball, but I don't remember any kind of jump ball," he said. "But it seems like everybody remembers how things happened a little differently."

"This was unbelievable," Jesky said after the game. "Never in a million years did I expect this. Last year the score was 95–78. That's a paradox for you, huh? Our kids handled themselves real well. We remained patient on defense and tried not to give them any openings.

"A game like this is more nerve-racking than when you're 50 points down," Jesky added. "It's a gamble. You're either going to win or lose on the last shot. Harry called a timeout with about 10 seconds left. We went to a triangle-

and-two defense: man-to-man on the Samz boys and three-man zone on the rest because I knew one of the Samzes would try to take the last shot.

"What should have been a great basketball game turned out to be a battle between two stubborn coaches," Jesky added. "I remember our next game against Goodman. It took us about three seconds to score. We weren't going through that again."

Jesky coached in the Saint Paul, Minnesota, area for nine years before his 14-year stint with the Bobcats. He has been the athletic director in Zeeland, Michigan, which is about 20 miles south of Grand Rapids, ever since. And even today he can't believe what happened that night. "We only played Crandon once that year," Jesky said. "Harry was a good coach and they had a good ball club. They were smaller and quick, and we didn't match up with them very well. We had a pretty good team that was averaging about 80 points per game, and we had Bill Counter, a guard who was averaging 33 points per game coming into that contest.

"It was weird," Jesky added. "You could have cut the tension with a knife because it slowly came down to which team would make the first mistake. I remember the crowd counting down. The kid in the corner couldn't get the ball to one of the Samz brothers, so he fired up a shot with about four seconds left. It skimmed off the rim and went straight down to the floor, where a bunch of kids scrambled for it. They called a jump ball, but there was only a second left."

Jesky said he still feels bad that the game was played the way it was. "It turned out to be a good win, if you're counting wins and losses," Jesky said. "But in hindsight, I wonder if we didn't steal something from the kids because they didn't get to really play. At halftime I told them that we needed to get the tip, go down and score to make it 4–1 and maybe they would start playing ball. But we missed the shot.

"I remember a lot of fans, at least at first because we were ahead, they were yelling at Harry to play ball. I guess you could say he took a lot of verbal abuse. But it was just one of those crazy things that happen. You know how stories change over the years, but I remember that game like it was yesterday."

Jesky shouldn't have been surprised, however, after recalling an incident before the game. "On the way to Crandon I remember telling my assistant [Bob Wolfe] that I was worried about the game," he said. "I thought that it was going to be a struggle. Bob had his own prediction. He said not to worry and that we'd win by 12 or something like that. I looked at Bob and said, 'Hey, I'll be happy if we win 2–1.'"

The contest gained national attention, getting mentioned on Paul Harvey's "The Rest of the Story" radio show, while *Sports Illustrated* was one of many media outlets that contacted Jesky.

In an article marking the 20th anniversary of the game, people still marveled at what they had witnessed. Marv Tollefson of Crystal Falls, Michigan, was one of the officials who worked the game. "Definitely the most unusual game I ever worked in 30 years of officiating," Tollefson said. "I remember going home and telling my wife what the score was and she didn't believe me."

Deward Ison, the remarkably underworked scorekeeper that night, was quoted as saying, "You wouldn't think a game like that would be exciting, but as it went on it got very exciting. The crowd really got into it."

Ben Samz, a senior who tallied the only point for the Cardinals, still lives in Crandon. Although his memories have faded considerably since then, he knows he was part of something unique. "It was a situation where we tried to stall them to bring them out, and they never came out," Samz said. "It wasn't our idea for it to end up 2–1, but it just worked out that way. They knew they couldn't beat us playing man-to-man."

But Samz said he knows the real reason Crandon lost the game: "We couldn't afford a pump, so the ball was flat and we couldn't make anything."

Baumgart also recalled lighter moments during the contest. "I remember hearing people's conversations and stuff, and normally you block all of that stuff out," he said. "They kept yelling, 'Let's play ball.' But once Crandon got into and stayed with that strategy, there was a lot more cheering. Regardless of the score, it was still a one-point game all the way, so it got to be pretty intense, especially at the end of the fourth quarter. Everybody was going crazy, and it got pretty chaotic at the end." ★

University of Wisconsin–Platteville Dominates Division III

Coaches don't like to hear terms such as dynasty bandied about. However, that's exactly what the UW–Platteville men's basketball team was in the period 1989–90 through 1998–99.

Under current Wisconsin Badger coach Bo Ryan, the Pioneers won an amazing 91 percent of their games, compiling a 266–27 record, the best in college hoops at any level, while claiming National Collegiate Athletic Association Division III crowns in 1991, 1995, 1998, and 1999.

The Pioneers lost two games in a row only once while playing in the rugged and talented Wisconsin State University Conference in which league foes handed them 20 of their 27 defeats during their remarkable 10-year dominance. That competition prepared Platteville for the postseason as the team of the decade made nine consecutive NCAA tournament appearances, including five trips to the Final Four, where the Pioneers finished off perfect campaigns in 1995 and 1998. While each of the four NCAA championship banners hanging in Williams Field House was memorable, the last one was perhaps the most gratifying because of what the Pioneers had to overcome.

Platteville lost four seniors from its 30–0 squad, including Ben Hoffmann and Andre Dalton. The Pioneers then overcame the absence of point guard Joel Beard, who committed just eight turnovers in 16 starts before being declared academically ineligible for the second semester. And they survived when Colin Gassner and Dan Wargolet missed significant chunks of time due to injuries.

And then there was the title showdown against Hampden-Sydney, a Virginia foe whose home court was only a hundred miles from the Final Four site, the Salem Civic Center, and one that the Pioneers had knocked out of the '92 and '95 tournaments.

Somehow, on March 20, the Pioneers found a way, pulling out a 76–75 triumph, the first double-overtime championship contest in the event's first 25 years. And they did it in front of a mostly hostile, record crowd of 4,461.

Coach Bo Ryan helps cut down the nets after his UW-Platteville men's basketball team wins its fourth Division III championship in 1999. (Photo courtesy of UW–Platteville)

RETIRED NUMBERS

The Milwaukee Bucks have retired the numbers of seven former players so far: Oscar Robertson (1), Junior Bridgeman (2), Sidney Moncrief (4), Bob Lanier (16), Brian Winters (32), Kareem Abdul-Jabbar (33), and Jon McGlocklin (14). McGlocklin was on the original team and is still with the organization as one of its TV announcers.

Gassner's patented back-door cut and reverse layup with 20 seconds left provided the winning margin and culminated the Pioneers' 30–2 season, although the Tigers (29–3) got off several shots in the waning seconds, including Jeremy Harris's 17-foot attempt that rimmed out at the buzzer. Gassner finished with 12 points and received plenty of help from all-tournament selections Mike Jones and Merrill Brunson, who scored 21 and 20 points, respectively. The latter earned tournament Most Valuable Player honors.

Jones, who also contributed game highs with 16 rebounds and seven assists, drilled his biggest field goal of the game when he nailed an unlikely three-pointer to tie the slugfest at 66 with 18 seconds remaining in the first overtime. "I thought I was open, got a good look and knocked it down," said Jones afterward. He had converted only two from beyond the arc all year, but it was the most important one in a seesaw affair that saw the Pioneers shoot a woeful four-for-21 from three-point range.

Then Platteville connected on five of six shots in the second overtime. Aaron Olson made a jumper, and Brunson scored two baskets within 30 seconds to give the Pioneers a 72–68 lead.

However, the Tigers tallied the next five points. Gassner and Harris then exchanged layups at the 1:19 and 48-second marks to set the stage for the dramatic ending, in a battle that featured 13 ties and no leads of more than seven points. That occurred when Platteville used a 16–3 spurt during a six-minute span to grab a 55–48 cushion with 8:11 left, after trailing 45–39 early in the second half. Brunson accounted for seven points in the run.

Then it was Hampden-Sydney's turn to grab the momentum, as T. J. Grimes and Chris Fox, who combined for 31 points in the game, turned the Tigers' deficit into a 61–59 margin with 1:26 showing in regulation. Platteville tied it at 61 after trailing 37–34 at halftime. "I have to give them all the credit in the world," Ryan said of the Tigers. "That was the best team we have ever beaten in the tournament. I thought both teams played extremely hard and played with a lot of class."

Ryan, who left for the University of Wisconsin–Milwaukee, then UW–Madison, after winning his fourth trophy in 15 seasons at the UW–Platteville helm, said he couldn't have been prouder of his team. "This group has accomplished more during the course of the year as far as getting better, persevering, handling things that have been thrown at them better than any team we've had," Ryan said after the Pioneers qualified for the Final Four. "I just hope we have a week left."

His players proved that they definitely had plenty left in their tanks, whipping William Paterson of New Jersey, 77–51, in the semifinals before their climactic victory in the championship tilt. Wargolet, a senior small forward, ignited the Pioneers that night. The Milwaukee Pius graduate scored Platteville's first 11 points, including three three-pointers, en route to 17 points.

Although he only chipped in four points against Hampden-Sydney, it was sweet nonetheless because he had injured the medial collateral ligament in his left knee during the parents' night game to end the regular season. "Our center, Mike Jones, had probably the game of his life, so we kept feeding it into him," Wargolet said via phone from his home in Greenfield, where the engineering major works for an electrical contracting company. "And then he stepped out and hit that big three-pointer. Merrill had a great game, and so did Blake Knutson (eight points). Colin, who probably would have started for any other team in the conference, came off the bench to make some baskets and then hit the game-winner, which says a lot for him. I only made one bucket, but it was great to play in that game.

STATEWIDE SUCCESS

Whether it's been called the Wisconsin State University Conference or the Wisconsin Intercollegiate Athletic Conference, its members have enjoyed as much or more success in NCAA Division III as any collegiate league in the nation.

Eight of the nine universities have earned national championships in at least one sport. Only once (1999–2000) since the 1982–83 campaign has the conference been shut out of a trophy.

UW–Platteville's men's basketball team won four titles in the 1990s, but that program isn't alone. University of Wisconsin–La Crosse has claimed seven women's gymnastics titles, nine men's indoor track championships, and seven men's outdoor track crowns. University of Wisconsin–Oshkosh has captured five women's outdoor track trophies and four each in men's and women's cross country. And University of Wisconsin–Stevens Point has won top honors in men's ice hockey four times.

"In all of the games we played against Division III schools, they were by far the best-coached team," Wargolet added. "They resembled a Bo Ryan team in how they played and executed, and that's why it was such a great game and so closely contested. At Platteville we weren't cocky, but we had an extreme confidence about us. We won games because we knew we could, and that's why we came out with a 'W' in almost every close game."

Indeed they did, and Wargolet said it was a special send-off for Ryan. "There was talk of Bo going somewhere else almost every year, and it sounded like a lock he'd go to the University of Denver after my junior year," Wargolet recalled. "Right before the '99 tourney there was an inkling that he was headed to UW–Milwaukee. With what he did there and now at Wisconsin, I can say that I played for him. He knows how to bring each kid's talents out, and that last championship team had a bunch of guys who liked playing together. And we hung out together off the court, playing Nintendo, having a couple of drinks at a bar or doing homework."

And in the 1990s, the Pioneers finished at the top of the dean's list in more ways than one. ★

Shullsburg Girls Snap Their Losing Streak

Six isn't such a big number, but when you're talking about years, well that's another story.

The Shullsburg High School girls basketball team ended a 102-game losing streak in February 1992. From left: seated, Angela Mulcahy and Theresa Woodworth; kneeling, Stacie Miller, Amy Doyle and Janelle Pahnke; standing, manager Adam MacNaughton, Gina Scott, Julie Teasdale, assistant coach John Heinberg, Jodi McGlynn, head coach Mark Lierman, Robin Krueger, Nikki Woodworth, and manager Michelle Ensch.

During that stretch, one in which embarrassing losses included a 104–18 shellacking at the hands of West Grant and a 75–15 setback to Bloomington, the Shullsburg girls basketball team and its fans endured 102 consecutive defeats. It is believed to be the longest drought in state high school history, surpassing the 86-game skid the Stockbridge boys team endured during the 1970s. Not since January 30, 1986, had these Miners tasted victory, a 57–47 decision against Elizabeth, Illinois.

WHAT A COMEBACK

On February 8, 2002, River Valley High School in Spring Green earned an 89–81 overtime victory at Dodgeville in boys basketball, rallying from 25 points down early in the fourth quarter. In this Southwest Wisconsin Conference contest, coach Jeff Johnson's Blackhawks outscored Chuck Tank's Dodgers 35–12 in the fourth quarter, drilling seven three-point baskets, to force a tie at 75–all to end regulation. River Valley then outscored the Dodgers 14–6 in the extra session. River Valley's 10 baskets from beyond the arc were one shy of the team record.

It was a highlight among highlights for the Blackhawks, who fashioned their first winning varsity season since 1979–80. Their 16–7 mark included a 9–3 league effort.

So when the 85-year-old gymnasium in this town of about 1,400 residents shook southwestern Lafayette County on February 13, 1992, no one could be upset. Tears of joy, relief, redemption, and vindication flowed all at once.

Shullsburg's girls had won a basketball game. The Miners used an 18–7 margin in the fourth quarter en route to a 46–33 victory over Prairie du Chien Martin Luther Prep. And needless to say, what erupted immediately after the buzzer was something special in this school five miles north of the Illinois border. "It was pandemonium," first-year coach Mark Lierman said after the game. "I stood up and bawled my eyes out. I was so happy for them." Most of his players were seventh-graders when the program had last won a contest. Senior Jodi McGlynn, who tied Gina Scott with team-high honors of 14 points, said nothing could equal the excitement of that moment and that accomplishment.

"It was the best feeling in the world," McGlynn said. "I could compare it to [winning] a state championship for us. It was a great feeling to leave the streak in the past. We had three games left and I really wanted to win one before I left. We really had the feeling that tonight was going to be the night. I didn't have the feeling [of victory] until there was about 30 seconds left. I tried not to look at the clock. That last quarter seemed like it lasted forever." That was nothing compared to what she had already been through for four years.

Senior forward Julie Teasdale couldn't believe what she had just been a part of.

"Everyone was just screaming at the top of their lungs," Teasdale said. "We practically got smothered."

Luther Prep entered the showdown with a 2–11 conference record, so the crowd, estimated between 250 and 300, knew the opportunity for something positive to happen was there. However, like the previous 102 outings, nothing came easy for the Miners. Shullsburg had lost 18 games already that season, including all 14 in the Blackhawk Conference.

Guard Amy Doyle, who finished with 10 points, stole the ball and raced in for a layup, giving the hosts a 28–26 advantage after three quarters. It catapulted Shullsburg in the right direction as the hosts dominated the final period.

Lierman, a 1981 graduate of Durand High School and a UW–La Crosse alumnus, took over the Miners that season after helping Shullsburg's boys capture the WIAA Division 4 state title in 1990–91. "I wanted to help them because they had stuck with it for so long, and that gave me something to work with," he said.

The perennial cellar-dwellers had painfully put up with jeers during games and while out in public. "They were getting beat by 50 to 60 points and it was a big joke to some boys," Lierman said. "The girls just sat there and took it. They had given up on themselves winning a game, but they would not quit the team. Man, that'd be hard to do."

Shullsburg had finished 3–17 under Vickie Dahl in 1985–86. With only one senior, the school dropped the varsity program the next winter, only to bring it back in 1987–88. The Miners went 0–18 under Marsha Kremer and 0–61 the next three seasons.

The only thing Lierman could do was stress the basics, drilling his players on conditioning and fundamentals. "I dream about it," Lierman said as the losing skid reached 90 games. "That will be the feeling of a lifetime. I just want to be able to look into their faces when they get that 'W.'" He finally got that opportunity on a Thursday night in February 1992.

"The streak has been a burden, no doubt, and it wasn't a lot of fun," Lierman said afterward. "But we've been saying all along that these girls are winners. We don't have any superstars, but if you play as a team, you can win."

Lierman and Shullsburg proved that and then some, qualifying for the state tournament four years later, finishing a 24–3 season with a second-place trophy at the UW Field House. For the Miners, it was their final season in their old gym called the Pit, and then they reached the ultimate site, the Barn.

Lierman had this to say after securing a trip to Madison: "When I came into the girls program, nobody wanted to work with them. They needed someone who cared. The kids have put their hearts into this whole thing. We're going to ride this out as far as we can."

They had finished 7–14 in 1992–93, 13–8 in 1993–94, and then 19–4 in getting to the regional finals of the 1994–95 season, where they suffered a 48–43 loss to eventual state champion Barneveld. But Shullsburg defeated Pecatonica, 62–45, which won state crowns in 1993 and 1994, and Randolph, 59–50, to advance to state. Senior Heidi Corley was an eighth-grader when Shullsburg ended its string of futility and was the leading scorer as the team beat Niagara, 50–42, before losing the championship game to Augusta, 57–49.

Lierman couldn't have been more proud of any squad, except, of course, the one that stopped six years of defeat. "I'm not the greatest coach, but I think I'm a good motivator," Lierman said via phone in 2003. "When I came in I stressed the basics, the fundamentals. I wanted to instill in them the idea that if they worked hard and stayed together that they'd see results." Lierman added that "I had seven seniors on my first team, so they had endured a lot, and that's part of the reason they stuck with it. They were tired of losing, but they were very resilient because they'd been through hell the previous five or six years."

McGlynn, a UW–Whitewater graduate, suffered through most of those setbacks and almost quit during her junior campaign. "My body started to give out before my stubborn attitude did," she said. "Between the ligament in my knee, to the sprained ankles, shin splints and groin pulls, after three years of injuries I was tired and hurt by my junior year. After I was laid up for several weeks on Christmas break of my junior year, I sincerely thought about hanging up my basketball shoes, but my mom changed my mind.

"I guess that is what parents are for, to make sense of the big picture," McGlynn added. "She never doubted anything I did, and I know I can attest for all of the players and say that our parents supported and believed in us even when we didn't."

So, McGlynn and her teammates trudged along, not wanting or being able to quit. And that set the stage for finally stopping the losing streak, something McGlynn said she sensed before and during the uplifting victory. "I remember that entire week as being nerve-racking," she said. "The media had caught wind of the streak, and there had been reporters at the school, showing up at practice and trying to get the next big story. I had done interviews, and I was beginning to feel the burden of the situation. Here I was, the captain of the team who had managed to play her four years of high school on the varsity and never managed to have any success, at least not measured in wins and losses. I refused to believe that I would graduate with a zero under the win bracket.

"I think for the first time all of us sat in the locker room before the game with an arrogance that I had never seen with any of the girls I had played with the past four years," McGlynn recalled. "It was a great feeling, and it poured onto the floor. We played a rather mediocre game as far as scoring, stats, etc. But we made the important, smart plays, the ones that made the difference."

McGlynn said the losing string was a bit embarrassing, but she added that it was actually worth going through. "There are a lot of teams and players that have fond memories, but there are only a few great ones that get to experience what we did that night and the next few days," McGlynn said. "Even if for a short period, we had the admiration and support of an entire community. It doesn't get much better than that."

So, if there is a moral to this story, it would have to include stick-to-itiveness and survival. "When we won that first game to break the losing streak, it was like we had won the state championship," Lierman said. "It was such a relief for the kids. If there's one video I have that I like to play the most, it's of that game because the spirit and emotion of finally winning was so genuine. I remember that fans were calling their families or friends at halftime because the crowd actually got bigger as the game went along.

"Then after we went to the state championship, which played up well in the media, us being a Cinderella story and everything about the itty-bitty school and everything. We had every reason to give up at one point, but our kids wanted so badly to be successful." ★

Anthony Pieper Breaks State Scoring Record

Anthony is his given name, but to most people who knew or admired him around the small logging and tourism haven of Wausaukee, he was called Andy.

Kids hounded Number 3 after games for autographs and pretended to be him during pickup games across the town of about 650 in Marinette County. During the early 1990s, Anthony Pieper was not only a household name in his school of 200 students and around the northeastern corner of the state, but throughout Wisconsin.

Then, at about 3:25 p.m. Saturday, January 16, 1993, the six-foot-three-inch guard became the most prolific scorer in the history of Wisconsin high school basketball. Pieper's three-pointer from the right wing swished through the net at the 7:05 mark of the second quarter, giving him 2,749 points, two more than Mickey Crowe had finished with 18 years earlier.

Teammates mauled him as the game against conference foe Suring was halted for several minutes. His coach and father, Gene, congratulated him and fans erupted inside the small gymnasium where Pieper had lived for hours on end, fine-tuning his game for several years to make his big dreams come true.

The senior finished the afternoon with a game-high 33 points, seven steals, four rebounds, and five assists in the Rangers' 74–38 triumph that kept

Anthony Pieper skies in for a dunk as a sophomore at Wausaukee High School in 1991, when he wasn't quite halfway to becoming the state's all-time leading scorer. (Photo courtesy of the Pieper family)

them tied with Crivitz at 6–0 atop the Marinette and Oconto Conference race.

Although it was a typical workmanlike performance for Pieper, the electric atmosphere and media buzz surrounding that game, that shot, that moment, separated it from any other during his sterling prep career.

Pieper got an early indication of what was in store for him. "What I remember most about that day had nothing to do with the game," Pieper said from his Madison office, where he works as a sales representative for Pitney Bowes. "I woke up around 9 or 10 that morning, and I remember looking out the window. We lived right across the street from the gym, and there was a line of people all the way up to our house and curled around down the street. They were already waiting to get in for the game. I have to admit that I got a little chill at that moment and knew that it was going to be an interesting day."

It only got more exciting and stressful as tip-off approached. "We had such a small court, and it seemed even smaller because of all of the media and the people standing around the sides," Pieper recalled. "You couldn't even stand out of bounds. It was a hell of an atmosphere, and it was a fun game to play in."

LAST OVER FIRST

One game away from a merciful end to the 1978–79 season, Bill Cofield's Badger men's basketball team was near the bottom of the Big Ten pack (they would finish tied for eighth place). So, few expected much from their season finale against fourth-ranked Michigan State.

However, Wisconsin ended its 12–15 campaign with an 83–81 victory over the Magic Johnson-led Spartans when guard Wes Matthews sank a 55-foot shot at the buzzer in the UW Field House. It was Michigan State's final setback of the season as it went on to win the NCAA championship.

While he wouldn't trade the record for anything, Pieper said the constant talk about it as he piled up points and neared the mark only added to the distractions and took away from his and the team's goal of returning to the state tournament. "It was nice to get it over with because then I could just get back to playing basketball," Pieper said. "My main goal was to win the state championship, so even though it was a nice career capper and everything, that was my last go-round and we wanted to get to Madison and win it all. We got there when I was a sophomore and laid an egg.

"I remember pushing and pushing so hard to get it over with that I couldn't do anything right for a while," Pieper added. "After making the record-breaking basket, I threw my arms up in the air as if to say it was finally over. I got a kick out of it, but I wanted to be humble about it. It was something to be very proud of, but not just for me, for my teammates. You can't do something like that without a lot of help. A lot of guys sacrificed a lot for me, and that's not easy for people to do. We had a talented team and great athletes, so I appreciated what they did for me."

Pieper finished his four-year varsity career with 3,391 points in 1989–93 and set the state's single-season scoring record with 1,063 points his senior year before playing at Marquette from 1994 to 1997.

No two people could be more proud than Pieper's parents, Gene and Sue, who have since moved to Florida. "That gym, which has been replaced, held about 600, so there were people standing all over the place," said Gene, who coached at Wausaukee for 27 years beginning in 1975–76. "It got lots of media attention. We even had a closed-circuit TV hooked up in the cafeteria for 20 or 30 people who couldn't get in to see the game."

As for the action itself, Coach Pieper said it wasn't much unlike many of the Rangers' games until the shot, of course. "Suring tried to stall, not because they didn't want Anthony to get the record," he said. "They knew he'd get it. But it was their only chance to beat us. We played a man-to-man, up-tempo style and liked to run. After the first quarter their delay game fell apart. After the game there was a media frenzy. We actually had set up a sort of interview area in our band room. I loved the whole situation because Anthony and our kids deserved the attention."

However, Anthony struggled at times in his role as superstar, especially early in his high school days when he didn't always handle the reaction from opposing coaches and fans, who thought he was cocky and came off as a showboater. He had to learn how to control his talents, and he matured during his last two years.

"The biggest problem I had with Anthony was when to take him out of games," Gene said. "We played good defense and had some pretty awesome teams, so many of our games were over by halftime. You want to be fair to the other kids and to the other teams, and especially because he's your son. But I have to be honest. He could have scored a lot more points. Frankly, he was often a man among boys and lots of times could turn it on and score at will. Many times I kept him in or put him back in and he refused to shoot. So it was a tough situation for everybody."

But nobody who knew Anthony begrudged him the record or the fame that came along with it because they saw how much time and effort he put into reaching that pinnacle. "I told him that I'd have been proud of him whether that was his 1,000th point or his 100th point," Gene was quoted after the contest. "But I guess when it's the history of Wisconsin, that's pretty awesome."

That it was. The basket shattered Crowe's mark, attained while he played for small JFK Prep in Saint Nazianz in Manitowoc County. Crowe's late father, Marty, was a Wisconsin Basketball Coaches Association Hall of Famer.

Despite personal problems that dogged him after his playing career, Crowe sent Pieper a letter the week leading up to the Suring game, telling him to "set his goals high, keep clean and don't let things get to you." "He said you can never set your goals too high," Pieper said after the game. "I'm going to take that to heart and do the best I can and get the farthest I can get."

Pieper had already arrived, and his high school statistics proved it in staggering fashion. He was selected first-team Associated Press all-state as a senior, when the WBCA named him Mr. Basketball. He later led Wausaukee to the Division 4 state title with a 69–57 triumph against future University of Wisconsin recruit Sam Okey and Cassville. He scored 22 points in the second half as Wausaukee pulled away from a 30–all deadlock at the intermission.

Pieper averaged more than 39 points per game his final season, adding eight rebounds and six assists to the high-powered Rangers' attack. He broke his one-year single-season record of 1,032 points to go out with a bang. He reached the 30-point plateau 66 times in his four-year career, including 10 games of 50 or more. He made 59.1 percent of his two-pointers, 34.7 percent of his three-pointers, and 78.7 percent of his free throws as a senior.

He tallied a high school career-high 59 in a regional championship victory over Gillett and added 42 points in each of the two state tourney games at the Field House. He was the *Green Bay Press-Gazette's* player of the year three times, and Wausaukee won three conference championships and compiled an 84–19 mark during Pieper's four years.

Pieper said the record would have been a pipe dream had it not been for his family and teammates, especially older brother Phil, who played at UW–Oshkosh for three years.

"My brother beat the hell out of me for about seven years," he said. "We started playing one-on-one when I was very young. We'd play games up to 10 [baskets], the best out of seven games. He'd whip me 10–0 every time. I don't think I scored on him until I got into eighth grade. Even when I'd get around him or make a good move, he'd tackle me. That taught me not to give up, how to be tough, that nothing would be easy."

"I was always taller and bigger for my age, but against him I was nothing," Anthony added. "That taught me that if I wanted to be better I had to play against bigger and better competition, to make it challenging or it wasn't worth it."

His sister, Anne, was a four-year starter at UW–Milwaukee, and his mother, who coached girls programs at Wausaukee and Crivitz, was his personal rebounding machine many times during his shooting marathons. "That's why all of that time I put in at the gym was quality time. It involved hard, intense workouts, stuff that was beneficial to me."

And it culminated with his special game that January afternoon. Or did it? *Milwaukee Journal* research done weeks after Pieper surpassed the supposed state mark discovered a 23-point error in Crowe's point total, meaning that Pieper had reached the summit a game earlier against Lena. "I didn't know anything about that," said Pieper, who also received all-state honorable mention in football as a defensive back his senior season.

It didn't and doesn't matter. The January 16 contest is considered the anniversary and the game that everyone will remember as the one in which their local hero made history.

He took his crew cut and goatee to Marquette, where he had signed a letter of intent during the early signing period in November of his senior season. He was the first player off the bench during his freshman season in which Marquette advanced to the NCAA's Sweet 16. As a sophomore, he scored a game- and career-high 31 points as the Golden Eagles defeated Penn State, 87–79, in March 1995 to advance to the National Invitation Tournament finals, where they lost to Virginia Tech. He finished his Marquette tenure with a 10.1 scoring average and 1,234 points, which ranked him 21st on the school's all-time charts.

Pieper then played for 4 1/2 years professionally, including overseas stops in Slovakia, Ireland, and Austria sandwiched around a stint in the IBA, after graduating from Marquette. His career ended in 2002, early in his second stint in Ireland, when he ruptured the patellar tendon in his left knee.

Despite playing major college ball and traveling the world, Pieper said what he cherishes most about his basketball career are the facts that Wausaukee took home the gold ball and that his name is still in the record books.

So, does he think anybody can reach his plateau? "They'd have to have the same things I did," Pieper said. "They'd have to play all four years and they'd need a coach who has as much confidence as my dad had in me, to have the freedom I had. And they'd have to have teammates who were as unselfish as mine were."

If that should happen, Pieper said he'd take it in stride. However, he'd like to hang onto the title as long as possible. "I definitely don't want it to be broken," he said. "It'd be a pretty nice thing to have for all of my life. It's been 11 years, and it's something that I can really appreciate more now, about what I accomplished, what we accomplished." ★

Badgers and Golden Eagles Reach Final Fours

They were Cinderella teams in the NCAA Tournament's big dance, but their glass slippers didn't fit when it came to the Final Four ball.

Wisconsin's Badgers of 2000 and Marquette's Golden Eagles of 2003 captured the imagination of hoops fans around the state and showed just how maddening March Madness can be.

Especially Dick Bennett's UW squad, which defeated four ranked teams during its whirlwind ride through the West Regional, including two in the top 10, to advance to the Final Four at the RCA Dome in Indianapolis.

However, the Badgers' dream run ended with a thud against Big Ten power Michigan State, which ousted the underdogs, 53–41, in the semifinals, en route to finishing 32–7 after claiming the national title with a victory over Florida.

BOYS AGAINST MEN

On March 12, 1922, the Delafield St. John's basketball team claimed it was the Western national prep champion after playing against mainly collegiate competition and losing only two games. Among the opponents that St. John's defeated were Oshkosh Normal, the Milwaukee School of Engineering, Lewis Institute, and the Wisconsin School of Mines.

It was the Spartans' fourth triumph against Wisconsin for the year, as the latter finished 22–14 after becoming the first team seeded number eight or lower to reach this point since 11th-seeded Louisiana State did it in 1986. Wisconsin joined UCLA (1980) and Villanova (1985) as the only number eight seeds to qualify for the Final Four, while number nine Penn advanced in 1979.

In front of 43,116, the Badgers melted in a contest against a foe that played the same stifling man-to-man defense but had more talent and offensive firepower to prevail. Wisconsin's output established a season-low for points. Junior Roy Boone scored almost half of them (18), and no other Badger tallied more than six.

Senior guard Jon Bryant, voted the Most Valuable Player of the West Regional, finished with only two points on one-of-five shooting from the floor. Junior forward Mark Vershaw entered play averaging a team-high 11.9 points but scored five on two-of-11 shooting. Spartans' senior Morris Peterson came up big, registering 16 of his game-high 20 points after the intermission.

The setback may have dampened fans' spirits, but not for long, because they hadn't seen anything like this since the last and only time Wisconsin had won an NCAA crown 59 years earlier.

UW's magical journey started with a 66–56 victory over Fresno State at Huntsman Arena on the University of Utah campus. It was the Badgers' first tourney victory under Bennett and second time in six appearances that he had won a tournament game. His unit helped followers forget the embarrassing 43–32 loss to Southwest Missouri State in the first round the previous season, as Bryant finished with a season-high 21 points on a career-high seven three-pointers.

The Badgers trailed by seven points early in the second half and had grabbed the lead before Bryant got hot, but he cemented the rally by nailing four consecutive treys. Andy Kowske, a six-foot-eight-inch junior forward, finished with 14 points and a personal-high 14 rebounds, including eight of the team's 16 offensive boards.

Duany Duany added 12 points, and junior point guard Mike Kelley chipped in seven points, six steals, and six assists. Kelley also was the top defender against Courtney Alexander, the nation's leading scorer at 25.3 points per game, who struggled mightily though recording a season-low 11.

Wisconsin then posted the largest upset of the tournament to that point and one of the school's biggest in history, knocking off top-seeded Arizona, 66–59, to give the Badgers their first spot in the Sweet 16 since the event expanded to 64 teams.

UW built a nine-point lead 10 minutes into the contest and kept squeezing. Forward Michael Wright, the Wildcats' top scorer, finished with two points and nine rebounds, while fellow sophomore Richard Jefferson scored 12 points but managed only five shots during his 24 foul-plagued minutes. And super freshman Jason Gardner added 10 points on three-of-11 shooting.

The Badgers' tenacious defense limited Arizona to four points and two-of-nine shooting during the first eight minutes of the second half while extending their advantage to 14 points. Four minutes later, the margin was 17.

Mike Kelley was the point guard and defensive catalyst for Wisconsin's surprising run to the NCAA's Final Four in 2000. (Photo courtesy of the University of Wisconsin)

Vershaw bounced back from a poor game to lead Wisconsin with 15 points, four assists, and three blocks. Kowske turned in his second straight double-double with 10 points and 12 rebounds. And junior forward Maurice Linton finished with 14 points, nine during the final three minutes. Bryant chipped in 12 points on four-of-eight shooting.

That meant a date with 28–5 Louisiana State, and the Badgers knocked the swagger out of the Tigers by halftime. Going into the showdown, LSU's players figured that a rugged Southeastern Conference slate had prepared them well for the Badgers. UW's defense proved them wrong during a 61–48 victory over the fourth-seeded Tigers.

Kelley again led the charge, compiling five steals, five assists, and defending LSU point guard Torris Bright, who finished with five of the Tigers' 23 turnovers. Bryant led Wisconsin with 16 points, nine in the second half, while Kowske and Linton added eight points apiece. Kowske, Linton, Vershaw, and Charlie Wills put the clamps on the Tigers' Stromile Swift and Jabari Smith, holding the duo to 24 points, and most of that damage occurred after it was too late.

That set up a confrontation against league foe Purdue, which was 24–9 after downing Gonzaga, 75–66. The combined 22 losses between the Badgers and Boilermakers were the most ever for two teams meeting in the Elite Eight. Wisconsin overcame the odds again, claiming its third victory in a row to win the season series 3–1 with a 64–60 triumph in the Pit at the University of New Mexico. Bryant provided most of the offense, tallying 18 points while canning five of nine from three-point range.

Kowske and Kelley joined Bryant on the all-tournament team. Kelley scored just five points, but his most important contribution was frustrating Purdue's Jaraan Cornell for the third consecutive game, holding the senior guard to three points on one of nine attempts. Kowske added 14 points and eight rebounds and held Brian Cardinal, who finished with 13 points, to no baskets during the last six minutes despite playing with four fouls. And Boone came off the bench to score 12 points.

While not as unexpected as Wisconsin's march, Coach Tom Crean's third-seeded Golden Eagles of the 2003 tourney hadn't grabbed many headlines since Al McGuire led Marquette to the 1977 championship.

In his fourth year, Crean had compiled a 79–40 record (.664) and led the Golden Eagles to their first Conference USA regular-season crown and back-to-back NCAA trips for the first time since the 1995–96 and 1996–97 campaigns.

And MU started its rampage to New Orleans against one of Crean's mentors, Ralph Willard and 14th-seeded Holy Cross. The Crusaders hadn't won an NCAA game since 1953, but for the third straight year it almost pulled off an upset of a higher-ranked team. The Crusaders lost to Kentucky in 2001 by four points and to Kansas a year earlier by 11.

Almost was the key word as point guard Travis Diener scored a career-high 29 points and Dwyane Wade added 15 points and 11 assists as Marquette pulled out a 72–68 verdict in the Midwest Regional at the RCA Dome.

The Golden Eagles improved to 24–5 after winning an opening-round contest for the first time since 1996, which earned them a matchup against sixth-seeded Missouri. Robert Jackson fouled out, which gave freshman forward Steve Novak a chance to shine in a thrilling encounter that went into overtime. The Brown Deer High School star broke the game open, converting three of four three-pointers in the extra period in helping Marquette shoot six of six from the field while hanging on for a 101–92 decision.

Missouri's Kevin Young cut the Golden Eagles' lead to 90–89 with 2:21 remaining in overtime, but Novak made his final three with the six-foot-nine Young in his face. That shot ignited an 11–0 burst during the next 1:39 to sew up the win.

Wade, who later was selected to the all-America team, took over in the Sweet 16 semis against number two-seeded Pittsburgh in the Metrodome in Minneapolis. The six-foot-five junior guard, who was later drafted by the Miami Heat and became one of the NBA's top rookies in 2003–04, was held to two points in the first half. But he showed off an assortment of drives, jumpers, and dunks to register 20 of the Golden Eagles' 43 points after the break. Wade made 10 of his 19 shots and carried MU to a 77–74 victory and into the Elite Eight.

WHAT'S IN A NAME?

In 1968, more than 14,000 fans participated in a team-naming contest for the new NBA franchise in Milwaukee, and R. D. Trebilcox of Whitefish Bay was one of 45 people who suggested the name "Bucks." His entry was eventually selected as the winner, with Trebilcox receiving a new car for his efforts. His reasoning for choosing that nickname: "bucks are spirited, good jumpers, fast and agile."

Marquette was ahead 73–72 in the final minute. The Golden Eagles ran the shot clock down to about 10 seconds, and then Wade, on the left wing, sliced through the Panthers to score with 25 ticks remaining.

As good as Wade had been against Pittsburgh, he was even better two days later. Kentucky, which had eliminated Bo Ryan's Badgers, 63–57, in the other semifinal, couldn't find an answer as Marquette ran away for an 83–69 victory and a ticket to the Final Four.

Wade scorched the top-seeded and number one-ranked Wildcats with a game-high 29 points on 11-for-16 shooting. He contributed 11 rebounds, game highs of 11 assists and four blocked shots, and added one steal in 35 magnificent minutes. Wade had posted a triple-double against a foe that had won its last 26 games.

However, Marquette's season (27–6) went from an emotional high to its lowest point as it suffered a resounding 94–61 setback to Kansas, which then lost the national title game to Syracuse, to finish 30–8 in the Louisiana Superdome. The demoralizing defeat was the fourth-biggest blowout in Final Four history, and the Golden Eagles' players were understandably down in the dumps afterward. "This will be in our minds forever," Diener said. "We're extremely disappointed not to be playing in the championship game. But no one can take away that we're one of the top four teams in the country."

Regardless of the collapse in front of a crowd of 54,432, the Jayhawks were simply the better team. Kansas led 17–14 with 13 minutes remaining in the first half before exploding for an 18–4 burst to enter the break with a 59–30 advantage. The Jayhawks then went on an identical 18–4 run to start the second half, which put things out of reach at 77–34.

Wade finished with 19 points, but Diener made only one of 11 attempts and committed eight turnovers. The Golden Eagles were successful on just three of 16 three-point attempts and shot 31 percent.

"We did not play the kind of game, certainly, that we're capable of," said Crean, "but at the same time, you should never take away the fact that this team won 27 games, and 53 over the last two years." ★

MORE RECORDS, STREAKS, AND AMAZING MOMENTS
COLLEGE BASKETBALL
Hoops Pioneer

It's no wonder that Christian Steinmetz Sr. became known as "the Father of Wisconsin Basketball." He was the Badgers' first all-American, earning honors after his senior season in 1905.

The team's captain set a UW single-season scoring mark with 462 points despite playing only one home game, which proved to be 23 more points than the combined total of Wisconsin's 18 opponents. His highlight that season came when Steinmetz was credited with scoring 50 points against Company G of Sparta, a 75–10 Wisconsin victory.

Steinmetz also connected on a record 26 free throws against the Two Rivers Athletic Club and established another mark with 20 field goals versus Beloit College. ★

Badgers' Back-to-Back Streaks

Walter Meanwell's UW men's basketball team turned in a string of success unmatched in school history. And it could have been even more impressive but for the University of Chicago.

The Badgers finished 15–0 in 1911–12 and went 14-0 the next season until dropping a 23–10 decision to Chicago in the season finale. They then fashioned another 15–0 campaign in 1913–14 and started 9–0 the next year before falling 24–19 to Chicago, giving them a 53–2 mark during that span. ★

Years of Service

Bill Zorn coached the University of Wisconsin–Eau Claire men's basketball team for 40 years in 1928–29 through 1967–68, compiling a 397-357 record that included 22 winning campaigns.

Following such a legend is never easy, but the Blugolds' next coach proved otherwise. Ken Anderson was in charge for 27 seasons, all of them with winning records. He posted an amazing 631–152 mark, which means his teams won 80.5 percent of their games with him at the helm. ★

Two-Sport Star

Kathy Andrykowski was the first female inducted into the Marquette University M Club's Hall of Fame in 1991. She earned four letters each in volleyball and basketball in 1977–80, but her hoops work is where she gained most of her accolades.

At the end of her playing days, Andrykowski held the top three single-season scoring marks in school history and still holds the top three seasonal averages in rebounding, including a standard of 16.8 in 1976–77. She played professionally in the United States and overseas. ★

HIGH SCHOOL BASKETBALL
Scoring Machine

Aaron Ritchay of Mellen High School is considered the top gun when it comes to scoring.

Sources credit the five-foot-seven guard as pouring in 87 or 88 points during a whopping 99–3 triumph against Butternut on December 23, 1916, which is still recognized as the single-game record in Wisconsin. The contest between these Ashland County opponents was played at Mellen on a court that measured approximately 50 feet long. Ritchay accomplished his feat during a period when the rules stipulated that there be a center jump ball after each basket was made. ★

Accepting Charity

Antigo's basketballers proved they were true marksmen in the 1973 Class A state tournament in Madison. The Red Robins defeated Kimberly, 52–42, for third place. In the process, Antigo finished with a free throw shooting record by making 55 of 64 attempts for a .859 percentage. John Muraski converted 24 of 27 attempts, including nine against the Papermakers. The Red Robins needed to be good from the line in that game because they only shot .274 from the field, converting 22 of 25 charity tosses compared to Kimberly's 10-for-21. Antigo's tourney mark still stands among teams that played at least three games.

Janesville Parker's 1971 champions top a list of six schools that have recorded perfect contests at the line, although they attempted 11 more than any other team that shares that honor. Bob Morgan's Vikings, who finished 19–7 after upsetting previously 24–1 Milwaukee King in the final, connected on all 23 tries during their 79–68 victory. ★

Beloit Shows the Way

Ninety-four schools have won boys state basketball championships, and Beloit is the king with seven, including three in succession from 1932 to 1934. The only other programs to equal that string are Marathon (1975–77), Milwaukee Vincent (1996–98) and Randolph (2002-04). Superior Central has the distinction of making the most appearances at the state tournament with 27, followed by Eau Claire (25), Neenah (24), Beloit (23), and Wisconsin Rapids (21).

The lowest combined score in a final since the event was recognized in 1916 was La Crosse Central's 10–4 win over Shawano in 1925, while the only time both teams registered single digits was the next year as Stevens Point edged River Falls, 9–7. The first time a school shattered the 50-point barrier was when Beloit whipped Hurley, 56–37, in 1947. The first overtime contest came in 1961, when Milwaukee Lincoln downed Rice Lake, 77–75.

There have been three double overtime dandies: Beloit's remarkable win over Neenah in 1969 that made Lamont Weaver a household name, Milwaukee Washington's 44–41 triumph over Fond du Lac in 1987, and Saint Croix Falls' victory against Columbus in 1992. The latter is the last time a final has needed extra periods to decide a winner.

Elkhorn's 1979 squad has the distinction of having the most losses by a state champion, finishing 13–12 after downing Prairie du Chien for its second consecutive Class B title. ★

Conference Domination

The Randolph High School girls team has controlled the Trailways Conference, winning 17 consecutive league championships from 1985 through 2001. Coaches Tim Omen, Dave Adel, and Cal VanBeek led the Rockets to their success.

Omen, who started in 1981, led Randolph to a 245–38 mark that included 11 conference crowns and five regional titles. Then the Rockets added five loop titles and three regional championships under Adel, who finished 100–13. And Randolph counted two conference trophies, plus one regional and one sectional trophy, among its accomplishments and went 38-9 with VanBeek at the helm.

The Rocket boys program has done just as well or better, winning 92 consecutive league tilts from February 1993 to December 1998. Randolph won 14 conference championships from 1986 to 2004. It also qualified for the state tournament nine times, taking home Division 4 trophies in 1996, 1998, 2002, 2003, and 2004 under Coach Bob Haffele. ★

Generals In Charge

When it comes to girls basketball, which started a state tournament in 1976, Milwaukee Washington and Janesville Parker have made 10 appearances while Durand, Fall Creek and Watertown have qualified nine times. Washington and Cuba City lead with five championships and Fall Creek and Kimberly have won four apiece.

Eight schools have won back-to-back trophies, but Washington is the only one with three straight titles (1994–96). Pam Kruse's squads also advanced to the finals the next two years but lost.

There have been 31 unbeaten title winners. Eight times there have been at least two undefeated teams, while the 2000 season culminated with Janesville Parker, Mosinee, and Flambeau finishing with 27–0 marks.

There have been only three overtime finals. Washington's first title team (1979) scored the most points in a tournament with 190 in three games, but the highest team average goes to Pecatonica in Division 4 at 70 ppg in two contests. However, it lost the 2002 final to Elkhart Lake-Glenbeulah. ★

FOOTBALL

Marquette Plays in the First Cotton Bowl

Nobody supposedly remembers who finishes second, which means the loser of the first Cotton Bowl game would probably be an answer to a good trivia question. For that matter, not many recall who won that contest either.

Well, on January 1, 1937, the showdown that became an annual affair and joined the ranks of college football's best New Year's Day traditions featured the unlikely matchup between Texas Christian and Marquette universities. TCU has never been an NCAA Division I powerhouse, and a lot of people have forgotten that the Jesuit school in Milwaukee fielded a gridiron program.

However, the Horned Frogs' starting quarterback was senior "Slingin'" Sammy Baugh, the all-American who later that year led the Washington Redskins to a 28–21 victory over the Chicago Bears to win the National Football League championship.

Meanwhile, Marquette, which was nicknamed the Golden Avalanche at the time, was enjoying perhaps its finest hour under Frank Murray, who had been the head coach since 1922. The northerners included such standouts as Ray "Buzz" Buivid, Ward Cuff, and the Guepe twins from Milwaukee, Art and Al.

Marquette had lost its final regular-season game, 13–0, to Duquesne; otherwise, it might have earned a bid to the Rose Bowl. On December 10, the Golden Avalanche accepted the invitation to visit the Lone Star State and the $6,000 guarantee that went

Ray "Buzz" Buivid was a star running back for the Marquette University football team that played in the first Cotton Bowl game in 1937. (Photo courtesy of Marquette University)

with it. TCU was the Southwestern Conference runner-up but had upset top-ranked Santa Clara, 9–0, to end its regular season at 8–2–2.

The teams hooked up for the first of only four times in front of 17,000 spectators on a blustery day in Dallas. Although the game hadn't earned much prestige, it boasted of having two of the finest backs in the country.

Buivid was a Port Washington native who had gained all-American laurels, finishing third in the 1936 Heisman Trophy balloting. His counterpart, Baugh, placed fourth in the Heisman voting.

Marquette had highlighted its season with a victory over the Eddie Jankowski-led Wisconsin Badgers, 12–6, a game in which Buivid tossed two touchdown passes to Art Guepe. Then Al Guepe intercepted a pass at the goal line to preserve the win in front of 32,000 at Madison's Camp Randall Stadium.

However, the Cotton Bowl appearance was the university's most memorable gridiron accomplishment, having been the only bowl bid in 68 years of Marquette football, which ended after the 1960 season. In the end, TCU and Baugh, despite subpar statistics, gained the upper hand in a 16–6 triumph.

The late Robert Hanel was the only sophomore on that Marquette squad. He didn't get to play in the Cotton Bowl, but pretended to be Baugh during Golden Avalanche practices. He apparently did his job well, as did the Marquette defense: Baugh completed only five of 13 pass attempts.

SLOWING DOWN THE MACHINE

Legendary Michigan coach Fielding Yost's famous "Point-A-Minute Machine" defeated the University of Wisconsin football team, 6-0, on November 1, 1902. The setback snapped the Badgers' 17-game winning streak in a game at Marshall Field in Chicago that drew more than 20,000 fans. Michigan finished the season unbeaten, scoring 644 points in 11 games for a 58.5 average.

However, Marquette's offense never got going against the Horned Frogs in a slugfest in which all of the scoring occurred in the first half. L. D. "Little Dutch" Meyer, an unheralded end who was a nephew of TCU coach Leo "Dutch" Meyer, booted a 33-yard field goal for a 3–0 lead. But Art Guepe scampered 60 yards with a punt return to give Marquette its only advantage of the game, 6–3. Meyer then registered the only score from scrimmage in the period, hauling in a 24-yard strike from Baugh and kicking the extra point for a 10–6 cushion to end the first quarter.

In the second quarter, Meyer again was on the receiving end, this time from Vic Montgomery, for a 16–6 halftime advantage that unfortunately— for frosty fans—ended the scoring.

In a *Dallas Morning News* article to commemorate the 50th anniversary of the game, a Horned Frog named Willie Walls was interviewed. He had been injured, which gave Meyer the chance to play and earn his place in Cotton

Bowl history. "I was in the hospital in Fort Worth, and I listened to the game on the radio," Walls said. "I yelled, 'Go get 'em L. D.' That little rascal sure could run. I was happy he got his chance. I had my big game the year before in the Sugar Bowl, when we kicked the — out of LSU, 3–2."

Meyer didn't see his performance as anything special. "Everything just seemed to fall into place," said Meyer, who played six years in the Major Leagues with the Chicago Cubs, Detroit Tigers, and Cleveland Indians. "When you had someone like Sammy Baugh you could do a lot of things. I just wasn't very big, only 160. The only thing I could do was catch the ball. With Sam, we beat a lot of people passing."

In accounts after the game, Golden Avalanche players lamented the team's lack of quality preparation time but admitted that they were the second-best team that day. "Our season was over before Thanksgiving," said Marquette end Lee Muth. "When we accepted the Cotton Bowl invitation in December, it was colder than hell in Milwaukee. We worked out in the field house a few times but did no physical work. Then we took a train to Oklahoma and spent eight or 10 days there. It was warmer but we still didn't do any contact work. In the Cotton Bowl, Buivid was really off. He and Guepe were good runners and Buivid normally was a good passer, but he didn't show it that day."

Muth also said switching from a six-man defensive front to combat Baugh's passing meant they didn't put enough pressure on the Horned Frogs' star. "Texas Christian was one of the best teams we've encountered," said Buivid, who played two seasons with the Chicago Bears. "But it wasn't better than Saint Mary's or Duquesne. Sammy Baugh, without a doubt, was the outstanding player we've met. Our short practice for the game was insufficient. Practicing against dummies and playing against 210-pounders are two different things."

Murray, who left to coach at Virginia but returned for four more years at the Marquette helm (1946–49), offered his assessment. "I was not disillusioned," Murray said. "From the beginning I strongly suspected that we would not be able to win. Practicing against dummies can by no means approximate actual scrimmage, and we could not scrimmage for fear of injury. Besides, Texas Christian had played up until two weeks of the game and we were handicapped by a five-week layoff."

Almost 1,000 fans greeted the Marquette players upon their return that Sunday night. They enjoyed it while they could, as the school managed only four more winning seasons after that year. ★

The Horse Romps for the Badgers

He was called a lot of things, including the famous nickname the Horse, but more than anything Alan Ameche was known as one of the greatest football

83

players this state has ever turned out. And perhaps his brightest moment occurred in 1954, when the Kenosha High School graduate became the first of only two Wisconsin Badgers to ever win the Heisman Trophy as college football's best player.

Ameche, who had finished sixth in the balloting a year earlier as a junior, accumulated 1,068 points to outdistance Oklahoma center-linebacker Kent Burris (838) and Ohio State halfback Howard "Hopalong" Cassady (810).

The rugged fullback scored nine touchdowns and gained 641 yards to win the honor. While the nine TDs were the most in his four-year starting career, his yardage and average per carry (4.4) were the lowest totals at UW. He had a season-high 127 yards on 17 carries and scored the winning TD against Michigan State.

He suffered an ankle injury against Northwestern and was less effective in the final two games of the season versus Illinois and Minnesota. Ameche only played three minutes against the Illini and hobbled for 26 yards on 13 carries in the battle with the Gophers but still scored twice. However, there was no mistaking how valuable the Italian Stallion was to the Badgers, who posted a 26–8–3 record during Ameche's tenure in the backfield.

Ameche ended his UW career as a three-time all-Big Ten selection and two-time all-American. He set a then-Rose Bowl record with 133 yards rushing, including a 54-yard jaunt, on 28 carries in the 1953 contest that the Badgers lost to Southern Cal, 7–0.

Wisconsin won the Big Ten title for the only time in 1952 during Ameche's career, and was ranked number one in the country early in the season before faltering to a 6–3–1 mark. That was the only time UW has topped the rankings in its history, but the Badgers were in the top 10 at some point during all four of Ameche's seasons. He is a member of the all-time UW team and was inducted into the College Football Hall of Fame in 1975; his number 35 jersey is one of four retired by the Badgers.

His other career numbers look like this: 157 carries for 824 yards (5.2) as a freshman, 233 for 1,079 (4.6) as a sophomore, and 165 for 801 (4.8) as a junior. He was the Big Ten's Most Valuable Player in 1954 and was the league's rushing champion in 1951 and 1952. Ameche was the NCAA's all-time leading rusher with 3,345 yards upon graduation.

Those accomplishments prompted Baltimore to make him the number-two overall pick in the 1955 NFL draft. He rambled 79 yards for a TD on his first play from scrimmage as a pro in a game against the Chicago Bears, but Ameche's most famous feat occurred when he scored the winning TD in the classic 1958 title game to give the Colts a 23–17 overtime win against the New York Giants.

Alan Ameche became the first of two UW players to win the Heisman Trophy, earning college football's highest honor in 1954. Ron Dayne became the second 45 years later. (Photo courtesy of the University of Wisconsin)

Ameche died at age 55 in August 1988, three days after undergoing open-heart surgery, but former Badger teammates can't forget the positive influence he had on them during one of the school's most glorious periods on the gridiron.

Dave Suminski was a starter at offensive and defensive tackle for the Badgers and played with Ameche in 1951–52 before suiting up for the Washington Redskins for one year and in Canada for four seasons. "One thing about Alan, for as long as I played with him or watched him, I don't remember ever seeing him fumble," said Suminski, who is retired and lives about 20 miles from his hometown of Ashland. "He was a good-size man in those days, but he had great lateral movement."

Don Voss was a standout end for UW's defensive unit known as the "Hard Rocks." He played in 1951–52 before a knee injury curtailed his promising career. "As a teammate he was very, very friendly and humble," said the Milwaukee Washington High School star who went into human resources work for about 20 years and then ran a travel business for 25 more before retiring. "He wasn't a braggart or never flaunted his talents. He was a good, fun guy with a sense of humor. Even though he started and established himself during his freshman year, he let his actions speak louder than his words.

"We always used to kid Al, we'd call him 'Spider' or 'Chicken' because his legs were quite slim despite his size," Voss added. "He had legs more like a track guy, but that was one of the reasons he was so shifty. Most fullbacks in those days were big, bulky guys all the way down to their toes, but Alan had quick feet. He was fairly fast for his size, hit the holes so quickly and had good balance."

In high school, Ameche set a Big Eight Conference record with 108 points in seven games as a senior in 1950. Kenosha went unbeaten and averaged more than 45 points per game as Ameche rushed for 831 yards on 102 attempts (8.1 average) and as he and his teammates outscored their foes 316–47. As a junior, he also led the league in scoring and earned all-state second-team recognition by the Associated Press.

DID YOU HEAR A WHISTLE?

The Wisconsin Badgers football team suffered a loss to Michigan at Camp Randall in 1923 by a 6–3 score in a game that official Walter Eckersall determined by his controversial "non-call."

It all started when Wolverines' quarterback and safety Tod Rockwell returned a punt about 20 yards before seemingly being tackled by two Badgers near the sideline at midfield. He was apparently down for a few seconds, got up and walked away from a group of players and then sprinted the rest of the way to the end zone to give the visitors a victory. Eckersall said he never blew his whistle to stop the play, and field judge Colonel Mumma said forward progress had not been stopped.

Eckersall was the *Chicago Tribune's* football writer and repeatedly defended his decision. He was escorted off the field by Wisconsin players for his own protection from fans' potential retributions. One fan was arrested after connecting with Eckersall's jaw, but the latter asked that the man be released.

Jim Temp knows all about Ameche's many athletic traits, which included running a 10.2 in the 100 and winning a state shot put championship. Temp played with Ameche all four years at Wisconsin, where was an offensive end before switching to defense for the Packers in 1957–60 after a stint in the Army. "He was a wonderful guy to play with," said Temp, who worked in the property and casualty insurance business for 43 years. "He got married in his sophomore year, so we didn't do a lot socially, but he was a great teammate. They went to the one-platoon system that one year, so he played linebacker behind me and didn't have to worry about making many plays."

The La Crosse Aquinas alumnus joined Ameche on the *Milwaukee Journal's* all-time all-state team in 1993. "His biggest strength was his strength," said Temp, who currently serves on the Packers' seven-member executive committee. "He didn't have outstanding speed or moves, but he'd run over people, especially defensive backs, and never missed a beat. He was the first guy on our team to wear a facemask. The first one they made for him, all you saw was his eyes and a slit for his mouth. He had such a big honking nose, and it would bleed from the beginning of the game to the end. They had to redesign the thing for him."

But there was only one Alan Ameche, whom Temp put in the same category as such rough-and-tumble ball carriers as Green Bay's Jim Taylor and Chicago's Rick Casares. "He treated everyone on the team with the same respect," Temp said. "He was a real tough guy on the field. In the pros, he was one of the more difficult guys I faced in my career. Off the field, he was happy-go-lucky and enjoyed a good time." ★

The 1963 Rose Bowl: The Badgers Come Close

Sportswriters had badgered University of Wisconsin football coach Milt Bruhn for supposedly letting his players enjoy too much of the glitzy Los Angeles area nightlife in the days preceding the 1960 Rose Bowl. What else could explain Wisconsin's humiliating 44–8 setback to Washington?

Regardless of the reasons, Bruhn didn't want to leave anything to chance when the second-ranked Badgers returned to Pasadena, California, three years later for the 49th version of the Granddaddy of Them All game, the first time that the top-two-rated teams in the country had appeared in this contest. His main precautionary maneuver was to keep his players secluded for two nights before the showdown against number one and unbeaten Southern Cal. His choice: the Order of Passionate Fathers Monastery.

Maybe his squad should have bunked there an additional night or two so they could have squeezed in a few more hallelujahs and Hail Marys. Wisconsin needed them, at least for the first 46 minutes. The Trojans waltzed to a 42–14 advantage after the first play in the fourth quarter.

However, that's when the Badgers and little-known senior quarterback Ron Vander Kelen finally came to life. The six-foot-one, 176-pound Green Bay native had completed a modest 91 of 168 attempts for 1,181 yards and 12 touchdowns during the regular season, with all-America end Pat Richter hauling in 38 receptions for 531 yards and five scores.

But the fourth quarter of this Rose Bowl game belonged to Vander Kelen and the Badgers, so much so that even today many fans treat them like the victors despite the fact USC actually held on for a 42–37 triumph.

Wisconsin started its magical 23–0 comeback run with an 80-yard, 12-play drive in which Vander Kelen completed eight of 10 attempts for 63 yards. The Big Ten champions climbed to within 42–21 with 11:51 left on tailback Lou Holland's 13-yard run.

Southern Cal fumbled on its next play from scrimmage, with Elmars Ezerins recovering for the Badgers. Wisconsin covered the 29 yards in five plays, including the final four-yard pass from Vander Kelen to Gary Kroner, to move

Wisconsin within two touchdowns at the 8:42 mark. The Trojans ate up some of the precious clock before turning the ball over on downs at the UW 32.

The Badgers marched again, this time to USC's 4 only to have Willie Brown intercept a pass in the end zone, Vander Kelen's third errant toss of the game. Wisconsin's defense held and gladly accepted two points when Southern Cal's center snapped the ball over punter Ernie Jones's head. Ernie Von Heimburg got credit for the safety, which inched the Badgers to within 42–30 with 2:40 remaining.

Richter then capped the ensuing 43-yard drive, which was set up by Ron Smith's 21-yard return of the free kick, with a 19-yard scoring reception with 1:29 left to make it 42–37.

DALE DOES IT

Future NFL defensive back Dale Hackbart scored on a quarterback sneak in the fourth quarter as Wisconsin rallied to down Minnesota, 11–7. The November 21, 1959, victory handed the Badgers their first undisputed Big Ten Conference football championship since 1912 and a spot in the Rose Bowl. Wisconsin's 5–2 league finish placed them a half-game ahead of Michigan State.

USC's Pete Lubisich, who had delivered the high snap on the punt a minute earlier, recovered Wisconsin's onside kick attempt. But the Trojans punted after losing 12 yards on three plays, with the Badgers' Ezerins almost blocking the boot. The game ended on Wisconsin's return.

Alas, Wisconsin's final prayer went unanswered at the foot of the San Gabriel Mountains near a gorge called Arroyo Seco. That afternoon's game lasted three hours, eight minutes after starting 12 minutes late because of television commitments. It ended in semidarkness because of the stadium's substandard lighting system, which was addressed several years later.

It only seemed appropriate, after Vander Kelen and the Wisconsin offense had kept the Trojans in the dark the final 14 minutes. The Badgers' signal caller finished 33-of-48, including 18-of-21 in the final quarter, with two scores for a Wisconsin and Rose Bowl record 401 yards. Richter set a record with 11 catches (for 163 yards) and the late score. His mark wasn't broken until J. J. Stokes of UCLA hauled in 14 receptions for 176 yards against Wisconsin in the January 1, 1994, Badgers' Rose Bowl victory.

Vander Kelen tried to explain his performance during an interview with the *Milwaukee Journal Sentinel's Badger Plus* magazine several years ago: "I've thought about it many times, what exactly happened to me that day. All I can say is it was one of those times in an athlete's career when everything all of a sudden came together. It didn't matter what play I called, whether we had blocking or not, I just couldn't do anything wrong."

He definitely electrified the partisan USC crowd. But he almost never got the chance, as he told a *Los Angeles Times* reporter on the eve of the Badgers' return to the Rose Bowl 31 years later. "As we fell further and further behind, [Wisconsin coach Milt Bruhn] was within an eyelash of yanking me out of that game and going with a younger, fresher player to give him experience," Vander Kelen recalled. "But then he decided to give me one more series."

Everyone involved with or who watched the game wouldn't have blamed Bruhn if he had gone to a backup with the score 42–14, but they're glad he didn't. "We were really embarrassed," Vander Kelen said of the Badgers' performance up to that point. "I called the guys around me. I said, 'Hey, we're a good football team. Let's score a couple of times, get respectable here. If we lose, let's lose with our flags flying.'

"Well, we scored a couple of quick touchdowns to make it 42–28. As you know, football is a game of momentum, and we had momentum. We ran the Trojans ragged." If only Vander Kelen could have jump-started the Badgers a little sooner, which is what the *Wisconsin State Journal's* headline said the next day: "Plucky Bucky Bows; Game Ends Too Soon."

Bruhn summed up the Jekyll-and-Hyde nature of the game. "They won the first half and we won the second. They got to us quickly in the first half and again in the second. What probably has to be called the turning point was when they hit us right after the half."

USC had grabbed a 21–7 halftime lead and extended it on the first play of the third quarter when Hal Bedsole took quarterback Pete Beathard's swing pass 57 yards for a TD. Vander Kelen's 17-yard scamper closed the gap again, but Beathard connected on two touchdown passes to give Southern Cal an insurmountable cushion. Or so it seemed.

Wisconsin gained only 67 yards rushing and earned 23 of

Badgers' quarterback Ron Vander Kelen led Wisconsin to 23 points in the fourth quarter of the 1963 Rose Bowl, but it wasn't enough as USC won the game, 42-37. (Photo courtesy of the University of Wisconsin)

its 31 first downs through the air. Meanwhile, Beathard completed eight of 12 passes, but four of them went for scores, and the Trojans rushed for 114 yards.

Wisconsin was whistled for seven penalties for 77 yards, including a controversial call that nullified a TD pass to Holland in the second quarter, while USC committed 12 infractions for 93 yards.

Southern Cal (11–0) finished number one in the polls and improved to 10–3 in the Rose Bowl, including a 7–0 triumph over Wisconsin in 1953. Meanwhile, the never-say-die Badgers (8–2) settled for number two, which is where both teams were when the day started.

Beathard set a record with his four scoring aerials: 13 yards to Ron Butcher, 57 and 23 to Bedsole, and 13 to Fred Hill. The Trojans' other scores came on runs from future Green Bay Packer back Ben Wilson and Ron Heller.

The Badgers questioned the loss of 25 seconds of time when, with four minutes remaining, the timer ran out to tell officials that the clock was wrong. Who knows what Vander Kelen and company could have accomplished with three or four more plays?

The 79 total points was a Rose Bowl standard that stood for 28 years, and USC coach John McKay said afterward that he was glad he had all 42 on his side of the scoreboard. "When it was 42–14, the kids were congratulating each other on the sideline. You would, and I would. Wisconsin is a great offensive team, the best we've played."

Years later McKay, who went on to become the Tampa Bay Buccaneers' first head coach, expanded on those thoughts. "Was I worried about losing the game?" McKay said. "Heck no, I was worried about getting killed. The USC alumni would have murdered me if Wisconsin had won. Seriously, what happened was this. I think myself and my coaching staff got a little too concerned about getting everybody into the game instead of winning the game. But that last Wisconsin touchdown got our attention. After that, our first-string offense went back out there and was able to get a couple first downs, reestablish field position and keep that big quarterback of theirs off the field."

Vander Kelen and Wisconsin never would have gotten that chance had they not rallied to edge Minnesota by 14–9 at Camp Randall and finish the regular season at 8–1. The Badgers and Gophers entered the contest with 5–1 league records, with UW sporting the conference's number-one offense and Minnesota fielding the top defensive unit. The host Badgers led 7–6 at halftime and luckily held on because 15-yard penalties twice thwarted deep Gopher drives, including one that eliminated a touchdown and forced the visitors to boot a field goal for a 9–7 advantage.

Future NFL Hall of Fame linebacker Bobby Bell was whistled for roughing the passer, giving Wisconsin new life because it waved off an interception.

Minnesota coach Murry Warmath protested and officials added on another 15 yards, which moved the ball to the Gophers' 13. Three runs later, Wisconsin had a 14–9 lead.

Regardless of how they got to Pasadena, Vander Kelen said the experience was one he and his teammates cherished. "For any college athlete to play in the Rose Bowl, in that setting, was absolutely tops," Vander Kelen said via phone from his Twin Cities office. "As a kid, I remember watching the Rose Bowl on TV, so to participate in the game was a thrill in itself."

And he gave thousands of fans a thrilling performance, something unexpected from a senior who had only played one varsity season before that. "I was on the varsity my sophomore year and got about 90 seconds of playing time as a defensive back in our game against Marquette," said Vander Kelen, who later became a backup signal caller for the Minnesota Vikings. "I hurt my knee in the spring and missed the fall of '60, and then I was out of school in '61 because of academic troubles. I'm so grateful that Milt Bruhn gave me the chance in 1962."

So were his teammates, including Richter, who earned all-America honors at end because of his frequent collaborations with Vander Kelen and who later served as Wisconsin's athletic director from 1989 to 2004.

The latter said the Badgers' Rose Bowl outburst might have surprised a lot of people around the country, but it wasn't news to him. "In those days there wasn't much throwing, so if teams got behind it was more difficult to catch up and make big comebacks," Vander Kelen said. "But Coach Bruhn had spent time up in Green Bay with [Vince] Lombardi and [Bart] Starr, so we used a lot of similar type plays and passed the ball more than most teams. So when things clicked, we could move the ball down the field in a hurry."

That's what happened in the fourth quarter against Southern Cal, and not even Vander Kelen could have predicted what he and the Badgers' offense accomplished. "Football is an unusual game in that you can be cold and nothing you do works," he said. "We had that touchdown called back, and instead of trailing only 21–14 we were down by two TDs at halftime. Then we couldn't do anything right offensively or defensively in the third quarter.

"But we knew we were a better team than that, and I think pride had something to do with it," Vander Kelen added. "We just decided to take it one play, one score at a time. We didn't rush anything, and everything clicked. It was one of those days. All of us felt that if we would have had three or four more plays we could have scored again, but we ran short of time."

That was the only thing the Badgers were short of that day. ★

Packers Win First Super Bowl

"I've had better days, but I never timed one better." January 15, 1967, was that kind of day for Max McGee of the Green Bay Packers.

Notorious for his off-the-field escapades—some true, some not—the 34-year-old reserve wide receiver was the unlikeliest of heroes on professional football's biggest stage. "I was sitting on the bench enjoying the shady side of the field for a while, because we normally sit on the sun side when we play in the [Los Angeles] Coliseum, and I heard somebody yell," the prankster McGee said of his unexpected role in what was called the AFL–NFL World Championship Game before it became known as the Super Bowl.

The call came from legendary coach Vince Lombardi because starter Boyd Dowler had aggravated an injury while attempting to block Kansas City linebacker E. J. Holub during the Packers' first offensive series. Dowler had damaged his shoulder landing in the end zone for the go-ahead score in the NFL title game. McGee would see the pigskin more times in this game than he had all season long, a year in which he caught a measly four passes for 91 yards and one touchdown.

All-pro quarterback Bart Starr and the Green Bay coaching brain trust stuck to their game plan, one in which they hoped to exploit what they considered a weak Kansas City secondary that featured the boastful Fred "The Hammer" Williamson.

And McGee was the beneficiary, even if it occurred by default. He scored the game's first touchdown on Green Bay's second possession on a nifty 37-yard pitch and catch from eventual game Most Valuable Player Starr, a play in which he plucked a potential interception away from Chiefs' cornerback Willie Mitchell.

"Let's face it, it was a rotten pass," McGee said in his customary deadpan manner. "You pay a guy a hundred thousand dollars to throw to a 25-thousand dollar end, you expect him to throw better than that. I wasn't going to go back and get killed by some linebacker. I thought sure somebody was going to intercept the ball, so I reached back to knock it down, to break up the interception. And when I did, the ball stuck in my hand. Just like that. Stuck right in my hand."

McGee corralled 11- and 16-yard gains and played hot potato with another pass, culminating a 56-yard march with a bobbling 13-yard score in the third quarter en route to seven receptions for 138 yards.

It was the first time since November 1964 that the Tulane University alumnus had hauled in two or more scores in a game, and his reception total equaled the output of his last two seasons; he caught three more passes in 1967 before retiring after the Packers' 33–14 triumph over the Oakland Raiders in Super Bowl II.

Paul Hornung, McGee's sidekick for many a late-night adventure, said his buddy should have been named the game's top player. "I told Bart that a hundred times, and he agreed with me," Hornung said. "That was the greatest performance by a guy who was out of shape. If Max had not been such a great athlete, he would never have done what he did."

Despite McGee's tremendous contest and Starr's performance, Green Bay's defense turned a precarious 14–10 halftime lead and possibly embarrassing setback to the AFL entry into a 35–10 triumph.

Kansas City signal caller Len Dawson had completed 11 of 15 attempts, including his final eight, for 152 yards and a TD in the first half against a unit that had led the NFL in pass defense for the third consecutive year.

Dawson had tossed a seven-yard scoring strike to fullback Curtis McClinton to end a 66-yard drive, which knotted the score at 7. He then directed the Chiefs down the field to set up future Packer kicker Mike Mercer's 31-yard field goal.

Green Bay had registered 47 sacks and picked off 28 enemy aerials while allowing only seven touchdown passes, the fewest by any team since the Cleveland Browns in 1956.

But then the Packers' smallest starter, five-foot-10-inch safety Willie Wood, turned the momentum, the game, and history around for Green Bay. The Packers' pass rush, aided by blitzing linebackers Dave Robinson and Lee Roy Caffey, forced Dawson into an ill-advised toss toward tight end Fred Arbanas in the flat. Wood, the former free agent quarterback/defensive back from the University of Southern California, grabbed the errant throw and raced 50 yards to the Chiefs' 5.

THE FIGHTING FAIRIES

In the two years before the Packers became part of the National Football League in 1921, they posted a combined 19–2–1 record and outscored their opponents by a combined 792–36. However, they couldn't solve their foes from Beloit, whose nickname was the remarkably unfootball-like "Fairies."

In 1919, Green Bay started the season at 10–0 before a November 23 contest along the Rock River. Beloit claimed a 6–0 victory at Fairbanks-Morse Co. field after a local referee called off three Packer touchdowns. Green Bay, accompanied by a large contingent of fans who came via train, said they were robbed and asked for a rematch, which Beloit apparently agreed to but canceled.

In 1920, again at Beloit in November, the Fairies belied their name and posted a 14–3 triumph, the last time the two parties tangled on the gridiron.

"Willie Wood probably would have made it to the Hall of Fame anyway, but I probably helped put him in by throwing that pass," Dawson said. "I've seen it on so many replays and it still looks just as bad."

Filling in for Hornung, who didn't perform because of a pinched nerve in his neck that would force his retirement, halfback Elijah Pitts scored the first of his two rushing TDs on the next snap and the rout was on. "We had to do a lot of regrouping between halves," Wood said afterward. "These things happen sometimes and you need a little coaching to get back."

No doubt Lombardi did some of his best "coaching" during that intermission, but several players said they couldn't blame their leader for letting off some steam. For two weeks he had heard from coaches and owners around the senior league that Green Bay had to defeat Kansas City to put the young pups in their place after seven years of verbal and financial wars over players.

Lombardi had set his Packers' camp up 90 miles to the north in Santa Barbara—after much wrangling with NFL commissioner Pete Rozelle—to

Green Bay receiver Max McGee takes Kansas City's Willie Mitchell for a ride on this reception that helped set up the Packers' final score in Super Bowl I. (Photo courtesy of Vernon Biever)

FLATTENED BY PLATTEN

Millions of Green Bay and Chicago football fans get fired up twice a year, but few, if any, have taken their frustrations as far as Packer backer Emmet Platten did on September 20, 1936.

The radio personality was no slouch, standing six-foot-four and weighing 230 pounds. Upset with an official's call that negated a Green Bay touchdown, Platten charged onto the field and punched Chicago's Ted Rosequist, who was trying to restrain him.

The Bears got the last laugh, whipping the Packers, 30–3, that day. However, that was Green Bay's only loss of the season as it avenged the setback and finished 10–1–1 en route to winning its fourth NFL championship, while the Bears settled for second place in the Western Division at 9–3.

Meanwhile, Platten avoided arrest and wrote a letter to the *Green Bay Press-Gazette* justifying his actions the day before at City Stadium.

prevent as many distractions as possible. Offensive right tackle Forrest Gregg said Lombardi warned his team not to be complacent.

"We didn't know a thing in the world about Kansas City," Gregg said. "We had never seen them play except on television. And Vince came out and talked to us [during] our first meeting. And he left no question in our minds that they had a great football team."

Linebacker Robinson concurred, saying that Lombardi treated this cross-country journey to sunny California like a business trip and those who failed to comply with his stringent rules would be dealt with harshly. "He told us this game was so big that if anything went wrong he would fine us $2,500 for a minor violation, such as being late for a meeting, and $5,000 for a major violation, like being caught for sneaking past curfew. That was unheard of." Luckily for McGee, Lombardi never found out about his Super Bowl Eve activities.

Meanwhile, the Chiefs had fashioned an 11–2–1 regular season and then scored 24 unanswered points in demolishing the two-time defending champion Buffalo Bills, 31–7, in upstate New York to establish themselves as a force to reckon with in protecting the AFL's honor.

Still, they were 13 1/2-point underdogs to the playoff-hardened veterans from the frosty north, who were looking for their fourth championship in six years.

The late Ray Nitschke said the immense pressure that Lombardi lugged around on his back for two weeks was evident. "It was the only time I ever saw Lombardi that tense and uptight," the ferocious middle linebacker said. "He was so tense and nervous about everything, he made us tense, and it carried over into the game, which is something he never did.

"I really believe Lombardi's mentality before that Super Bowl affected us so much that we played poorly in the first half," Nitschke added. "But it was more than that. We were nervous and the Chiefs were good. They were even better than we'd thought they'd be. Heck, look at the players they had—Lenny Dawson at quarterback, [linebacker] Bobby Bell, and some others. And three years later, they won the Super Bowl, so they were definitely tough and very well coached by Hank Stram."

The game was attended by 61,946 fans in the 100,000-seat Coliseum and watched by an estimated 65 million TV viewers—NBC and CBS had broadcast rights as part of the merger agreement that would begin in 1970. Everyone wondered what was happening as the Chiefs stayed with 12-2 Green Bay, which had turned back the Cowboys, 34–27, in what many observers felt was the real title contest January 1 in the Cotton Bowl in Dallas.

Frank Gifford, a former pupil of Lombardi's while playing for the New York Giants in the 1950s, said the scrutiny had taken its toll. "During the five minutes or so I talked to him, he held onto me and he was shaking like hell," Gifford said of his pregame interview with the coach.

Regardless, the Packers overcame those troubles in the second half, limiting Kansas City to 58 total yards and 0-for-6 on third down conversions while forcing six punts. That was more typical of Green Bay's defense, which had allowed only 163 points during the regular season, 49 fewer than the second-stingiest unit of the Los Angeles Rams.

The Packers' offense also unloaded its balanced attack, which had scored the fourth-most points (335) in the league. Green Bay churned out a workman-like 130 yards rushing, wearing down the much bigger Kansas City defenders and quieting their critics.

That included Williamson, who had talked about how his dreaded forearm and clothesline tackling would silence the Packer receivers. He was knocked unconscious in the fourth quarter while trying to stop rookie running back Donny Anderson and was hauled off the field on a stretcher. "Everybody was laughing at him," Green Bay left guard Fuzzy Thurston said of Williamson's antics that paid off better for him in Hollywood after his playing days. "What a goofball. He kept yakking all week. Nobody was concerned about him."

Green Bay let Williamson and his mates do the talking and concentrated on its preparation, which was evident in how the Packers' passing game chewed up big chunks of yardage, and that didn't include Starr's 64-yard scoring connection to Carroll Dale after a play-action fake in the first half that was brought back when the officials penalized Green Bay for illegal motion.

The Starr-to-McGee tandem sliced up a Kansas City defense that had helped the Chiefs claim nine consecutive triumphs. "Max's experience and ability to rise to the occasion was evident," Starr said of his number-one target. "He ran patterns extremely well. He would set the defender up and when he made his break, he could get separation from him. It was very easy to complete passes to him because of the way he ran his routes."

Starr wasn't too bad either. Despite throwing his first interception in 173 attempts, he finished with 250 yards on his usually efficient 16-of-23 passing. It was an exclamation point on a season that had seen the 17th-round draft pick from Alabama win MVP laurels after tossing 14 TDs and only three interceptions while compiling a 105.0 quarterback rating.

Jerry Mays saw firsthand from his position along the Kansas City defensive line. "The Packers and the Packer mystique beat us in the second half. . . . They beat the hell out of us."

After celebrating his team's superiority, Lombardi put an end to reporters' constant badgering about how the two leagues compared, saying that Kansas City didn't measure up to the top teams in the NFL, comments he later regretted.

However, on this day, he and his Packers had earned the right to be proud of their accomplishments. "It wasn't only Packer prestige, but the whole NFL [that] was on the line," Lombardi said. "We had everything to lose and nothing to gain."

Except a world championship and a trophy that was later named after him. ★

The 1967 Ice Bowl

It began innocently enough at the Green Bay 32-yard line on a frigid New Year's Eve day in 1967, but what transpired during the next 4:41 at Lambeau Field has been replayed thousands of times and elevated to the status of a religious experience.

No disrespect is meant to John Elway and the Denver Broncos' 98-yard march at Cleveland in 1987 and Johnny Unitas and the Baltimore Colts' late-game and overtime heroics in the 1958 title game. However, the Packers' 12-play, 68-yard drive to decide what has become known as the Ice Bowl stands out as the ultimate drive in National Football League history.

Future Hall of Fame quarterback Bart Starr had thrown 17 interceptions and only nine touchdown passes during the regular season, one in which the Packers had managed a 9–4–1 record despite fielding an aging, injury-plagued roster.

Starr and his teammates put those frustrations behind them during that one march, a journey that culminated an unbelievable contest against the Dallas Cowboys and Mother Nature's fury, a victory that gave Green Bay an unprecedented—and still unequaled—third consecutive league championship with a 21–17 triumph.

The drive started after safety Willie Wood returned a punt for 9 yards, unfolding this way:

- First down and 10 at the Green Bay 32 with 4:50 left: halfback Donny Anderson catches a pass from Starr for 6 yards in the right flat.

- Second and 4 at the Green Bay 38 with 4:27 left: fullback Chuck Mercein runs right for 7 yards.

- First and 10 at the Green Bay 45 with 3:57 left: Starr completes a pass to flanker Boyd Dowler across the middle. Dowler is injured when his head slams onto the ice-covered and concrete-hard ground.

- First and 10 at the Dallas 42 with 3:30 left: Anderson is dropped for a 9-yard loss by Cowboys' defensive end Willie Townes, who splits between pulling guards Jerry Kramer and Gale Gillingham.

• Second and 19 at the Green Bay 49 with 2:52 left: Starr's delay pass to Anderson picks up 11 yards.

• Third and 8 at the Dallas 39 with 2:00 left: Anderson hauls in another pass in the right flat, this time for 9 yards.

• First and 10 at the Dallas 30 with 1:35 left: Mercein makes a nifty catch and 19-yard run in the left flat.

• First and 10 at the Dallas 11 with 1:11 left: Mercein fires through a gaping hole for 8 yards. His path is created when Dallas all-pro tackle Bob Lilly follows the pulling Gillingham and Packer left tackle Bob Skoronski seals off Marquette graduate George Andrie, finishing off two of the most crucial plays in the series. Starr said the latter play was perhaps his best call under pressure in his career. Green Bay calls its first timeout.

• Second and goal at the Dallas 3 with 54 seconds left: Anderson gets 2 yards.

• First and goal at the Dallas 1 with 30 seconds left: Anderson is stopped for no gain, and the Packers call their second timeout.

• Second and goal at the Dallas 1 with 20 seconds left: Anderson slips and miraculously hangs onto the ball, getting stopped for no gain again. Some players from both teams said they thought it was a touchdown. Replays also showed that Anderson could have fumbled as he and Dallas middle linebacker Lee Roy Jordan fight for the ball. Green Bay calls its third and final timeout.

• Third and goal at the Dallas 1 with 16 seconds left: Starr calls a "31 wedge," a play in which Mercein would plunge forward behind center Ken Bowman and right guard Kramer, who double-team Cowboy defensive tackle Jethro Pugh. However, Starr doesn't tell anyone in the huddle and decides to keep the ball himself because he's closer and would have better traction than his running backs.

Packer coach Vince Lombardi's only opinion on the topic: "Run it and let's get the hell outta here."

LET IT SNOW

Sunday, December 1, 1985, dished out perhaps the worst weather conditions ever for a pro football encounter in Green Bay. However, the Packers acted like kids in beating up the shivering Tampa Bay Buccaneers, 21–0, in the Central Division contest. Only 19,856 fans made it to Lambeau Field that day as a blizzard unleashed more than a foot of snow before the game and didn't slow down much afterward.

That's exactly what Starr did. Had the gutsy call failed, Green Bay probably wouldn't have had enough time to set up for a potential game-tying field goal on fourth down, an outcome that would have traumatized Cheeseheads nationwide. Instead, it etched Starr's name and those of his teammates into the record books and NFL lore. It also made "Frozen Tundra" a household phrase, appropriate for what the elements dished out that day for the 48th NFL title game.

A sellout crowd of 50,861 braved temperatures that plummeted to near minus 20 degrees and wind chills of minus 50 by the time shadows cast an eerie darkness over the scoreboard at the south end zone where Starr sneaked across the goal line.

The afternoon slugfest epitomized everything that football stands for: courage, resolve, and most importantly, for players and fans, survival. It meant layers upon layers of clothes, butane heaters, Saran wrap, and plastic garbage bags.

Lombardi's "electric blanket" heating coil system that had been installed six inches under the playing surface before the 1967 season was useless once the mercury plummeted below 20 degrees, so moisture that had accumulated between the ground and tarps on the field eventually froze, creating a playing environment better suited for hockey.

The Packer cheerleaders, the Golden Girls, made a brief appearance before kickoff and hightailed it to their dressing room for the rest of the day. Referee Norm Schachter and his officiating crew, who donned ear muffs, gloves, and whatever else they could find at the local sporting goods store, weren't that

Packer fullback Chuck Mercein (30) was an unsung hero during Green Bay's victory over Dallas in the NFL Championship game better known as the Ice Bowl. (Photo courtesy of Vernon Biever)

lucky: umpire Joe Connell lost part of his lip after trying to blow his whistle to signify the start of the game.

Surrounded by a surreal, enveloping cover of steam coming from throughout the stadium, a great football game unfolded between two teams that had squared off in Texas a year earlier, with the Packers advancing to Super Bowl I with a 34–27 win.

Dallas had killed Cleveland, 52–14, to win the Eastern Conference championship, while Green Bay had overcome a 7–0 deficit to whip favored Los Angeles, 28–7, in the Western title showdown at Milwaukee's County Stadium. The Rams had tied Baltimore for the Coastal Division crown at 11–1–2 but had outscored the Colts in their two meetings to qualify for the postseason.

Lilly said no one could have imagined what would happen that day, especially after December 30 had been a nice day with temperatures around 30 degrees. "I played in a lot of games where it was zero degrees or a little above, and it never bothered me," Lilly said. "We'd have heaters at the game and you'd come off the field and be kind of warm. And we had heaters that day, but we never got warm. Never. We just froze to death. I think we thought more about the weather that day than about the game."

Mercein echoed those sentiments, although he and the Packers were much warmer afterward. "It was like playing inside a meat locker," said Mercein, who had been claimed off waivers from the New York Giants and had gained only 46 yards in 14 carries during the regular season. "I'll never forget the feel of the football. I've never felt leather that cold."

Dallas offensive tackle Ralph Neely didn't feel some other things. "You always want to play your best, but all I wanted to do that day was get inside and get warm," Neely said. "I took my foot and put it in front of one of those big ol' kerosene heaters . . . My shoe was burning, but I couldn't feel anything."

Despite all of that, the Cowboys, who hadn't played in Green Bay since 1960 and hadn't defeated the Packers in the regular season or playoffs, were optimistic of ending their foes' storied run of success.

Dallas sported a high-scoring offense, while Green Bay, which didn't feature the famed backfield of Jim Taylor and Paul Hornung in 1967, was also without the services of injured ball carriers Elijah Pitts and Jim Grabowski.

So, it was easy to see why the Packers mixed in more passes than usual despite the weather. Starr connected with Dowler for a 7–0 first quarter lead, capping a 16-play, 82-yard drive that lasted almost nine minutes and benefited from two Dallas penalties. The march featured a 17-yard pass to Anderson, a 17-yard toss to Carroll Dale on a third-and-9 play, and a 15-yard pass to Dale that gave the hosts a first-and-goal at the Cowboys' 9 as they evenly split up their running and passing plays.

The conditions negated Dallas's speed at the skill positions and therefore took away some of its playbook. One of the most vivid memories of that game shows Cowboys' lightning-fast wide receiver "Bullet" Bob Hayes with his hands tucked inside his pants when he wasn't a target.

In the second quarter, one of the hot air blowers on Green Bay's sideline ran out of gas, the billowing smoke sending players scurrying for what comfort they could find. However, that didn't slow down the Packers' arsenal as Starr hit Dowler again, this time from 43 yards out on a third-and-1 call that Starr had become famous for during the decade, giving the hosts a comfortable 14–0 cushion.

THE TOWN TEAM ERA

During the 1930s, more than 25 Wisconsin cities were homes to professional or semipro football teams. The Green Bay Packers played preseason games against such foes as the La Crosse Lagers, Merrill Fromm Foxes, Chippewa Falls Marines, and Fort Atkinson Blackhawks, which included encounters in Chippewa Falls and Merrill.

Later in the second quarter, Green Bay cornerback Herb Adderley returned an interception to the Dallas 32. But an Andrie sack for a 10-yard loss ended a threat that could have blown the game open.

Dallas's defensive front four then turned the game around. Townes hit Starr on first down from the Green Bay 26, and Andrie scooped up the loose pigskin and rumbled in for a seven-yard TD to cut Green Bay's advantage to 14–7 with 4:04 left in the first half.

The Cowboys were forced to punt on their next possession, but Wood fumbled the ball, giving the visitors a first and 10 at the Packers' 17. Green Bay held Dallas to Danny Villanueva's 21-yard field goal for a 14-10 score.

The visitors had grabbed the momentum despite not registering a first down in the second quarter, and the defensive tide continued in the third. Pugh's sack halted Green Bay's first drive after the intermission, and the Cowboys moved to the Packer 18.

However, Green Bay linebacker Lee Roy Caffey came up huge. He forced Dallas quarterback "Dandy" Don Meredith to fumble while scrambling deep in Packer territory, with Adderley recovering at the Green Bay 13. Later in the quarter, Caffey sacked Meredith for a nine-yard loss on a third-and-5 play from the Packer 30 to force a futile 47-yard field goal attempt that came up short. Green Bay's offense had been stymied, gaining only 8 yards and one first down in the third quarter.

Dallas started the fourth with a gadget play on second and 5. Halfback Dan Reeves surprised the Packers with a 50-yard option pass to Lance Rentzel to give the Cowboys a 17–14 lead with 14:52 remaining. The right-handed Reeves, formerly a college quarterback at South Carolina, ran the play to his left, lofting his pass to a wide-open Rentzel, who had to wait for the wind to quit playing with the ball before he could corral it.

Green Bay, which had only three first downs in the third and most of the fourth quarters, moved into range for kicker Don Chandler, but in the miserable conditions, he missed a 40-yard field goal attempt with 9:44 left.

Dallas ran off almost five minutes of the clock while earning two first downs before punting to set the stage for the famous drive.

Green Bay won the first down battle 18-11 but only outgained the Cowboys 195–192, although Dallas managed just 142 besides the long option play for their final score. Don Perkins led Dallas's running game with 17 carries for 51 yards, while Meredith completed 10 of 25 passes for 59 yards. Hayes, who had 49 catches for 998 yards and 10 scores in the regular season, was limited to three receptions for 16 yards. Starr finished 14 of 24 for 191 yards but lost 76 yards on sacks. Anderson led the ground attack with 35 yards on 18 carries.

One elderly man died of a heart attack during the game, and the brutal conditions took their toll on those working that day. NFL Films cameraman Art Spieller was stationed in an opening in the metal scoreboard above the south end zone. "I felt my life was going to come to an end in Green Bay and I was going to freeze to death in that scoreboard and no one would know I was there."

But in the end, Lombardi and his Packers had cemented their place among the great dynasties of pro football. "This was our greatest one," Lombardi said of his team's fifth crown in seven years. "This is what the Green Bay Packers are all about. They don't do it for individual glory. They do it because they love one another."

Mercein said he would never forget that last drive. "To see it must have been great, but to be in it and feel it was just something else," the Milwaukee native said. "Thank goodness I was able to contribute. Everybody gave everything they had. We knew what we had to do."

Dallas coach Tom Landry was stunned at how the contest ended. "I can't believe that call, the sneak," Landry said. "It wasn't a good call, but now it's a great call. I thought Starr would roll out and, depending on what he saw, throw to an open receiver or just toss the ball out of bounds to stop the clock and give them time to get Chandler on the field. If the play had failed, the game would have been over. There's no way they'd have gotten off another play."

But that's one small part of why this game has created so many myths and legends and why it remains forever etched in the minds of football fans across Wisconsin and the nation. ★

Packers Outlast Redskins in a Monday Night Marathon

It's debatable whether Green Bay defensive coordinator John Meyer was being funny, sarcastic, or both after his unit allowed 552 yards the night of October 17, 1983. Regardless, he was definitely accurate in his description of what happened during that *Monday Night Football* contest between Bart Starr's struggling Packers and Joe Gibbs's defending National Football League champion Washington Redskins.

"Our function today was to play defense while the offense caught its breath," Meyer said after the Packers escaped with one of the most thrilling victories in team annals, a 48–47 decision that remains the highest-scoring *MNF* showdown in history.

It was a microcosm of many contests at Lambeau Field in the 1980s: the Packers often finished around the .500 mark when their offenses unleashed enough firepower to outscore opponents that usually ran roughshod against the Green Bay defense.

But it was appropriate for these two teams. Green Bay finished the season with 429 points (it allowed 439), a team record that stood until the Super Bowl XXXI champions registered 456 in 1996, while the Redskins tallied 541, an NFL record that lasted until Minnesota reached 556 in 1998. Still, nobody who attended and none of the millions who watched on television could have envisioned a shootout like this, but they're oh so glad they got to see it.

Quarterback Lynn Dickey (12) retreats into the pocket during the Packers' thrilling 48-47 victory over Washington in 1983 in what is still the highest-scoring "Monday Night Football" game. (Photo courtesy of Vernon Biever)

The Redskins entered the game with five consecutive victories after a season-opening setback to Dallas. The visitors didn't lose again until being demolished by the Los Angeles Raiders in the Super Bowl.

In what proved to be Starr's final campaign as head coach, Green Bay's roller-coaster season had gotten off to a 3–3 start (they finished 8–8). That included two 24-point setbacks in the last three weeks before facing Washington, a heavy favorite.

Green Bay entered with the league's worst defense, so the fact that the hosts allowed 47 points wasn't surprising. However, despite the power of the Packers' attack, scoring 48 against the 'Skins was startling. The outcome provided the fifth-most points scored in any NFL game.

Washington kicker Mark Moseley missed a 39-yard field goal as time expired to give Green Bay the victory in front of 55,255 fans. The Redskins had moved 46 yards with no timeouts left to set up the game-winning attempt.

The game was tied three times in the first half and the lead changed hands on six occasions in the final 10:15. The combatants accumulated 1,025 yards in total offense as the Packers scored seven of 10 times they had the ball and the Redskins got points on nine of 12 possessions.

Washington quarterback Joe Theismann finished 27-of-39 for 398 yards, Moseley connected on four field goals, and halfback Joe Washington contributed 80 yards rushing and nine catches for 57 yards.

IT'S FOOTBALL OR ME

Daisy Goldstein found out firsthand just how fanatical supporters of the Green Bay Packers can be. In 1931, the Oshkosh woman sought and was granted a divorce from her husband, Hyman, because she said she couldn't compete with the team for his attention. She testified in circuit court that he neglected her to follow Curly Lambeau's team around the country.

But Hyman could claim just cause. The Packers were good that year, winning their third straight NFL championship.

Meanwhile, Green Bay signal caller Lynn Dickey answered his counterpart almost pass for pass, recording a 22-for-31 performance for 387 yards. Tight end Paul Coffman caught six passes for 124 yards and two touchdowns.

Green Bay kicker Jan Stenerud made the deciding three-pointer from 20 yards out with 54 seconds remaining. Gerry Ellis's 56-yard catch and run set up the field goal.

After the emotional, topsy-turvy evening, Starr credited his offensive coordinator. "The play calling of Bob Schnelker was the finest I've seen in a lifetime and the execution of it was a close second." Part of the strategy had Dickey passing on 16 first down plays. "It's no big secret that we're not a great running team," Dickey said later. "I think he [Schnelker] wanted to be real aggressive from the start." The Redskins were 26th against the pass and first against the run coming into the game.

Green Bay's five offensive scores came after drives that lasted four minutes or less, including quick-striking marches of 74 yards in 37 seconds, 80 yards in 35 seconds, and 39 yards in 15 seconds. However, the first score of the game came when Green Bay outside linebacker Mike Douglass scored on a 22-yard fumble return.

Washington responded with a six-play, 55-yard drive that ended when tight end Clint Didier recovered a fumble in the end zone. Stenerud then put the Packers on top with a 47-yard field goal, but Moseley booted his first, a 42-yarder after two Green Bay sacks, to knot things at 10 after the first quarter.

Dickey and Coffman collaborated on a 36-yard pitch and catch for a 17–10 Green Bay lead, but Washington fullback John Riggins smashed in from a yard out after his 36-yard jaunt set up the score for another deadlock.

Halfback Eddie Lee Ivery tossed a 35-yard option pass to Coffman to the Redskins' 9, and the latter scored on a pass from Dickey for a 24–17 margin. Moseley's 28-yard field goal left Green Bay ahead 24–20 at halftime.

Ellis's 24-yard scamper pushed Green Bay's cushion to 31–20 after Dickey found future Hall of Fame flanker James Lofton for a 40-yard gain. Washington shaved its deficit to 31–23 on Moseley's boot after an offensive interference penalty negated a TD.

The Redskins then blocked a punt that led to a touchdown to make it 31–30, and the visitors moved ahead 33–31 after another Moseley field goal with 10 seconds left in the third quarter.

Harlan Huckleby returned the ensuing kickoff 57 yards to the Washington 39. Ellis's 32-yard catch to the 7 set up tight end Gary Lewis's two-yard TD run on a reverse as the hosts regained the lead at 38–33 with 14:45 left.

The onslaught continued as Theismann's 25-yard pass to Art Monk set up Riggins's one-yard plunge to cap an eight-play, 70-yard drive and a 40–38 score at the 9:57 mark. Green Bay then covered 68 yards in six plays, including a 31-yard pass from Dickey to fullback Mike Meade on a third-and-13 call, for a 45–40 lead.

Joe Washington's five-yard TD catch concluded another long march, this time 72 yards on nine plays, as the Redskins grabbed what proved to be their final lead, 47–45, with 2:50 left. Then, on a third-and-10 play from the Green Bay 36, Dickey and Ellis hooked up for the 56-yarder to the Washington 8.

The Redskins dominated in time of possession, 39:05 to 20:55. Riggins churned for 98 yards, while Charlie Brown caught six passes for 91 yards and Monk added five for 105 as Washington won the first down battle, 33–23. Green

Bay's output included Ellis's four receptions for 105 yards and Lofton's five for 96 as the Packers averaged 9.1 yards per play to Washington's 6.4.

Starr then urged his players to remain on the field to enjoy the revelry with Green Bay fans. "I wanted them to stay out there and salute the crowd, which was instrumental tonight," Starr said. "The crowd was really tuned on and it was a brief way to say thank you." Green Bay defensive end Ezra Johnson said it was a special night and that the Packers deserved to win. "We got pride," Johnson said. "We got desire. We got heart. We proved what caliber of team we got."

Despite coming up short, Theismann, currently an analyst on ESPN games, said he couldn't believe what had transpired during the past three-plus hours. "I don't think I was on the bench more than four or five minutes at a time," said Theismann. ★

The First of Three: Badgers Take 1994 Rose Bowl

Pasadena, California, long had been used to the hoopla and pageantry surrounding the annual New Year's Day celebration that culminated with the Rose Bowl game. However, residents had never been invaded by a red army like this, as tens of thousands of Wisconsin Badger fans converged on their city in late December 1993.

Decked out in T-shirts, hats, and any other Bucky Badger paraphernalia available, they came from across the country to cheer on their favorite team in its tussle against the UCLA Bruins. The $46 tickets were selling for as much as $500 and Wisconsin supporters were grabbing as many of them as they could get their hands on because it was their university's first trip to the granddaddy of bowl games since 1963. An announced crowd of 101,237, of which an estimated three-fourths were wearing red and white, attended the contest. Unfortunately, more than 2,000 UW backers were steaming because Southern California brokers oversold the game, leaving them with nonrefundable plane tickets and no passes for the 80th Rose Bowl showdown.

And then there was the game between the ninth-ranked Big Ten cochampion Badgers and the number 14 Bruins, who had overcome an 0–2 season start to claim the Pac-Ten crown.

Even though Wisconsin entered with a 9–1–1 mark and UCLA finished the regular season 8–3, the Bruins, playing on their home field, were labeled a seven-point favorite. Despite the odds, the Badgers controlled most of the action and escaped with a thrilling 21–16 triumph, only the second bowl win in the 104-year history of the Wisconsin football program and its first in four tries in Pasadena. And Wisconsin capped its unbelievable campaign with the unlikeliest of heroes clinching the verdict, six-foot-two, 200-pound sophomore quarterback Darrell Bevell.

Quarterback Darrell Bevell celebrates with teammates after scoring the winning touchdown in Wisconsin's 21-16 triumph over UCLA in 1994, giving the Badgers their first Rose Bowl victory. (Photo courtesy of the University of Wisconsin)

Bevell had set several team and league passing marks that year, but what made his big contribution so unique was that he used his legs to do it. Less than fleet of foot, Bevell eluded the rush of Travis Kirschke and headed down the left sideline. He got a crucial block from flanker J. C. Dawkins at the five-yard line and reached paydirt to give the Badgers a 21–10 advantage about four minutes into the fourth quarter. "Considering how many guys were coming at me, I was amazed I was still on my feet at the 5," Bevell said afterward. "I've never run 21 yards at one time in my life. If you asked anybody on this team who they would least expect to do something like this, I guarantee they'd say me."

If anybody would have been Wisconsin's hero in the running game, it would have been tailback Brent Moss, who was later picked the game's Most Valuable Player for his 36-carry, 158-yard afternoon, featuring two touchdowns that gave the Badgers a 14–3 cushion at halftime.

He couldn't believe what he saw on the second-and-8 play. "Yeah, I was surprised when Darrell took it all the way in," said Moss, UW's workhorse, whose longest gain of the game was 17 yards. "I thought he might run out-of-bounds."

It was Bevell's only rushing attempt in an encounter in which he completed 10 of 20 pass attempts for an economical 96 yards with one interception. His scoring play was supposed to be a pass to the right side. "Depending on the coverage, I was going to try to hit the tight end or fullback, but both of them were covered, so I didn't have much choice but to scramble," Bevell said.

UCLA had pulled to within 14–10 on Ricky Davis's scamper 52 seconds into the final quarter. However, Davis fumbled, one of five times the Bruins coughed up the pigskin, on UCLA's next possession, with Mike Thompson's recovery putting the Badgers 34 yards away from the end zone. Bevell reached that destination four plays later.

However, Terry Donahue's Bruins didn't cave in, clawing back to within 21–16 when UCLA quarterback Wayne Cook hit receiver Mike Nguyen with a five-yard pass in the right corner to cap off a 15-play march that featured 14 passes. But Cook's toss for a two-point conversion failed with 3:38 remaining. Then the Bruins, who were forced to use their three timeouts on defense, stopped the Badgers on downs at their 38.

BLIZZARD BALL

Many later referred to it as the Snowball game, a November 7, 1925, Big Ten football showdown in which Wisconsin defeated Iowa, 6–0, in Iowa City. An estimated 10,000 fans braved the blowing snow, which wiped out the sideline and yard markers. The teams combined for 40 fumbles, including 18 in the first quarter. "Red" Kreuz scored the game's only touchdown in the fourth quarter after Wisconsin took over on the Hawkeyes' 11-yard line after a punt.

Cook later connected with standout wide receiver J. J. Stokes for an 18-yard gain to the UW 18. On first down with 15 seconds left, Cook ran up the middle instead of throwing the ball away to stop the clock. Thompson tackled him, and time ran out before the Bruins could get off another potential game-winning play. It was Donahue's first setback in four Rose Bowl visits and ended the current San Francisco 49er executive's eight-game winning string in bowl games.

Tackle Carlos Fowler and nose guard Lamark Shackerford led the Badgers' defense that held UCLA, making its first appearance in the game in eight years, to a field goal until the fourth quarter. The upset victory capped a merry-go-round season for Wisconsin, which had shaken the label as Big Ten doormat in four years under coach Barry Alvarez. The Badgers survived an unexpected defeat to rival Minnesota, a stampede of students onto Camp Randall Stadium that injured 70 people after their win against Michigan, and a trip to Tokyo, where they beat Michigan State, 41–20, to tie for the conference title and earn the Rose Bowl berth.

Alvarez said afterward that the positive result came because the players believed in each other and themselves. "They believed in the plan that we gave them," Alvarez said during postgame interviews. "Regardless of the doubters, regardless of whether we were underdogs or favorites, regardless of what people said or what they had to overcome, they believed in one another."

And it didn't take long for the Badgers to start the celebration. Mike Brin had been one of the heroes from the Michigan crowd mishap and made snow angels on the big red rose at the 50-yard line. Scott Nelson proposed to his girlfriend, Becky Bliefoth, after interviews with members of the media. Others danced the polka and the UW's famous marching band jazzed up the partisan crowd with its West Coast version of the Fifth Quarter.

But none of that would have been possible had the Badgers not dominated the scoreboard in the first half. UCLA moved ahead 3–0, but Wisconsin retaliated with a 10-play, 78-yard drive that Moss ended with a three-yard TD run with 11 seconds left in the first quarter. After the foes exchanged interceptions, Stokes fumbled to put Wisconsin in business at the UCLA 32. Moss's second score, after three plunges from the 1, made it 14–3 at the intermission.

WHAT A TURNOUT

Milwaukee Pulaski and Milwaukee Bay View high schools drew what is believed to be the largest crowd to ever attend a prep football game in Wisconsin. That happened when 19,500 fans piled into Marquette Stadium in the fall of 1949. Pulaski won the contest, 30–0.

Wisconsin could have put the game out of reach on its first offensive series of the second half, but Moss was stuffed on a fourth-and-1 play from the Bruins' 9.

The heated confrontation turned ugly after a lot of trash talking and mild skirmishes earlier in the game, when a fight after that crucial UCLA defensive stand resulted in two players from each team being ejected: Bruin safeties Marvin Goodwin and Donovan Gallatin, UW's top receiver Lee DeRamus, and fullback Mark Montgomery.

The Bruins marched up and down the field to the tune of 500 total yards, but they couldn't compensate for their miscues, which included nine penalties for 95 yards.

Cook, who missed practice time because of the flu and had difficulty talking, ended up 28-of-43 for 288 yards. He had the one interception and lost two fumbles in Wisconsin territory. The all-American Stokes corralled a school record 14 catches for 176 yards, a Rose Bowl mark, as UCLA won the air battle by almost 200 yards and had 31 first downs to Wisconsin's 21. The Badgers committed 12 penalties for 89 yards but rushed for 250 yards.

However, the numbers didn't matter, except for the final score. The win put Wisconsin's program in the national spotlight and gave the Big Ten a boost after league teams had lost 19 of the previous 24 Rose Bowls.

Bevell said that victory cemented Wisconsin's place among the quality programs, not only in the Big Ten but also across the country. "That game and win were very special to me and many of the other guys," Bevell said in a 2003 phone interview from Green Bay, where he is the Packers' quarterbacks coach. "It was the school's first Rose Bowl win, and that carried over into recruiting and everything that Coach Alvarez and his staff did. People had seen and heard about what we had accomplished, so it meant the program was headed in the right direction."

However, Bevell said getting to that point meant gaining respect, something the Badgers definitely didn't have going into that trip to Pasadena. "I remember during the coin toss. The official says to Joe Panos, who was going to call it, that the coin had UCLA on one side and Washington on the other. Joe said to them, 'It's Wisconsin.' But if you listen to the TV replay, you can hear them say Washington. So that whole time we didn't feel like we were getting the respect we deserved. That kind of put the capper on it."

Yet as the Badgers had proved during their sometimes tumultuous season, this was one game, and it was the only one that mattered at the moment. "It's a cliché, but our coaches preached that the next game was the most important one, and that's how we approached the season," Bevell said. "We never got ahead of ourselves. We couldn't afford to anyway. The coaches kept us focused, and that's how we were able to put Wisconsin on the map. We helped build that winning tradition." ★

Packers Blitz Patriots in Super Bowl XXXI

Green Bay registered 12 scoring plays of 50 yards or longer during the 1996 regular season, so it shouldn't have come as a surprise to anyone reading the box score the morning after Super Bowl XXXI in New Orleans.

League Most Valuable Player Brett Favre threw touchdown passes of 54 yards to Andre Rison and 81 yards to Antonio Freeman in the first half, and Desmond Howard broke the game open in the third quarter with a 99-yard kickoff return to seal the Packers' 35–21 triumph over the New England Patriots.

General Manager Ron Wolf was the architect, coach Mike Holmgren served as the foreman, and the Packers executed the blueprint perfectly, recapturing the moniker America's Team while making victory in the Big Easy look so simple.

An estimated 800 million people worldwide watched this version of the Green and Gold erase almost three decades of "the Pack will be back" talk, creating its own legacy and putting itself alongside the storied franchise's greatest teams from the glorious past.

No doubt the game action on the Superdome carpet gave fans dozens of plays to remember, but what Cheesehead could forget the other sights and sounds that surrounded the game:

- Favre sprinting off the field, his helmet held high, after connecting with Rison for the TD on Green Bay's second offensive play.

- The jubilant quarterback leaping into the arms of his linemen after helping give Green Bay a 27–14 halftime cushion.

- Reggie White's victory lap around the stadium floor with the Lombardi Trophy in tow and cameramen falling over each other trying to catch him on film.

- Don Beebe grabbing the game ball and threatening to wear his uniform on the plane after winning his first NFL title in five trips to the big dance.

- Santana Dotson embracing his father, Alphonse, a former AFL defensive lineman.

- Holmgren being carried across the field on his players' shoulders—including ex-Wisconsin Badger and Wausau native Jeff Dellenbach—in a sea of confetti.

- And longtime radio announcer Jim Irwin's words after counting off the final seconds, "What a moment. Oh man, is this good? Is this heaven, or what?"

If it wasn't, it sure was close. And it didn't take Green Bay long to give its supporters a slice of it, bolting to a 10–0 advantage behind Favre's toss to a wide-open Rison on a post pattern and Chris Jacke's field goal after cornerback Doug Evans's interception.

Just when it looked like another NFC blowout, New England quarterback Drew Bledsoe spearheaded the 14-point underdog Patriots. Mixing a variety of screens, play-action passes, and enough doses of running back Curtis Martin to keep Green Bay's pass rush honest, the Patriots closed out the highest-scoring first quarter in Super Bowl history with a 14–10 margin.

THAT'LL SHUT HIM UP

Sometimes fans in the Green Bay Packers-Chicago Bears rivalry take things to extremes. Just ask John Cochara, a Packers fan from Antioch, Illinois. Chicago supporters apparently couldn't take his cheering during one of Green Bay's victories in the 1995 season, so they duct-taped Cochara to a stop sign outside of Casey's Cabin Tavern in Spring Grove, Illinois. A local policeman finally came to his rescue.

Green Bay became the first team since Don Shula's unbeaten Miami Dolphins of 1972 to lead the league in most points scored while allowing the fewest. And the Packers showed that kind of mettle the rest of the way, proving they were indeed the best team that season while making Titletown proud.

No one knew that better than Beebe, who had suffered gut-wrenching setbacks in four consecutive attempts at getting his hands on the Lombardi Trophy while suiting up for the Buffalo Bills. "I've been there five times, and in the four losses we just did not handle adversity," Beebe said. "This team is able to do that. We came out smokin', and then they went up 14–10 on us. That's adversity. Now what do you do? Do you still keep your emotions up? Sure. That's what this team did. That's what I think a true champion does."

Favre's dart to a streaking Freeman down the right side and behind safety Lawyer Malloy gave the Packers the longest-scoring play from scrimmage in Super Bowl history, and more importantly a lead they wouldn't relinquish again. After Jacke's second three-pointer, Favre scampered in to give Green Bay a 13-point advantage. "I was licking my chops when I saw that safety walk up," Freeman said of the go-ahead touchdown. "Eighty-one yards later, we are in the record books."

Green Bay lost 7 yards on a fourth-down play at the New England 36 to give the AFC contingent hope in the third quarter, as Martin culminated the Patriots' next drive with an 18-yard run to trim their deficit to 27–21.

However, that was only a hiccup along the road, as Howard, the former University of Michigan Heisman Trophy winner, silenced the New England fans 17 seconds later with his TD jaunt, strutting across the goal line to highlight a record-setting performance that included 154 yards on kickoff returns and 90 more on punt runbacks.

Favre's pass to Mark Chmura for a two-point conversion closed out the scoring, and Green Bay's number-one-ranked defense, which established an NFL standard by giving up only 19 TDs during a 16-game schedule, did the rest.

Reggie White sacked Bledsoe on consecutive plays en route to a record three takedowns, as the Packers allowed only one first down after the decisive score. The unit harassed Bledsoe into a 25-for-48, 253-yard day that included four interceptions and five sacks.

"You watch year in and year out, and Super Bowls are won on big plays," Bledsoe said. "The Packers made more big plays than we did, they didn't turn the ball over and they basically played a fairly mistake-free game. . . . Unfortunately, we weren't able to play to the same level."

No one else did during 1996, either. Green Bay raced to an 8–1 record despite the dreaded *Sports Illustrated* cover jinx September 2 that predicted the Packers would celebrate Mardi Gras in style late in January.

Green Bay safety LeRoy Butler pulls down New England quarterback Drew Bledsoe during the Packers' 35-21 victory in Super Bowl XXXI in New Orleans. (Photo courtesy of Vernon Biever)

But mounting injuries, especially to the Packers' receiving corps, helped give opponents reasons for optimism. Green Bay stumbled badly at Kansas City and Dallas and was headed toward a third consecutive defeat on its final leg of a long November road trip when Evans turned in what many believe was the most crucial play of the season. He intercepted a Tony Banks slant pass and returned it 32 yards for a TD, stopping the bleeding and igniting a second half rally against the lowly Saint Louis Rams that catapulted the team to a five-game winning streak to end the year.

Despite losing number-one ball catcher Robert Brooks for the season with a severe knee injury against San Francisco on October 14 and left tackle Ken Ruettgers's retirement from chronic knee problems after the loss to the Cowboys, Freeman returned from a broken forearm and Chmura overcame an arch injury for the stretch run.

The Packers ran roughshod over the competition, outscoring their last five foes by an average of 32–9 to earn home-field advantage throughout the playoffs. They carried that momentum throughout the postseason, clobbering the NFC West's top two teams at Lambeau: San Francisco (35–14) in the rain and mud, and Carolina (30–13) in frigid conditions with wind chills that reached 20 below zero.

But weather is seldom a problem for the Packers, not when compared to some of the other roadblocks individuals had to overcome to make preseason prognosticators correct, particularly Favre. In May, he went public about his addiction to the painkiller Vicodin and spent 45 days in a rehabilitation center in Kansas. His brother, Scott, was at the wheel during an accident that killed one of their best friends, Mark Haverty, in July. In September, his sister was arrested for being in a car during a drive-by shooting.

With typical Favre confidence, he told the world what to expect in the coming months. "I'm going to beat this thing and I'm going to win the Super Bowl," he said. "All I can tell people is if you don't believe me, bet against me, because eventually they'll lose." If the rest of the league wasn't listening, they sure heard it loud and clear during and after the Battle in the Bayou.

The death of close buddy Frank Winters's brother a few days before the biggest game of their lives dampened Favre's spirits and flulike symptoms hindered his practice routine, but the gunslinger wasn't about to hang up his pistols.

Much of the pregame hype concerning the Packers' sideline had to do with the fact Favre grew up in Kiln, Mississippi, about an hour's drive from New Orleans. But none of that rattled Favre, who passed for 246 yards and no interceptions in leading the Packers back to the Promised Land.

Besides, a lot of the media blitz leading up to the game was aimed at the Big Tuna, New England coach Bill Parcells. He orchestrated some of it to keep the pressure off his team, but most of it related to rumors about him leaving and taking over the New York Jets' fortunes, which he ended up doing, and his previous two Super Bowl wins with the Big Apple's other team, the Giants (1986 and 1990).

Denver (13–3) was the odds-on favorite to represent the AFC, but the second-year Jacksonville franchise upset Buffalo and the Broncos on the road to reach the championship contest. New England whipped Pittsburgh and then ended the Jaguars' Cinderella run with a 20–6 victory.

The Patriots were a confident bunch, but why wouldn't they be? Nobody figured they could knock off the Green Bay juggernaut, so New England players took advantage of their spot on the Super Bowl stage.

The Packers talked a good game too, but once the whistle blew, they backed it up. New England slowly realized that it couldn't match Green Bay's star power or its firepower. And that started with return ace Howard. He had taken three punts back for touchdowns during the regular season and one more to paydirt versus the 49ers. His first try against the Patriots, he returned 32 yards to set up Green Bay's first scoring drive. He then covered 34 yards to set up Jacke's second field goal.

Howard had floundered in Washington and Jacksonville before Green Bay picked him up during the summer. He almost didn't make the team until a return TD against Pittsburgh helped secure a final receiver spot during an injury-plagued exhibition season, but the shifty Howard became the first special teams player to be named the Super Bowl's top performer. "I won the Heisman coming out of college and being a very young athlete I thought I could never have the feeling of ecstasy that I had to be presented with that award, but this here is definitely the next level," Howard said while holding up his MVP hardware.

After blowing a lead in the fourth quarter at Dallas in the NFC Championship matchup the year before, Green Bay picked up several other key acquisitions that played a big role in the Super Bowl season: defensive tackle Dotson, Beebe, left tackle Bruce Wilkerson, and safety Eugene Robinson. Tight end Keith Jackson played a full season after being obtained in a trade with Miami the previous year. Rison, a talented receiver who'd been labeled a malcontent at other stopovers during his career, provided a much-needed target during the injury spree.

And a host of young players were growing up, namely those from Wolf's magnificent 1995 draft, including cornerback Craig Newsome, fullback William Henderson, linebacker Brian Williams, Freeman, running back and special teams demon Travis Jervey, and guard Adam Timmerman.

Throw in White, Favre, Chmura, Sean Jones, Winters, Gilbert Brown, LeRoy Butler, the backfield tandem of Edgar Bennett and Dorsey Levens … the list goes on and on. "We finally got here," Butler said. "It was a long road. It was a little bumpy along the way, but we got here. That's all that matters now."

Packer fans, former stars who roamed Lambeau, and, of course, Lombardi's ghost could rest easier now that sanity had returned to the NFL and Green Bay had brought Vince's trophy back home.

Holmgren, who had to settle for number two in the press behind Parcells for two weeks, also moved out from behind the huge shadow of the last man to lead the Packers to the title. "We've reached the top of the mountain," Holmgren said. "In a couple of days, we'll start talking about how we get back up there again. But for a couple of days I'm really going to enjoy this."

His sometimes unruly prize pupil, Favre, also found a sense of vindication. "I've been through a lot of tough times this year and a lot of good," Favre said. "They kind of equal themselves out, and you take the good with the bad. To win this, it's unbelievable."

"I'm very greedy," Favre added. "Now I want to win more [Super Bowls]. I see what other players have talked about once you win one. We want to come back and win another one. But we want to enjoy this for a while."

Faithful followers continued the celebration upon the team's journey back north, sitting for several hours in 17-degree cold and 10-below-zero wind chills along the motorcade route of team buses to catch a glimpse of their heroes or going inside Lambeau Field to listen to their victorious warriors address the crowd from a makeshift stage.

Holmgren said the reception was something he and the organization grew to expect. "Seeing all of those people and the outpouring of affection was overwhelming," Holmgren said. "People were all over. There were little bitty kids all the way up to grandmas and grandpas. It was something very special."

Perhaps nothing summarized the 1996 Green Bay Packers more than this offering written by Sam McManis of *Knight-Ridder*: "Sentiment ran thick Sunday, thick and rich as a fat wedge of cheddar affixed to one's cranium. You'd have to have a heart as hardened as a longtime Cheesehead's arteries not to feel something for these Green Bay Packers, who finally accomplished what their forefathers last did 29 years ago.

"They are Super Bowl champions once more. They lovingly passed around the trophy named after the franchise's former coach, Vince Lombardi, as if it were the family crest restored to its rightful place on the mantle. And maybe they're right. Maybe order in the football universe was restored now that Green Bay's claim as 'Titletown USA' is no longer merely a nostalgic notion from bygone days." ★

Ron Dayne Romps to Collegiate Rushing Record

It was a routine play in the University of Wisconsin's offensive attack called the 23 Zone.

However, November 13, 1999, wasn't a typical day in Badgers' history, and seldom did running back Ron Dayne settle for the ordinary.

The bruising 250-plus pounder entered this Big Ten Conference regular season finale against Iowa at Camp Randall Stadium needing 99 yards to surpass Texas's Ricky Williams as the all-time leading rusher in college football annals. Dayne, a New Jersey high school star before coming to Madison, shattered the year-old mark on his 14th attempt on the call that was designed for him to run left. But it's an option in that he can decide to go anywhere, so he broke it over right guard. He juked Hawkeyes' free safety Shane Hall and ran over cornerback Joe Slattery before cornerback Tarig Halman finally dragged him down after a 31-yard romp near the Wisconsin bench.

Badgers' coach Barry Alvarez, relegated to duty from the press box because he was recovering from knee replacement surgery, said the moment—which occurred with 4:32 left in the second quarter—couldn't have turned out much more special. "It would not have been appropriate to be a two-yard gain, a little mush into the middle," Alvarez said. "One of our base plays we put in the first day [of camp], where he reads it, makes the cut to a seam and then comes out the back end, runs through a couple of tackles. The only thing that would have been better is if he'd have gone to the end zone with it."

That might have mattered to the 79,404 in attendance, but Dayne was happier about the 41–3 victory that improved the Badgers to 9–2, clinched an undisputed Big Ten title for the first time since 1962, and earned the hosts their second straight trip to the Rose Bowl.

It was that team-first approach that carried Dayne throughout his days after he replaced 1,000-yard rusher Carl McCullough during his freshman season. "It's going to be great," Dayne said as the Badgers prepared for Iowa, who ended their season at 1–9. "First, got to get the win. I've been saying that all season. Once we do that, the record might come during the game, unless we turn into Florida State and start throwing it."

NO-DATING GAMES

Part of the reason Jack Ryan was hired as the University of Wisconsin football coach in 1923 was that he came from Dartmouth, an all-male university at the time. Of Ryan's hiring, UW Athletic Director Tom Jones said, "We have lacked man spirit in this school for the last four years. We have been fighting the coeds of the school. Jack Ryan comes from a man's school." One of the rules Ryan laid down was that his players could date only on Sundays.

It didn't work. His teams went 5–6–4 in two years, and Ryan left his position.

That obviously never happened, as Dayne rushed 27 times for 216 yards to reach 6,397 for his career. And whether he would admit it or not, his effort put an exclamation point on his date with the Heisman Trophy, which he won December 11 and became the second Wisconsin player so honored after Alan Ameche did it in 1954.

In the process, Dayne became the first running back to win three Big Ten Conference rushing titles. But it was strictly a formality, because he had rushed for more than 100 yards by halftime in five of the team's first 10 games, and few doubted that the same thing wouldn't happen against the hapless Hawkeyes.

Dayne gained only 37 yards on his first 10 carries, causing restlessness among those in the faithful packed house and with the wall of blockers in front of him. "It was definitely on all of our minds," said Mark Tauscher, the right tackle and current starter with the Green Bay Packers. "In the beginning it was kind of a struggle. I think it was maybe getting to us a little bit that we were getting 2, 3 yards a shot and weren't breaking any. Then we got a few big hits and the tension eased off a little bit and we started going."

When Dayne broke loose, there was little Iowa's defense could do to prevent the inevitable as Tauscher, Chris McIntosh at left tackle, Bill Ferrario at left guard, Casey Rabach at center, and Dave Costa at right guard started to dominate the line of scrimmage.

Dayne's 37-yard run was the key play as UW grabbed a 20–3 lead, and then he broke the record on a first-and-10 call from the Badgers' 17 on a drive that wide receiver Chris Chambers capped with his second TD catch for a 27–3 halftime cushion.

Because Iowa was keying on stopping Dayne, UW quarterback Brooks Bollinger found running and passing lanes, rushing for 96 of his 113 yards and completing seven of eight passes for 115 yards before the intermission. It became Dayne's fourth 200-yard outing of the season and the 11th of his career. His high was 339 yards against Hawaii as a freshman.

Tauscher helped open up the hole but said it was a team effort, which had carried the Badgers all year, that earned the record. "It's nice that it came back my way, but it's a tribute to the whole front seven that got it done."

As for the star of the moment, Ferrario said that Dayne responded to the attention and accolades in his usual ho-hum manner, although he was smiling a lot. "He just said, 'Great blocking.' The same thing he says every other play. 'Great job out there.' It's just as much ours as it is his."

And it allowed UW to go on and become the Big Ten's first back-to-back Rose Bowl champion, which is what Dayne said about getting to Pasadena all along. "That's because we get a ring for that," Dayne said. "I just get my name on the books for breaking the record."

Wisconsin running back Ron Dayne became the NCAA's all-time leading rusher as the Badgers pummeled Iowa in 1999. (Photo courtesy of the University of Wisconsin)

Wisconsin finished with 424 yards rushing and controlled the clock for 37:46, so newspaper headline writers had it easy the next day. One in the *Wisconsin State Journal* read "Historic Dayne" and a special section about his accomplishments was titled "What a Rush: UW's Great Dayne." He also had his name emblazoned on the façade of the upper deck at Camp Randall, which was revealed during the postgame celebrations. As usual, Dayne struggled to find the words. "I didn't know what to say," Dayne said. "I was just so happy and grateful. I'm still kind of amazed and dazed."

That's how he left the Hawkeyes and most opponents during his four-year rampage on gridirons around the country.

Dayne, whose childhood idol had been former New York Jet and Washington Redskin star John Riggins, also had the honor of having a streaker run across the field shortly after the record-setting play, wearing nothing but a number 33 painted on his chest and a red bandana.

But that wasn't the most lasting image that people took away from that game and what Dayne meant to the university. "How can you forget that big smile?" Alvarez wondered aloud. "He just lit it up. I went down on the sidelines and you see him smiling and trying to work his way over to me. It was very meaningful and something you always have that picture in your mind."

Dayne said that was what he'll always remember. "The moment I most remember is when Coach came down on the field and I got to hug him and say, 'We finally got it done.' " ★

MORE RECORDS, STREAKS, AND AMAZING MOMENTS
PROFESSIONAL FOOTBALL
The First of Many

On December 8, 1929, the Green Bay Packers clinched the first of their NFL-record 12 championships, and they couldn't have picked a better team to do it against, dominating archrival Chicago for the second time at Wrigley Field and third time that season.

Lawrence College graduate Eddie Kotal, a halfback, scored two of the team's touchdowns during the 25–0 victory, giving the visitors their third consecutive shutout over Chicago that year and fourth in a row spanning two seasons.

Green Bay finished 12-0-1, which placed them just in front of the New York Giants, who had fashioned a 13–1–1 mark with their only setback being 20–6 to Green Bay. It also proved to be the first of three straight league crowns for the Packers under Earl "Curly" Lambeau. ★

Nobody Like Him

Packer wide receiver Don Hutson established a National Football League record that still stands, scoring 29 of Green Bay's 41 points in the second quarter during a 57–21 drubbing of the Detroit Lions. A crowd of 20,463 watched the Packers' offensive explosion at State Fair Park in Milwaukee on October 7, 1945. The University of Alabama product and future Hall of Famer hauled in four touchdown passes and booted five extra points in the quarter.

Hutson hauled in a 59-yard reception from Roy McKay for his first score and then reached paydirt from 45 yards out on a pass from Irv Comp. He then grabbed TD tosses from McKay from 17 and 6 yards, respectively.

Hall of Fame receiver Don Hutson, with the ball, set several team and NFL records during his career in 1935-45, which included scoring 29 points in one quarter against Detroit in his final season. (Photo courtesy of Vernon Biever)

Green Bay's other two scores in the quarter were also big plays: Comp's 46-yard pass to Clyde Goodnight and Ted Fritsch's 69-yard return of an interception, one of six errant passes the Packers picked off that day.

Hutson had scored three touchdowns in a game six times, but his four-TD effort tied Joe Carter of Philadelphia, who had set the standard 11 years earlier against Cincinnati.

Number 14 finished with 31 points for the game, which put him second to Ernie Nevers's unbelievable 40 for the Chicago Cardinals against the crosstown rival Bears in 1929. ★

He Was Golden

Paul Hornung led the Green Bay Packers in scoring five times, including four consecutive seasons beginning in 1958. Not only did he top Vince Lombardi's first three squads in Titletown, but the halfback from Notre Dame led the National Football League all those years, scoring 94, 176, and 146 points, respectively, as the most versatile threat in team annals. The Golden

Boy scored 15 touchdowns and booted 15 field goals and 41 extra points during his record-setting 1960 season.

Hornung's 176 points still hold the top position in league history, although Saint Louis kicker Jeff Wilkins (163) and Kansas City running back Priest Holmes (162) came close in 2003. Kicker Gary Anderson, playing for Minnesota in 1998, came the closest with 164 points on 35 field goals and 59 PATs.

What makes Hornung's effort so remarkable is that he did it in 12 games, while the latter three needed 16. ★

COLLEGE FOOTBALL
Leg Up on the Competition

Patrick John O'Dea, known as the Kangaroo Kicker, was an Australian who starred for the Wisconsin Badgers football team in 1896–1899. His specialties were drop kicking field goals and punting.

O'Dea booted a 65-yard field goal during a snowstorm against Northwestern in 1898 and unleashed a 110-yard punt versus Minnesota in 1897. His tremendously powerful right leg also connected on 14 field goals in the 1897 campaign. He kicked four in a game against Beloit College in 1899, a contest in which the fullback also rambled 100 yards for a touchdown.

Badger fans got an early example of what to expect when O'Dea got off an 85-yard punt on his first play with the team in a battle against Lake Forest in 1896. ★

Knocking Off Number One

On October 31, 1942, Wisconsin surprised Ohio State, the top-ranked team in the country, 17–7, with a record crowd of 47,000 on hand at Camp Randall Stadium. Elroy Hirsch, in what proved to be his only season for UW, made the game's big play. His 59-yard run set up the Badgers' first touchdown.

Wisconsin finished 8–1–1 and was ranked third in the final Associated Press poll, while the Buckeyes won the national championship. Wisconsin tied Notre Dame and lost a controversial 6–0 decision to Iowa that year. It was the first of three times that UW has beaten the number-one team; the others came against Northwestern in 1962 and Michigan in 1981. ★

Toast of the Town

On October 11, 1969, the Wisconsin Badgers ended 2 1/2 years of futility, snapping a 23-game winless streak with a 23–17 triumph over Iowa.

What made the thousands of screaming students, who marched toward the State Capitol afterward, so happy was that the Badgers had overcome a 17-point deficit in the final quarter. Fans blocked traffic, drank beer, and cruised around State Street in their vehicles, many of them chanting "We're No. 1!"

That was going a little overboard but understandable considering Wisconsin had finished 0–9–1 in 1967 and 0–10 in '68, the only two times in school history, except for the 0–2 squad of 1889, the Badgers had gone winless. Wisconsin, which had tied the Hawkeyes (21–all) in '67, hadn't won since closing the 1966 season with a 7–6 triumph over Minnesota.

Neil Graf's 17-yard strike to Randy Marks was the game-winner with 2:08 remaining, as Neovia Greyer's interception in the final minute snuffed out Iowa's last bid. ★

HIGH SCHOOL FOOTBALL
Running Wild

Star back Rollie Williams, a future standout at the University of Wisconsin, and the Edgerton High School football team defeated North Milwaukee, 13–6, in its 1916 season opener and then downed Marquette Academy, 6–0.

Not impressive, you say? Those were just warm-ups. Edgerton added eight more shutouts to end the season 10–0, outscoring their opponents 339–6 overall. Included in that unbelievable run were triumphs against Janesville (99–0), Fort Atkinson (78–0), and Milton College (48–0). Williams's top game came against Janesville, when he scored nine touchdowns. ★

Skinny Scores—A Lot

On Saturday afternoon, October 23, 1926, Gilford "Skinny" Skenadore, a 136-pound back, scored 66 points as Nicolet High of West De Pere whitewashed Kewaunee, 126–0, in a high school football game.

Skenadore's total is still recognized as the state record for most points in a single game. Skenadore scored eight touchdowns and converted all 18 of his team's extra point attempts on a wet, muddy field at Legion Park in De Pere.

His exploits included four punt returns for touchdowns as Nicolet scored four times in each of the first three quarters, and then tacked on 42 points in the final quarter as seven players reached the end zone in the game.

An account in the *Green Bay Press-Gazette* said that Nicolet outweighed its foes by an average of 40 pounds to the man, "and the extra poundage gave them a great advantage on a field that became a sea of mud and water after rain fell in the first quarter."

As for Skenadore's magnificent performance, the article summed it up this way: "The Nicolet forwards opened big holes and the backs shot through them and then wiggled away from tacklers who tried to stop them. All of the Nicolet backs rammed the Kewaunee line at will, and Skenadore was especially clever at sidestepping an opponent who loomed up ahead of him to negotiate the distance to goal."

Skenadore also starred in basketball and track, where he competed as a runner and hurdler. He graduated in 1928 and continued his athletic career at Haskell Institute and La Crosse Teachers College. ★

Winning with Win

Under the direction of coach Win Brockmeyer, the Wausau High School football team compiled a 72–2–4 record during the 1940s. Included was a then-state record 46-game winning streak that ended September 27, 1946, with a 13–7 loss to Ashland.

Brockmeyer served as head coach from 1939 to 1970 and finished with a record of 230–33–10. His squads won or shared 26 Wisconsin Valley and Big River conference titles. In 1939 he was 7–1. In 1940, Wausau went unbeaten and outscored its opponents 299–12, shutting out every foe until the season finale. They also went unbeaten in 1941, 1943, and 1945. He coached future National Football League Hall of Fame inductees Elroy Hirsch and Jim Otto. ★

Raider Power

Coach Harry O'Mealy directed the Two Rivers football program to a remarkable level seldom matched in state high school history. In 1943–46, the Raiders compiled a 30–2–1 record in which the only setbacks occurred in his first three games at the helm. The unbelievable run featured a 30-game unbeaten string (29–0–1) and 24-game winning streak while dominating the Northeastern Conference.

Two Rivers capped O'Mealy's run with 7–0–1, 8–0, and 9–0 teams that registered 14 shutouts and a 0–0 deadlock against rival Manitowoc. Those teams outscored their foes by an average of 25.2 to 3.5 points per game. The 1946 squad scored 260 points, a school mark that stood for 33 years, until Jerry Bonino's 11–0 Division 3 state champions tallied 290. ★

Gridiron Greatness

The high school football playoff system started in 1976 and has grown exponentially since, including more than 200 schools in seven classes.

The most successful teams have been Monroe, Menomonie, and Osseo–Fairchild with five championships each. D. C. Everest, Darlington, Edgar, and Lancaster are right behind with four. Lancaster (2000–02), Manitowoc (1984–86), Monroe (1990–92), and Two Rivers (1980–82) claim three straight titles. Antigo won two of the first three and three of the first seven Division 1 trophies, while D. C. Everest (four) and Marshfield (three) have helped give the Wisconsin Valley Conference 10 champions through 2002.

Darlington's 1995 winners put on the most explosive scoring show in finals history with a 63–6 triumph over Hurley in the Division 5 showdown. The

Redbirds set records for most points in a quarter (30) and a half (42), largest winning margin (57) and most touchdowns (nine). Doug McGowan set a record with five TDs in that game.

Other individual title game records include Steve Hougom of Westby with 362 yards rushing in 1986, Tom Fitzgerald of Spooner with 230 yards passing in 1991, and Scott Bestor of Platteville with 150 yards receiving in 1983. ★

No Passing Fancy

At six-foot-nine, Jeff Skemp was an imposing figure on the gridiron. On Friday night, September 27, 2002, he towered over all of Wisconsin high school quarterbacks when the Southwestern junior set state records for completions (44) and yards (612) in a thrilling 40–39 win against Riverdale at Hazel Green. Skemp attempted 70 passes as the Wildcats ran only four times. Skemp connected for five touchdowns, including a six-yarder to Jeremy Droeszler with 23 seconds left.

Three of Skemp's targets shattered the 100-yard barrier: Chad Burkholder had 15 catches for 198 yards and one score, Ben Wiederholt added 11 receptions for 129 yards, and Ryan Budden contributed eight catches for 121 yards and two TDs.

Skemp's yardage total bettered the mark of Lomira's Steve Steer, set in 1965, when he threw for 551. His completion record was three more than Dave Geissler of Chippewa Falls McDonell had in a 1981 contest. ★

Through the Air

Records of the Wisconsin Football Coaches Association through 2002 show that the most pass-happy school in history is Chippewa Falls McDonell. Quarterbacks for the Macks hold four of the top five season yardage totals, and all of them were established in the 1980s.

Ben Gardow held the number one and two positions with 3,507 and 3,393 yards in '87 and '89, respectively, until Kenosha Saint Joseph's Danny Freund passed for 3,428 in 2003. Fifth in line is McDonell's Dave Huffcutt, who made a state record 512 attempts while passing for 3,244 yards in 1986. And Todd Harrings sits at number six with 3,156 yards in 1984. Franklin's Ben Hemple is fourth at 3,372 from 2003.

Gardow's 35 touchdown tosses in 1989 was the best, one more than his 1987 total, which was equaled by Fennimore's Brent Nelson in 2001. Freund tossed 40 TDs and Hemple threw 39 in '03. Tony Stauss of Racine Horlick bettered Gardow's standard for completions by 10 when he connected on 295 passes in 1999. Gardow also topped the career charts with 1,348 attempts, 712 completions, 87 touchdowns, and 9,056 yards through 2002. ★

On the Ground

Through 2002, five Wisconsin high school running backs have reached the 400-yard plateau in one game. Jim Baier of Elmwood set the standard with 401 yards during a 1961 contest and then reached 400 yards in a game the next season.

Those performances stood until 1998, when Jesse Wendt of Chetek rumbled for 415 yards. In 2001, Joe Bosak of Dodgeland reached Baier's mark with 401 yards. However, Jake Lindsey of Washburn raised the ceiling with his 24-carry, 442-yard showing in 2002.

The season rushing champion is Kenosha Saint Joseph's Adrian Davis, who marched through defenses 430 times for 3,422 yards and 43 scores in 2001. Jake Morris of Elk Mound still holds the season TD record with 49, which he set in 1992.

When it comes to career totals, Luke Hagel of Random Lake reached the end zone a remarkable 112 times from 1995 to 1998. Hagel's 6,495 yards were second to Hilbert's Mike Firkus, who accumulated 6,707 in 2000–02. Hagel, who also did some work as a place-kicker, holds the top two season scoring totals with 317 in 1997 and 301 the next year, and heads the career list with 802 points. ★

On the Receiving End

Several players have distinguished themselves atop the state's high school receiving charts, and that started with Mineral Point's Gabe Filardo and Eau Claire Regis's Nick Simon. Filardo hauled in 182 passes in 1988–90, while Simon topped the career yardage list with 2,661 in 1996–99.

But then Kole Heckendorf of Mosinee (2000–03) took over. His totals of 235 catches for 3,831 yards top the Wisconsin charts.

Ryan Pachniak of Stratford had the single-game mark by four yards over Ryan Rohlinger of West Bend East. Pachniak raced for 296 yards on eight catches, an amazing 37 yards per reception, in a 2001 game. That bettered Rohlinger's effort from 1999.

However, Mosinee's Eric Vehlow tied the state's single-game receiving yards mark when he hauled in nine passes for 307 yards and three touchdowns during a 50–36 loss to Medford in the second round of the 2003 playoffs. He equaled Auburndale's Jordan Zimmerman, who caught 11 passes and scored three times only two weeks earlier.

Meanwhile, the single-game record for most catches is shared by Tony Cera of Wauwatosa West and Rick Baier of Chippewa Falls McDonell. They snared 18 passes each in 1983 and 1987, respectively.

Only three receivers have ever reached one hundred receptions in a season, and two of them occurred in 2002. Heckendorf established the standard with

116—to lead the nation for another season mark of 1,714 yards (14.8 average)—while Kevin Laemmrich of Menasha Saint Mary's Central finished with one hundred catches. Baier was the only other individual to climb that plateau with 106 receptions in 1987.

Heckendorf moved past Greg Bracey of Milwaukee Vincent for most touchdowns in the state when he caught the 32nd of his prep career during the 2003 season. ★

Defensive Domination

In the dictionary, the entry for the word stingy should be accompanied by a picture of Coach Gary Hanson and his Cashton High School football team, at least during the 1980s. That's because the Eagles won 75 of 87 games in the decade for an .862 winning percentage, and the squad's defense was the key. Cashton outscored its opponents 279–0 in 1980 but didn't qualify for the WIAA playoffs, which were determined by computer ratings at that time.

The postseason selection process changed the next year, but the Eagles didn't. They allowed only three points and claimed the Division 6 state championship. ★

Winning Wonders

Thirty-five high school football coaches have reached the magical 200-victory plateau during their illustrious careers, and 12 of them are still active through 2003, including the top three and four of the top five.

Bob Hyland of Fond du Lac Saint Mary's Springs heads the charts with 298 victories. Next in line are Milwaukee Marquette's Dick Basham with 293 and Stevens Point Pacelli's Bob Raczek with 281. The late and legendary Win Brockmeyer of Wausau is fourth with 265, and Edgar's Jerry Sinz rounds out the top five with 256.

Brockmeyer, whose totals include six years in Minnesota, has the best winning percentage at .845 (265–43–14). Retired Mayville coach Alex Hilber was second at .833 (224–45), and the only other two who've won at least 80 percent of their outings are Sinz (256–59 for .813) and Basham (293–72 for .803), although D. C. Everest's Wayne Steffenhagen, ninth in wins, is knocking at the door (231–58 for .799). ★

GOLF

Andy North Wins U.S. Open—Twice

"The guy who wins will keep the ball in the fairway. The way to win will be to stay close, say three or four behind. It's hard for me to believe anyone will win here by leading from opening day. You could even be behind by four or five with nine [holes] to play. These last five are good holes. They could turn a tournament around."

Andy North's assessment on the eve of the 1978 U.S. Open championship couldn't have been much more accurate. The best part was that he took his words to heart and claimed his first of two major titles—both U.S. Opens—during an injury-riddled PGA Tour career that saw him win only three times.

But nobody can take away what he accomplished the weekend of June 15–18, 1978, at Cherry Hills near Denver, especially considering he had overcome a bout of food poisoning the week before.

Currently a commentator for ESPN and a part-time Champions (Senior) Tour participant, North was 28 and competing in his sixth season when he controlled most of the action on the 7,083-yard course in which wind played a significant factor, particularly during the final round.

He opened up a four-stroke advantage midway through the fourth day, with J. C. Snead, nephew of the legendary Sam Snead, and two-time PGA Championship winner Dave Stockton his closest competitors.

North suffered a double bogey at the par-3 15th hole, which allowed his nearest pursuers to inch within one stroke, and Hale Irwin and Tom Weiskopf climbed within two shots while sitting in the clubhouse. However, North registered pars on the 16th and 17th holes and then only needed a bogey on the 18th after Snead and Stockton bogeyed the same hole to give North a two-shot margin.

In his 2002 book, *The Long and Short of It*, North recounted what was going through his mind before the most important hole of his career. "It's really hard finishing a hole on any day, much less when every shot is as critical as in a major," he wrote. "So here I am with this one-shot lead, and now I'm right where I dreamed of being as a kid. I kept thinking to myself, 'Let's figure out a way to make par and win this championship.'"

He accomplished it—barely. North hit his drive into a deep rough and found himself in the same spot short of the green after his second shot. His third attempt landed in a green-side trap. He blasted out to within four feet of the cup and drained the putt after backing away twice. "It wasn't nerves," said the Madison native who won back-to-back WIAA state titles in 1966–67 at Monona Grove High School. "The wind was gusting. I was trying to find a hole in the wind so it wouldn't rock me on my putting stroke."

IT TOOK ONLY 13 SHOTS

Paul Hughes accomplished something, actually two things, that nobody else is known to have done. The 74-year-old Waunakee resident became a local and national celebrity when he registered a hole-in-one and bowled a 300 game within 24 hours.

At about 12:30 p.m. Monday, October 13, 2003, Hughes grabbed an eight-iron and found the cup on the 149-yard fifth hole at Pleasant View Golf Course in Middleton. The 11-handicapper finished with a 76 after his feat on the Prairie nine.

Paul Hughes of Waunakee made a hole-in-one and bowled a 300 game within a 24-hour period, believed to be the first person to accomplish the feat. (Photo courtesy of Paul Hughes)

Hughes then lit up the lanes at the Bowling Green Complex in Middleton the next day. Starting at 10 a.m., he converted 12 consecutive strikes in front of a crowd that had reached 300 by the time he was finished.

He was interviewed by the *Los Angeles Times* and *USA Today* and bowled a strike during an appearance that was shown on NBC's *Today Show*. Hughes said the 300 game was the highlight because it took a dozen quality attempts instead of just one swing of his golf club. A South Dakota man reportedly accomplished the feat in July 2000, but his efforts were 26 hours apart.

North entered action 10th on that year's money list and earned $45,000 for his effort in which his final shot avoided an 18-hole playoff. His 3-over-par 74 gave him a 1-over-285, which marked the 20th time since 1941 that the Open winner had finished above par. Irwin had led after the first round with a 69, followed by North, Snead, and 18-year-old Brigham Young University competitor Bob Clampett, all with 70s.

North recorded his second consecutive 70 to reach 2-under and grab a lead over Jack Nicklaus, Gary Player, and Snead, while Lee Trevino was one of those lurking three shots back. North capped the second round with a 35-foot putt on the 18th, only the fourth birdie on the 480-yard, water-guarded par-4.

His 71 gave him a three-round score of 211, one shot ahead of Player. Snead and Stockton were at 214. North repeatedly recovered from danger, including about a 50-foot putt on the 18th that preserved his lead.

None of that mattered as North, whose wife Sue was expecting their second child in August, earned the hard-fought victory and trophy. "It was perfectly straight and uphill," North said of the historic putt. "If you wanted a putt to win the Open or the Masters, this was the putt. I said to myself, 'Listen, sport. This is what it's all about. Now show them what you are made of.' And then I made a good stroke and it went in."

WIN A GOAT
On May 9, 1912, the Sinnissippi Golf Club in Janesville started a contest in which competitors played for each other's goats.

North said in his book that it was a week full of great memories. "At the time I was 28 years old and I not only got to play with the great players of the game as partners [including Nicklaus and Player on the last two days, respectively], but I got the chance to win in front of them. I felt as if I was a Pinocchio of sorts and had proved myself to be a genuine professional in their eyes."

He sure did. And North, whose third and only other Tour triumph came at the 1977 Westchester Classic, became the 15th player to win more than one Open crown when he conquered Oakland Hills outside Detroit in 1985, joining such greats as Nicklaus, Ben Hogan, and Bobby Jones.

Hogan had dubbed the course "the Monster," but North again persevered in tough weather conditions, bolting into contention with a second-round 65 and a rain-soaked 70 in the third. North, who had undergone elbow surgery in 1984, moved two strokes ahead of Dave Barr, T. C. Chen, and Denis Watson with two holes remaining.

Like seven years earlier, North made it difficult on himself with an interesting finish. At the par-3 17th, his tee shot ended up in a large, deep bunker right of the hole. Not even able to see the green, North rolled his second shot near the flag and tapped in for a par.

That meant that North needed only to bogey the 18th. His approach was short, but he chipped on safely and two-putted for the victory, netting $103,000 on Father's Day after trailing Chen by two strokes entering the final day.

Chen's famous double-hit and 8 on the par-4 fifth hole helped knock him spiraling backward down the leader board and out of contention.

North proved his '78 crown wasn't a fluke, turning in rounds of 70, 65, and 70 and assumed control on the back nine as his 4-over 74 left him 1-under for the tourney, the only one to finish under par. "There were days that I wondered if I'd ever win again, but I've always been a survivor," North said after his par on the tough par-3 17th had given him a one-shot cushion that increased to two strokes as he approached the 18th green. "I've always believed that if you just keep working hard, some good stuff might happen." ★

MORE RECORDS, STREAKS, AND AMAZING MOMENTS
PROFESSIONAL GOLF
Teeing Them Up

Johnny Revolta, who grew up in Oshkosh, won 13 events on the professional golf tour, by far the most of any competitor with Wisconsin ties. But none was bigger than his performance October 23, 1935, when he won the PGA Championship. Revolta defeated former champion Tommy Armour, 5 and 4, in the final round of the match-play event at Oklahoma City's Twin Hills Golf Course.

Revolta and Don Iverson of La Crosse were the only winners on the PGA or LPGA tours before Andy North claimed the first of his two U.S. Open crowns in 1978.

Wisconsin currently boasts four winners in Edgerton native and Madison resident Steve Stricker, Madison native and resident Jerry Kelly, Appleton product J. P. Hayes, and Madison native and resident Sherri Steinhauer. Martha Nause of Sheboygan, who is retired, won three times on the LPGA Tour between 1988 and 1994. ★

Beating the Babe

Nineteen-year-old Mary McMillin of Green Bay stunned the golfing establishment and sporting world when she upset Babe Didrikson Zaharias in the semifinals of the Western Amateur golf tournament in Cleveland on August 16, 1946.

The two were even at the turn, but McMillin, who had downed defending champion Phyllis Otto in her major tourney debut three days earlier, won four of the next six holes en route to her 2 and 1 victory.

McMillin, a stenographer, holed four putts of between 12 and 35 feet to prompt Zaharias to say, "I kept waiting for her to fall off, but she didn't fall. I've never seen such putting. She seemed to be in sort of a daze, but it's a nice daze to be in."

However, McMillin's run ended in the finals as Louise Suggs won handily, 11 and 10, the next day. ★

She Likes It Overseas

Sherri Steinhauer of Madison pulled out the women's British Open golf tournament championship held in Lytham Saint Annes, England, by one stroke, August 16, 1998. She finished the weekend with a 4-over-292 score. That wasn't enough for Steinhauer though, as she returned the next year and successfully defended her crown. ★

AMATEUR GOLF
Long-Ball Hitter

Ned Allis won 10 state amateur championships during a career that spanned 60 years. But perhaps his greatest achievement might have been one round he played in 1913 at the Milwaukee Country Club. On a spring day, Allis fired a round of 29 on the tough front nine. Then 20, Allis went on to lead Harvard to a national collegiate title in 1914.

A legendary long hitter, Allis made Western Golf Association history in 1914 by hitting a 306-yard drive. If he had used one of today's distance balls and an oversized driver, there is no telling how far that smash might have traveled. Allis starred in several U.S. Amateur tourneys and Western Amateurs, and many of his battles came against Billy Sixty and Chick Evans, also greats of the era. ★

Among his many feats, Milwaukee native Ned Allis won the Intercollegiate Golf Association tournament September 12, 1914, while representing Harvard University. (Photo courtesy of Western Golf Association)

Linked Together

In the 31 Wisconsin state girls golf tournaments held from 1972 to 2002, only 14 schools claimed championships, so obviously there have been some streaks involved. Madison West and La Crosse Central have the most titles with five, while Appleton West has four crowns. Madison West won the first five meets under the direction of three coaches. Madison Memorial then won three of the next four trophies before Appleton West dominated four of the next six tourneys under Coach Mary Beth Nienhaus. La Crosse Central took over in 1990 with its first of four consecutive number one finishes and added its fifth in 1998.

Individually, four golfers grabbed back-to-back medalist honors: Chris Regenberg of Madison Memorial in 1976–77, current PGA regular Sherri Steinhauer of Madison Memorial in 1979–80, Ellen Mielke of Appleton West in 1985–86, and Erika Brown of Madison La Follette in 1989–90. However, Heather Suhr of Racine Case is the lone three-time champion, having claimed medalist status in 1996–98, all at University Ridge. ★

Regents Are Kings

The Madison West Regents have won the most state boys golf championships with 15 and have crowned the individual medalist on nine occasions. Racine Park is second with seven team titles.

Individually, Bill Heim of Green Bay Preble (1986–88) and Jeremy Lyons of Glenwood City (1997–99) are the only three-time champs. Eight others have turned the trick twice: Edward Lock of Lake Geneva in 1927–28, Steve Bull of Racine Horlick in 1950 and 1952, Rick Radder of Madison West in 1961–62, Andy North of Monona Grove (and PGA tour fame) in 1966–67, Mark Voeller of Whitewater in 1988–89, Kent Higley of Eleva-Strum in 1989–90, Scott Cole of New Richmond in 1993 and 1995, Chad Kovaleski of New Richmond in 1999 and 2000, and Matt Bark of Washburn in 2000–01. ★

HOCKEY

Badgers Win Their First Frozen Four

In 1973, legendary coach Bob Johnson helped put the University of Wisconsin hockey program on the national map when it captured the first of three NCAA championships under Johnson.

And one of the key performers for Badger Bob was Dean Talafous, who recorded 133 points for the Badgers from 1971 to 1974. However, none of Talafous's scoring accomplishments came close to the drama and excitement surrounding his feats the weekend of March 16–17, 1973, which included the winning goal in the national championship game.

But that's skipping a little too far ahead because Wisconsin wouldn't have reached the final had it not been for Talafous's Frozen Four heroics the night before. The sophomore scored with five seconds left in regulation to tie Cornell in the semifinals. The Badgers had trailed 5–2, but Talafous tallied again with 33 seconds remaining in the first overtime period to lift Wisconsin into the final against Denver. He scored the tying goal on an assist from Dennis Olmstead and the game-winner on a rebound of Steve Alley's shot.

UW fell behind 4–0 four minutes into the second period against Cornell. The Badgers closed to within 4–2 but couldn't prevent the Big Red from regaining a three-goal edge 40 seconds into the third.

Johnson pulled goalie Dick Perkins with a minute remaining in regulation to give the Badgers a six-on-five advantage—Talafous was the last skater on the ice. "Dennis [Olmstead] took a shot, and Cornell tried to shoot it out of the zone," Talafous said afterward. "But the puck hit Dennis in the chest and dribbled down. He shot it over to me, and I knocked it in."

Talafous also reacted nonchalantly about his contributions on the game-winner. "Olmstead dug it out of the corner and passed to Steve Alley," Talafous said. "Alley shot and I think the goalie made a save. The puck went off to the side and I got it."

However, he and the Badger attackers may not have gotten that opportunity had it not been for UW goalie Perkins, who made the play of the overtime while thwarting a two-man breakaway that kept things knotted up.

"We never lost our poise," said Johnson, who went on to compile a 367–175–23 overall record for a .670 winning percentage and later became the only coach to win NCAA and Stanley Cup titles (1991 with the Pittsburgh Penguins). "We had to get some spunk, some momentum, and we had to get it ourselves."

And Talafous helped provide it as the Badgers then claimed the title on St. Patrick's Day in the Boston Garden to conclude a 29–9–2 campaign. Wisconsin had tailed off late in the year but regained the momentum during its magical postseason run. The Badgers eliminated bitter rival Minnesota, which had earned a 2–1–1 regular-season series advantage, by 8–6 and 6–4 scores in the Western Collegiate Hockey Association playoffs. UW then squeezed past Notre Dame (4–4, 4–3) in a total-goals format to qualify for the national tournament.

The headline for the Sunday, March 18th *Wisconsin State Journal* read: "UW Hockey Team No. 1." That it was, after the Badgers' 4–2 triumph against Denver. Dave Pay scored to give UW a 1–0 lead, but Denver tied it after one period and grabbed a 2–1 cushion in the second.

However, Tim Dool tied the score a second time. Then Talafous came up clutch again, registering what proved to be the game-winner later in the second period en route to earning Most Valuable Player laurels. "What a way to go out," Talafous said afterward. "Every guy on the team played his best game. I don't know about my being the MVP. They could have drawn my name out of a hat."

The Hastings, Minnesota, native makes the same contention today. "That experience taught me what it takes to become a championship team," Talafous said in a phone interview. "I was the only one who went on and played much professionally, while Denver maybe had eight or nine guys who did. We didn't have as much talent as most of the teams in the postseason, but we had character, good role players, and guys who competed and hustled all of the time. We didn't win the league title, but we worked hard. It was an amazing run. A lot of guys deserved credit for me winning the MVP award."

SUPER BOBCATS

John Mayasich and Paul Johnson, members of the amateur Green Bay Bobcats, were two major reasons the United States pulled off shocking upsets to claim the Olympic gold medal in hockey in 1960. Mayasich registered an assist, while Johnson scored the winning goal as the Americans stunned co-favorite Canada, 2–1, at the Games in Squaw Valley. The United States then defeated the Soviet Union and Czechoslovakia to claim its first gold medal in the sport.

Dean Talafous was named the most valuable player of the NCAA hockey tournament as Wisconsin earned its first hockey title in March 1973. (Photo courtesy of the University of Wisconsin)

Talafous knows of what he speaks. Despite a disappointing five-year tenure as coach of WCHA member Alaska–Anchorage that ended in 2001, he was an assistant at Minnesota and then won a national championship and coach of the year honors at UW–River Falls before taking over the Seawolves.

And he said Johnson was the driving force behind any success he and the team enjoyed. "First and foremost, Bob Johnson was Mr. Positive," said Talafous, who runs hockey training centers in Eagan, Minnesota, and Hudson, Wisconsin. "He definitely believed in miracles, and we learned never to think about winning or losing but rather about playing hard and never giving up. So even when we got behind against Cornell, we had confidence.

"Another one of his great qualities was that he made it fun, whether it was at practice or in the games," added Talafous, whose son, Pete, played for the Badgers in 2002–04. "He was positive even after losses, and he told us that if we continued to work hard things would work out in the end. He developed skills in each individual and wanted us playing our best at the end of the season, and that's why he won championships. He was a pretty special coach."

Talafous said March 1973 was just as special, particularly for a 19-year-old who didn't really fathom what the Badgers had accomplished. "Looking back on it, it was probably good that I was young and naïve," Talafous said. "That way we just went out and played. It really didn't sink in until years later when I saw the pictures or listened to the tape. But we won the national championship in the Boston Garden with thousands of Badger fans there.

"Most rinks didn't even hold that many people back then, so it was amazing how many fans followed us," Talafous added. "People out there couldn't believe it. I remember after the victory that everybody, and there must have been 3,000 to 5,000 fans, went down to a pub and [Athletic Director] Elroy Hirsch gave his little pitch about winning the championship and then bought a round of drinks. It was an amazing thing."

And the Badgers repeated the accomplishment in 1976–77 and 1980–81 under Johnson and in 1982–83 and 1989–90 under Jeff Sauer. ★

Mark Johnson and the Miracle on Ice

The United States' victory over the Soviet Union in the 1980 Olympic Games, better known as the Miracle on Ice, evokes vivid memories for most Americans. Everybody remembers announcer Al Michaels's call of the unbelievable outcome. And most people think about U.S. captain Mike Eruzione scoring what proved to be the winning goal in the 4-3 semifinal victory. Or what about goaltender Jim Craig celebrating with an American flag draped around his neck?

However, for many college hockey fans around these parts, those Games had a decided Wisconsin flavor to them. That's because University of Wisconsin all-American Mark Johnson played an integral role en route to the United States earning a gold medal. In addition, former Badger teammate Bob Suter and ex-Milwaukee Admiral star Buzz Schneider were members of that magical squad.

While Eruzione's heroics stand out, his place in the spotlight wouldn't have happened if not for Johnson's play at center on that February 22. Johnson, a Madison native who wore number 10 for the U.S. team, scored two goals as the Americans pulled off one of the biggest upsets in the history of Olympic hockey.

Not only had Russia won every gold medal since the United States' surprising triumph in 1960 at Squaw Valley, but the Soviets also had whipped the U.S. team, 10–3, the week before the Games.

In a *Madison Capital Times* article commemorating the 20th anniversary of the Miracle on Ice, Johnson said he didn't even consider the unlikeliest scenario—that the U.S. would take home the gold. "Walking into Lake Placid, no

WITH THE WIND

John D. Buckstaff of Oshkosh was a legendary ice-boating skipper. Along with crewmates Douglas Van Dyke and Emil Hinz, he once reached a speed of 143 mph on Lake Winnebago in 1938 in the boat *Debutante III*. That feat earned him a spot in the *Guinness Book of World Records* and is still considered the official world record. Buckstaff also won several Stuart Cup trophies, considered the most coveted award in ice sailing. His most famous boat was *The Flying Dutchman*.

one could at that time sit down and say, 'I'm dreaming about winning a gold medal,' because it just wasn't realistic," Johnson said. "It wasn't part of a dream, even a fantasy. And yet, we watched it transpire and become reality. That's why 20 years later you've got to pinch yourself. It's mind-boggling."

However, Johnson let his play do the talking. He scored a goal with one second left in the first period, chasing veteran Russian goalie Vladislav Tretiak. Dave Christian had fired a shot from beyond the blue line that Tretiak had blocked. Johnson got the rebound about 20 feet from the net, faked twice, and scored to tie the contest at two.

Then, against Russian backup goalkeeper Vladamir Myshkin, Johnson knotted the game again at three in the third period. Eighty-one seconds later Eruzione put in the game-winner as the United States handed the Soviets their first hockey loss in 12 years.

About his first goal, Johnson said afterward that he was in the right place at the right time. "The rebound popped out and I was fortunate to put it in. I never thought about any part of an open net. You can't do that. If you do you'll miss. Lady Luck played the role here."

Luck or not, Johnson's talent was evident as two days later he scored another goal as the U.S. beat Finland, 4–2, to clinch the gold medal after rallying from a 2–1 deficit after two periods.

In the championship game, Johnson and Rob McClanahan scored goals in the third period as the United States grabbed the trophy in front of 8,500 fans at Olympia Field House. Finland was ahead 1–0 and moved in front 2–1. Phil Verchata tied it and then McClanahan tallied the winner on an assist from Johnson with 3:35 remaining. "I was working the corner, and I saw Robby about 6 feet in front," Johnson said of his assist to McClanahan. "I was lucky to get it to him."

The Madison Memorial High School star said he couldn't believe what happened. "I never thought we'd be this close," said Johnson, named college hockey's player of the year in 1978–79 as a junior for the Badgers. "When we beat the Russians, we thought we had a chance. This is . . . I don't know how to describe it. I'm just in awe."

Johnson finished with five goals and six assists in seven games to lead the Americans, who entered the competitions seeded seventh among the 12 teams. He later played 11 years in the National Hockey League with five teams, including six postseason appearances. "I don't have the English vocabulary that really gives you an essence of what that moment was all about," Johnson said in the *Capital Times* story.

"There was a lot of political hatred," he recalled about the still raging Cold War and turmoil surrounding U.S. hostages in Iran. "We were just hockey players. I didn't learn about all this stuff until afterwards. It wasn't on our plate then. We were just playing hockey and fulfilling dreams of playing in the Olympics."

And even today, Johnson said he gets the chills every time he watches replays of the games. "We knew how good the Russians and other teams were, so going into the tournament we weren't even thinking about winning a medal or anything like that," Johnson said from his office at Camp Randall Stadium, where he was winding down his second season in charge of the nationally ranked Wisconsin women's hockey team. "We just tried to play as hard and well as we could, and with the right breaks and everything maybe we could have a chance at a bronze or silver.

"Then after we beat the Russians it was the first time we really controlled our own destiny," Johnson added. "At that point we could sense that it was a once-in-a-lifetime moment for us."

The Americans took advantage, and Johnson was a principle reason why. "Coach [Herb] Brooks gave me a lot of responsibility, so I knew I needed to play well," Johnson said. "I was fortunate enough to score big goals in big games."

The Miracle on Ice, unlike so many other spectacular sports stories, has not faded from the public's memory. In 2004, Johnson and his Olympic teammates grabbed the nationwide spotlight with the release of the Disney movie *Miracle*. The former Badger star was portrayed by Eric Peter-Kaiser.

However, it was nothing like being there. "We had skilled players from all over the country who became a team and good friends," Johnson said. "Coach Brooks felt from Day One that he would keep his distance and not get too close to any individual players. But he had a vision. Through preparation, hard work and playing together, he pushed all of the right buttons. And that's how we realized that vision." ★

MORE RECORDS, STREAKS, AND AMAZING MOMENTS
COLLEGE AND AMATEUR HOCKEY
Marquette Hockey

Marquette University put together one of the leading teams in the country during the late 1920s and early 1930s, playing its home games at an outdoor rink at the intersection of West Clybourn and North 15th streets. The roster of the Hilltoppers—this was before the Warriors and Golden Eagle days—featured two standouts from Canada, Donald McFayden and Pudge MacKenzie. McFayden, a 1972 inductee into the school's Hall of Fame, earned all-America acclaim after leading Marquette to intercollegiate championships in 1928–30. He helped lead MU to a 9–0 victory over Wisconsin in the program's first outing in 1927. ★

HIGH SCHOOL HOCKEY
Icing Their Foes

Vic Levine knows his ice hockey, and he knows how to win. He had been the head coach at Madison Memorial for 26 years through the 2002–2003 season, leading the Spartans to six of the school's eight state championships and five runner-up finishes.

Madison Memorial's eight titles are second only to Superior's 11, which included winning an unprecedented three in a row in 1994–96. Memorial has enjoyed unbeaten strings of 44 (43–0–1) and 42 games (40–0–2).

Levine, who has fashioned a 465–125–17 mark, has coached many fine players, but none better than Mark Johnson, who went on to fame with the University of Wisconsin and as a member of the 1980 United States Olympic champions. In high school, Johnson scored 273 points in 65 games, including 158 goals. His best season was 1975–76, when he registered 121 points in 22 games. ★

SKIING AND SKATING

The Birth of the Birkie

February 24, 1973, began pretty much the same as most winter days in Hayward, where residents greeted another bitter cold Saturday morning with cups of coffee or other warm pick-me-ups of choice. Except that things were a little different down at Wannigan Pancake House, part of Historyland, a summer tourist attraction just east of town. That's because an odd assortment of 35 bundled-up cross-country skiers had gathered on the ice of Lumberjack Bowl, not knowing that they were about to make history.

One of the onlookers was Tony Wise, who owned the Telemark alpine ski area at Cable, the destination for these brave souls in the first of what would become the American Birkebeiner. Among the participants were Wayne and Jacque Lindskoog of the Minneapolis area, who had been introduced to distance races of this nature while watching a film at a meeting of the North Star Ski Touring Club. "We were charter members of the club, so we probably had as much skiing experience as anyone," Jacque said in Tom Kelly's 1982 book *Birkie Fever.* "We were probably among the first 200 skiers in the Twin Cities and had only been skiing for a few years.

Jacque Lindskoog was the only woman to participate in the first American Birkebeiner event, which was held in February 1973 but wasn't officially open to women until 1975. (Photo courtesy of the American Birkebeiner)

"We basically thought it would be fun," she told Kelly. "We had done a lot of skiing in the Porkies [Michigan's Porcupine

Mountains] and some long-distance ski touring. The Birkebeiner was a culmination of the things we had been doing." So, it was an afterthought when Jacque joined the men in the 50-kilometer Birkebeiner instead of the 22-kilometer women's race.

She opened a lot of eyes by not only completing the event but also clocking a 4:33.35, even though women weren't officially eligible to enter the Birkie until 1975. "There was never an intent to crash the race or to liberate it," she said. "I just picked up my bib and raced. I didn't even think about it. In fact, I probably never would have said anything, but after the race my friends said that something should be done to recognize women." It didn't take long for Lindskoog to become a household name, at least in northwestern Wisconsin.

In 1974, Jacque was listed in the men's age 20–34 class. She finished in 4:53.30, which placed her 18th in the division and in the top half overall. Today, the competition is one of 14 races that make up the Worldloppet international circuit and draws more than 9,000 entrants and 20,000 spectators.

Jacque, in her 60s, lives in a log cabin near Hayward but lost Wayne to cancer in 2002. She has missed only a couple of Birkebeiner races since the beginning. "It is a bittersweet race for me," Lindskoog said in a *Milwaukee Journal Sentinel* article on the eve of the 30th annual Birkie in 2003. "But I think it is really important for me to do it because Wayne will no longer be here to do this race. The community up here has been so supportive. I feel alone, but the Birkie has kept me focused."

She hopes to keep the family tradition alive as long as she can, and she has placed a picture of Wayne at the highest point along the course. "It reads, 'Birkie Founder, No. 8,'" she said. "It has got the American and Norwegian flags on it. That picture is on the top of the hill. It will stay there until it blows down."

It all started with a cannon shot at 9 a.m. that February day in 1973. Sweden's Eric Ersson won the initial race that gray morning, traversing a course that followed snowmobile routes and makeshift ski trails in 2:48.16. Competitors reached the chalet at Mount Telemark all afternoon, causing alpine skiers to wonder why people kept emerging from the nearby woods.

Another competitor, Charles Weydt, had gotten lost more than once and was the last one to cross the finish line, 9 1/2 hours later. That didn't prevent Weydt from returning, as he entered the Birkebeiner or Kortelopet for years afterward.

Now 65, Weydt lives with his father Charles Sr. in Woodruff, and recalls the initial journey fondly. "I had old hickory skis and bear claw bindings," he said via phone interview, chuckling at the sight he and others must have created. "The skis were much wider back then. I had old leather boots that I used for downhill skiing at the time. I think my gear weighed something like 36 pounds.

"It was the first time I attempted anything like that," Weydt added. "The route followed old snowmobile trails, so the conditions were pretty primitive. Somehow I got off the beaten path and was forced to double back."

However, Weydt said it was a wonderful experience that has fostered his enthusiasm for returning many times since. "I never would have dreamed that it would evolve into what it has," he said. "It was something I did on a whim and really didn't know what to expect. I got more appropriate skis and gear the next year. I feel good about being one of the pioneers."

Weydt's story is a prime example of what the spirit of the Birkebeiner is all about. ★

Eric Heiden Skates to Five Olympic Firsts

Nobody before or since has reached the pinnacle that Eric Heiden did during the 1980 Winter Olympic Games in the hamlet of Lake Placid, New York. The Madison native earned five individual gold medals and defeated five former world record holders, establishing four Olympic records and one world mark in sweeping the men's speed skating events.

The irony is that on the eve of Heiden's final race to glory, the United States men's hockey team won the Miracle on Ice, a 4-3 semifinal triumph over the heavily favored Soviet Union en route to winning the gold and overshadowing Heiden's 14:28.13 world standard in the 10,000 meters.

Even though he and his sport of choice were much more popular in Europe, Heiden preferred to stay in the background, sliding into obscurity after retiring, at age 21, from competitive skating. He didn't want his picture on a Wheaties box or the pressure that such publicity and media attention invariably heave upon athletes.

Instead of such burdens upon his shoulders, he's spent most of his time since then fixing them—and elbows, knees, and ankles. Heiden, like his father Jack, who still resides in Madison, became an orthopedic surgeon. He works in Sacramento, California, where he has insulated himself as much as possible from his athletic prowess and the fame that indelibly tags along.

However, whether he likes it or not, Heiden can't erase what he did that Saturday morning, February 23, and the days before that final trip around the oval in the Adirondack Mountains, a place that had hosted the Games in 1932. "Over time, I have begun to appreciate more and more what I have done," Heiden told the *Madison Capital Times* in December 1999 after a six-member panel of experts named him the male Winter Olympian of the twentieth century. "I always thought it was possible for another athlete to do it. I guess it becomes more impressive with no one able to equal that."

His remarkable feat earned him the Sullivan Award as top American amateur athlete that year and included Olympic records in the 500 (38.03 seconds), 1,000 (1:15.18), 1,500 (1:55.44), and 5,000 (7:02.29), while his sister and occasional training partner, Beth, joined in the family fun by claiming a bronze medal in the 3,000 meters.

Heiden landed on the cover of *Sports Illustrated* and *Time* magazines, but he shunned numerous endorsement opportunities and the paychecks that went with them. "Maybe if things had stayed the way they were, and I could still be obscure in an obscure sport, I might want to keep skating," he said at the time. "I really liked it best when I was a nobody."

But he definitely wasn't just anybody. The spotlight shifted to his competitive cycling pursuits. He was selected an alternate for the 1984 Olympic team and then won the U.S. Pro National Championships in 1985. Heiden competed in the Tour de France in 1986, where he suffered a concussion in an accident during the 18th stage, ending his pedaling career.

Heiden had completed three years at the University of Wisconsin by the time his Olympic career concluded. In 1981, he transferred to Stanford, where he received his bachelor's degree and then attended medical school, graduating in 1991. He works at the University of California-Davis sports medicine clinic, is a team physician for the Sacramento Kings and Sacramento Monarchs, and worked with the U.S. speed skating teams during the 2002 Games in Salt Lake City, Utah.

He told the *San Francisco Chronicle* in September 2002 that many people would be surprised if they heard what his biggest achievement in life is. "It would be easy to say what I did at the Olympics. Speed skating was fun, but I don't look at it as my life's work. Medicine is," said Heiden, whose wife, Karen, is a hand surgeon and an assistant professor of orthopedic surgery at the University of California–Davis.

Like most of his memories, the hardware from Heiden's magnificent 10 days in Lake Placid almost 25 years ago is stashed away. The gold suit he wore is in the Smithsonian Institute, his skates and two of his medals are collecting dust in a closet at home and the other three pieces of gold are in a cedar closet at his parents' home.

Still, the grace and power Heiden displayed during his unforgettable Olympic run can't be forgotten. He stood above everybody else, being challenged only in the 500 before shattering the 10,000-meter record by more than six seconds and beating his closest competitor, Piet Kleine of the Netherlands, by 7.9 seconds. "During the race I thought about getting into a rhythm, and in the middle I tried to turn off my mind. Then I started to think about how tired I was and how good it would be to have it over. It hurt.

"But this is the best race I could have won," he added about his fifth gold.

"I skated well. I've trained hard to do it. To beat someone in the 10,000 is pretty special."

The whole experience was not too shabby for somebody whose first love was hockey. He was a forward at Madison West High School at the same time future UW standout Mark Johnson—one of the U.S. hockey team's heroes in those 1980 Games—was starring at Madison Memorial. That endeavor didn't work out, so Heiden switched his goals and dreams to speed skating, a sport in which he placed seventh in the 1,500 and 19th in the 5,000 in the 1976 Games in Innsbruck, Austria.

"It was a great time in my life," Heiden said in a 2002 article in the *Capital Times*. "The Olympics, gosh, I skated five races as well as I could have expected. Physically and mentally, it was a pretty draining 10 days."

TALL ORDER ACCOMPLISHED

Beth Heiden had no choice but to stand in the shadow of her famous brother, Eric, during and after the 1980 Winter Olympics. After all, she stood only five-foot-two and weighed about 105 pounds. However, that didn't stop her from claiming her small piece of fame at Lake Placid, New York.

She grabbed a bronze medal in speed skating's 3,000 meters, a remarkable and memorable accomplishment considering most of her competitors were six inches taller and 50 pounds heavier in a grueling sport in which strength and stamina are so important.

But Heiden had proven that she was up to the task. She had claimed four gold medals and the all-around title at the 1979 World Championships in the Netherlands. In the Olympics, she proved that wasn't a fluke by finishing fifth in the 1,000 and seventh in both the 500 and the 1,500 despite a sore ankle and tough conditions. "At my size, skating outdoors was tough," she told the *Los Angeles Times* in a retrospective look at the Games in 2002. "Cutting through the wind made things harder for me."

But Heiden said that hasn't diminished what she did and the wonderful experience she had. "If I look at it now, speed skating wasn't a good choice for me, not at my size," she said. "My brother and I started out as figure skaters because we had a house on the lake [in Madison]. But Eric and I spent most of our time at figure skating practice racing around the rink. And it's still always a thrill to see an Olympic opening ceremony."

Don't forget special. No one knows that better than Beth, who lives in Palo Alto, California. "To come back each time for five races with your head together, to step out on the ice five times, to be mentally and physically ready and to successfully execute a good race is really amazing," she said in the *San Francisco Chronicle* article. "I can't imagine that anybody will ever be able to do that again."

Dan Jansen, another Wisconsinite who would later gain Olympic fame, agreed. "He had a huge impact on my career," Jansen told the *Chronicle*. "He was probably the reason that I stayed with skating. I was 14 when I saw what Eric did in 1980. It was simply the greatest feat in Olympic history."

Voted number 63 among the top one hundred greatest athletes of the twentieth century by ESPN in 1999, Heiden won more gold medals in the 1980 Olympics than Finland, Switzerland, West Germany, the Netherlands, Italy, Canada, Great Britain, Japan, and France combined, accounting for five of the U.S.'s total of six.

"Medals really aren't anything special," Heiden said after his final spirited 25-lap race. "It's much more satisfying to go out and do your best. But it kinda boggles my mind. I thought I'd win one or two, but more than that was out of the question." ★

Dan Jansen Prevails, Wins Olympic Gold

A movie titled *A Brother's Promise* was made about his life, and although the Dan Jansen story featured a storybook ending, his ultimate triumph may not have been so memorable had it not been for several nightmarish chapters along the way.

The speed skater burst onto the Winter Olympic stage with a fourth-place finish in the 1984 Games at Sarajevo, Yugoslavia, finishing 16 hundredths of a second away from capturing the bronze medal.

Jansen, a native of West Allis, was considered the top sprinter in the world and thus favored to take home gold in the 1988 Olympics in Calgary. However, he fell in his signature event, the 500 meters, hours after learning that his sister, Jane, had died from leukemia. The devastated Jansen fell again in the 1,000 meters a few days later. The world record holder couldn't shake the gigantic storm cloud, managing only a fourth place in the 500 during the 1992 Games at Albertville, France. He started strongly but faltered to 26th place in the 1,000.

That meant the 1994 gathering in Lillehammer, Norway, would be his last Olympics, his final opportunity to bring home a medal that had so painfully eluded him for so long. Jansen and Sean Ireland of Canada were the second pair of skaters in the 500, a bad sign for those who believe in such omens; Jansen had been in the same group in 1988 and 1992.

In his 1994 book *Full Circle*, Jansen recounted how he wanted to be aggressive. But as luck would have it, Ireland false-started and perhaps threw Jansen out of his rhythm. Jansen started in the inside lane and clocked a 9.82 in the first 100 meters (his world record was 9.75) and his best stretch was usually the final 250 to 300 meters.

However, one or two strides into his last turn Jansen's left skate slipped and his hand touched the ice. Jansen was the only man to have broken the 36-

second barrier up to that point, clocking a 35.92 on December 4, 1993, and went even faster (35.76) in the world championships a few weeks later. Yet his 36.68 was only good enough for eighth place. The gold medal time was 36.33. He had stumbled in a slow race, and this meant the best 500-meter skater on the globe would not medal in his specialty.

Loved ones and fans worldwide were stunned and didn't think Jansen could handle another disappointment like this one, on the sixth anniversary of his sister's death.

SPEED TO BURN

Maddy Horn was born in Michigan and moved to Beaver Dam as a small child, but her home was on the ice. She became a three-time women's United States outdoor champion in speed skating, winning titles in 1937, 1939, and 1940. She was inducted into the Speed Skaters Hall of Fame in 1966.

But somehow, some way, the human spirit finds a way. And four days later, on February 18, Jansen proved it in the 1,000 meters.

Jansen didn't feel right during warm-ups and his timing appeared to be off. But instead of dwelling on it he put in some time on the stationary bike and did a little jogging while repeating the phrase, 'I love the 1,000,' periodically.

The youngest of Harry and Geraldine Jansen's nine children started on the outside in the fourth pair, standing next to Japan's Junichi Inoue. Anything less than 17 seconds after 200 meters is considered flying, and Jansen had clocked a 16.71. But as millions had witnessed time and again during the past decade of Olympic mishaps, Jansen couldn't avoid making a mistake. On the second to last turn, about 300 meters from the finish, he slipped and his left hand shot toward the ice as he came within an inch or so of stepping on one of the lane markers.

However, the crowd noise was deafening as Jansen crossed the finish line. His first thought was that he had won a medal, but when the contact wearer's eyes finally were able to focus on the scoreboard clock, he couldn't believe what he saw. It read 1:12.43 and had the letters WR next to it. Jansen had established a world record, which was .58 seconds better than he'd ever skated that distance before. He raised his arms, closed his eyes and covered them with his hands. The time stood. Dan Jansen had become an Olympic gold medalist.

No one will ever forget the victory lap he took with eight-and-a-half-month-old daughter Jane, named after his sister. More than 12,000 people serenaded them with "The Skater's Waltz." It was one of the most heart-warming scenes in Olympic history, if not in all of sports.

"I never lost hope," Jansen said afterward. "I just didn't want to expect anything anymore. Again after the 500 here, which I should have won and was expected to win, this time I said, 'You have to just go skate.'" His coach, Peter Mueller, said his pupil dug deep when he had to. "He kept coming back," Mueller said. "That's what makes him a special guy. Sometimes the good guys do win."

For the emotionally and physically drained Jansen, it was as much relief as it was joy. "I have forever to think about what I've done, but right now I'm glad it's over," he said. "Of course, I'm glad of the result, but I'm so happy for my family. More than anything I wanted this for them."

Jansen was named the Sullivan Award winner for 1994 after giving the Tonya Harding/Nancy Kerrigan Olympics the feel-good story of the Games.

Today, Jansen lives in the Charlotte, North Carolina, area and is heavily involved in the Dan Jansen Foundation, which raises money for leukemia patients, youth sports programs, and educational and scholarship awards. He is a motivational speaker and sometime television commentator.

Nothing will top that night in Lillehammer, as Jansen recalled in his book, which is subtitled *An Olympic Champion Shares His Breakthrough Story*. He wrote: "I know it will never leave me. The circumstances that had brought me to that moment, with the whole world watching, had essentially begun with Jane's death on February 14, 1988. And here we were, six years later, another Jane in my arms, tasting victory at last. I had, indeed, come full circle." ★

MORE RECORDS, STREAKS, AND AMAZING MOMENTS

More Olympic Winners

When it comes to Olympic medals for speed skating, Eric Heiden and Dan Jansen easily come to mind. But a few other Wisconsin natives have also achieved glory in the event. On February 11, 1976, Madison native Peter Mueller, who later became Jansen's coach, won the 1,000 meters for a speed skating gold medal at the Winter Olympics in Innsbruck, Austria. Another Madison native, Dan Immerfall, had claimed a bronze medal in the 500 meters two days earlier.

In the 1998 Games in Nagano, Japan, Chris Witty of West Allis brought home a silver medal for her showing in the 1,000 meters and captured a bronze in the 1,500.

Although not a Wisconsin native, Bonnie Blair spent so much time training in the state that she might well qualify. She took a gold in the 1988 Olympics in the 500 meters and repeated that feat in 1992, along with a win in the 1,000 meters. Four years later, she repeated those two victories. ★

Taking One for the Team

In 1947, Milwaukee fireman Del Lamb was fired from his job because he missed work to compete in the United States Olympic speed skating trials.

Lamb took the weekend off despite being warned beforehand about the potential ramifications. He qualified for the American squad but lost his appeal to the city's fire and police commission. ★

SOCCER

Heather Taggart Shines in Goal

"Watching that goalkeeper flying around, I thought it would take a miracle to beat her," North Carolina coach Anson Dorrance said. "That was one of the best collegiate goalkeeping performances I've ever seen." The legendary Tar Heels' mentor was referring to University of Wisconsin goalie Heather Taggart. And it was saying a lot considering that North Carolina had just defeated the Badgers, 3–1, to claim its 10th national championship on that Sunday, November 24, 1991.

The senior from Millard North High School in Omaha, Nebraska, had led the sixth-ranked Badgers, 15–2 entering the postseason, to their fourth consecutive NCAA tournament bid. Wisconsin had secured a first-round bye for the second straight year in the field of 12 after ending its regular season with victories over Santa Clara and University of California-Santa Barbara, which both also qualified for the postseason.

UW was ranked second in the East Region and opened against seventh-rated Hartford at Breese Stevens Field in Madison. The Badgers' only losses were to Virginia, another qualifier, and Colorado College, the top seed in the West Region. Wisconsin earned its lofty position in part because of seven victories over teams that held top 20 rankings when they faced the Badgers.

And Taggart had been a major reason why, having rolled up an unbelievable résumé during her four-year run. She was selected the women's collegiate freshman Player of the Year by *Soccer America* magazine in 1988, had participated in the U.S. Olympic Sports Festival in 1989, and gained Associated Press first-team all-America status in 1990–1991.

But her heroics in the Badgers' net weren't enough for them to pull an upset, as the Tar Heels won their sixth straight trophy and ninth in 10 seasons while finishing 24–0.

UW coach Greg Ryan said his team left everything on the field and then some, but came up short. "We knew what we were up against," Ryan said afterward. "We wanted to give North Carolina everything we had, and we did that.

We wanted to show up and play them a hard game. We did and they beat us. You have to respect them."

North Carolina, which has gone on to claim 17 of 22 NCAA crowns through 2003, scored in the first minute of the title game and the first minute of the second half en route to the victory in front of a crowd of 3,800 on its home turf.

GIRLS FINALLY GET THEIR CHANCE

The Wisconsin Interscholastic Athletic Association held its first state tournament of any kind for female athletes in 1970. An estimated 500 girls representing 45 high schools gathered in Beloit for a swimming meet.

Taggart, who reached the Final Four with the Badgers her freshman year, said getting into the postseason was a goal since the beginning of the year. "We were hoping to get back to the tournament, but once you get this far anything can happen." And it almost did for the underdogs against the powerful Tar Heels.

Kari Maijala's penalty kick produced UW's lone goal and was only the second that North Carolina had allowed in 10 finals games. However, the hosts made the crucial plays when they needed to. On the first goal, Taggart and defender Tanya Russ collided, letting the ball go into the net. UW had allowed only five goals all season until the championship matchup.

The Badgers opened tourney play against Hartford, which it had defeated, 1–0, in the regular season. Margaret Kopmeyer made a key defensive play in the second half to help Amy Warner's first-half goal stand up, as Wisconsin again claimed a 1–0 decision. Taggart tried to smother the crucial kick only to have it go through her legs, but Kopmeyer deflected it and the shot missed the post by inches.

In the semifinals, UW squared off against nemesis Colorado College, which had knocked the Badgers out the year before, 2–1, on penalty kicks. Maijala's 25-yard shot with about 10 minutes remaining was the only goal as UW survived in action at Chapel Hill, North Carolina, after a CC foul for the 1–0 win. Midfielder Jennifer Hill took a free kick to Maijala. "[Hill] played the ball a little far for me, so I had to reach for it," Maijala said. "Luckily I got some topspin on it and it snuck in between the goalie and the post."

Ryan said it was another gutsy performance. "We knew when we got it in that we just had to hold on for 10 more minutes to win the game," he said. "We put lots of pressure on them at the end of the game. We never let them get into their rhythm."

Colorado College got off three shots in the final 10 minutes and outshot UW by a 9–7 margin overall, but it didn't matter because the Badgers had

Sparked by the play of goalie Heather Taggart, the Badgers qualified for the NCAA soccer tournament all four years she played at the UW. (Photo courtesy of the University of Wisconsin)

advanced to face North Carolina, which had downed Virginia, 5–1, in the other semifinal showdown.

Taggart said she was more pleased with her team's success than her own against Colorado College. "I played average," said Taggart, who faced eight shots in goal. "I didn't feel like I played that well but well enough that the team won. Our defense really limited their opportunities. It was a great game, a really tight game. We have a tense rivalry with them."

"We were pretty loose coming in," she added. "We felt that we could play with Colorado College."

Taggart was too modest as her career statistics at UW prove. She led Wisconsin to four consecutive NCAA tournaments, finishing with national and team records for most career shutouts with 52 1/2. She established a school mark for fewest goals allowed with 37 and most saves registered with 310.

Despite all of those glowing numbers, Taggart said in a phone interview that she and her Badger teammates played for the love of competition and much loftier goals. "As does any athlete who's played individually or as a team, we strived for excellence and played to win a national championship," said Taggart, a physician with Alegent Health Care in Omaha who still plays soccer and ran her first marathon in 2003. "We had lost in the Final Four when I was a freshman and had played in the NCAA Tournament all four years. So to get back to the final and have a chance to play against the most successful program ever certainly was a challenge and a privilege. We had worked really, really hard to get there." ★

MORE RECORDS, STREAKS, AND AMAZING MOMENTS
Riding the Wave

After the Milwaukee Wave joined the American Indoor Soccer Association as one of six charter members in 1984, the franchise failed to reach the postseason during its first three seasons. It finally accomplished the feat after the 1987–88 campaign; the Wave then moved into the new Bradley Center for the next season and posted its first winning record at 24–16.

Several up-and-down seasons followed, until, under the direction of Keith Tozer, the Wave became one of the elite squads. Milwaukee overcame several playoff disappointments after compiling the league's best mark at 28–12 in 1997–98, winning its first title. The Wave then claimed back-to-back crowns in 2000 and 2001, becoming the first AISA team to do so in nine years. ★

Shutout Rampage

Jim Launder's University of Wisconsin men's soccer team completed a 20–4–1 season in 1995 with seven consecutive shutouts, including its 2–0 victory over Duke on December 10 to win the NCAA championship. During the season, the Badgers registered 17 shutouts, five better than the school's previous best.

In the title game, Lars Hansen and Chad Cole scored and Jon Belskis made two saves in the competition at Richmond, Virginia, culminating in only the second time UW had advanced to the quarterfinals. Hansen scored at 8:12 of the first half, giving him three game-winning goals in the tournament and four for the season. ★

Blue Dukes Tops in Girls Soccer

The girls state soccer tournament started in 1983, increased to two divisions in 1997, and expanded to three in 2003. Whitefish Bay won the first three crowns and has earned seven overall heading into the 2004 campaign. The Blue Dukes won three straight Division 2 events in 1998–2000. Madison West has four championships to its credit, while Monona Grove and Wauwatosa East have grabbed three. Monona Grove's came in succession from 2001–03.

Overall, Whitefish Bay has made 14 state appearances, with Neenah qualifying for 12 and Madison West for 11. ★

Marquette, Whitefish Bay on Top

Since the Wisconsin Interscholastic Athletic Association began a boys state soccer tournament in 1982, expanding to two classes in 1992 and to three in 2002, Marquette University School and Whitefish Bay have claimed four championships, while Cedarburg and Madison West have earned three. Marquette is the only school to have won four straight crowns, accomplishing the feat in 2000–03. Whitefish Bay, Neenah, Sheboygan County Christian, and Madison West have done it in back-to-back seasons. ★

TENNIS

Frank Parker Wins Back-to-Back U.S. Opens

To say that Milwaukee native Frank Parker lived an interesting life would be an understatement.

He was a ball boy at the Milwaukee Town Club when noted tennis coach Mercer Beasley spotted him and became his mentor. Parker later created controversy when at age 22 he married Beasley's former wife, Audrey, who was almost twice his age. They remained married until she died in 1971 at age 75. Parker worked as assistant director of special effects for MGM in Hollywood and served in the Army during World War II in special services. Because he was stationed in California, he still participated in many tournaments during his tour of duty. On the court, there were few as graceful as Parker, the ultimate sportsman.

His accomplishments started early, as he won the national boys championship at age 15 in 1931. He won a national junior title, the national clay court crown three times and a national doubles title. Parker lost in the semifinals at Wimbledon in 1937 but won a doubles title there in 1949. He claimed the top prize in the French Open in 1948 and 1949 and was a member of four Davis Cup teams in 1937–48. His record of 17 straight years in the United States Lawn Tennis Association's top 10 was unsurpassed until Jimmy Connors reached 18 consecutive years in 1988. For his myriad achievements, Parker was inducted into the International Tennis Hall of Fame in 1966.

Despite the success, one void remained for much of that time—a singles title at the U.S. Open, a competition that was then called the U.S. Nationals and only open to amateurs. Parker had participated and come up short every year since 1932, but as the number-one-ranked player in 1944, his dream finally came true that Labor Day, September 4.

Stationed at Muroc Field in California, the fourth-seeded Parker's tourney play that season had been limited to the Pacific Coast doubles title earlier in the year. But his lack of activity didn't seem to bother Parker, who defeated third-seeded Bill Talbert for his first Open championship, winning 6–4, 3–6 (only the second set he had lost during the tourney), 6–3, 6–3 in front of an estimated 8,000 spectators at the 63rd event.

Parker, who held a rank of sergeant with the Army Air Force, had whipped Bruce Thomas 6–0, 6–2; downed Victor Seixas 6–1, 6–4; and dominated Eastern Junior winner Charles Oliver 6–2, 6-4 (he trailed 3–2), 6–1 in the first three rounds.

In the semifinals, Parker had run away from Donald McNeil, the fourth-ranked player during 1944 and the titlist from 1940, after splitting the competitive first two sets. He won 6–4 after breaking serve twice during a 3–0 start, and then McNeil roared out to the same three-game margin en route to evening the match with a 6–3 decision. Parker controlled the next two sets by 6–2 scores to advance to the final at the West Side Tennis Club in Forest Hills, New York.

NO MERCY

John Whitlinger of Neenah played no favorites on June 22, 1974, when, playing for Stanford University, he claimed the National Collegiate Athletic Association singles crown with a four-set verdict over teammate Chico Hagey. Whitlinger lost the opening set 6–1 but rallied to post 6–3, 6–3, and 6–1 margins for the title in Los Angeles.

In the championship showdown against Talbert of Indianapolis, Parker again won in four sets after playing to a draw in the first two, jumping on top 6–4 before falling 6–3.

Talbert, who had defeated top-seeded Francisco Segura of Ecuador in a grueling five sets, including an 8–6 setback in the fourth, couldn't find an answer to Parker's consistent arsenal in dropping the final two sets. A crucial point came in the third set when Parker broke Talbert's service to grab a 5–3 cushion en route to regaining the lead.

Parker raced to a 4–0 advantage in the first game only to see Talbert rally back to within a game. But Parker won at love on his service to clinch the 6–4 victory. In set two, Parker again jumped out quickly, this time 2–0. But Talbert rebounded for a 4–2 lead and won the final two games to knot things up.

The first two sets had only taken an hour to play, but action slowed down in the third as both players held serve through six games for a 3–all tie. Parker again held serve and then forced the issue, setting up a break point at 40–30 in Talbert's next service. Talbert hit into the net, giving the crucial game to Parker, who then got a break in the next game. With the score 30–all, Parker slipped, but Talbert missed the shot and hit into the net again to give the set to Parker.

What proved to be the deciding set started the same as the previous one, with both foes holding serve through four games. But then Parker broke Talbert and overcame a double fault to gain the upper hand at 4–2. Parker broke serve again to climb one game from victory but handed it back to Talbert to make it 5–3. Then with Talbert serving again, Parker won the last two points at 30–all to claim his long-awaited title.

"I rather thought that I'd be playing Segura in the finals, and he might have given me more trouble because he's beaten me once [out of three matches]," Parker said in the afterglow of his triumph. "No, I didn't fear McNeil. He has never beaten me either. Anyway, it was Talbert and that's that."

Parker followed his effort with another dandy performance in the 1945 Open, claiming his second consecutive crown with a 14–12, 6–1, 6–2 victory against Talbert to finish off a run in which he didn't drop a set. The top-seeded Parker flew 7,500 miles from Guam to defend his title, playing the final match on Labor Day again, this time September 3, with a near capacity crowd of 12,000 looking on the day after World War II ended.

Talbert had strained his hamstring in beating Segura in three sets in the semifinals the day before, and it worsened during one of his doubles matches that same day. He led the draining first set 10–9 and was ahead 40–30 on Parker's serve, but he couldn't turn the tide.

Talbert had a perfect record and had won all 10 tournaments he'd entered that season, but his injury and participating in three other matches that day were too high a hurdle to overcome.

Parker followed a first-round bye with an easy 6–1, 6–2 victory and rolled even more impressively in the third round, 6–1, 6–0. He handled seventh-seeded Seymour Greenberg, a left-hander, 6–2, 6–3, 6–2 in the fourth round, setting up a semifinal against number six Elwood Cooke, whom he overcame 6–1, 8–6, and 7–5.

In his rematch, Talbert was up 2–0, leading 40–15 and seemingly headed to a big lead in the first set. However, Parker rallied to knot things at 2. Talbert enjoyed the same cushion in the fifth game but faltered as he had in game three. Talbert broke back to even things at 3, and then each held service through the next 18 games, making it 12–all after Parker overcame a 30–0 deficit on his serve in the 24th game.

That's when the momentum finally shifted. Talbert's two errors on his backhand led to Parker's break and a 13–12 lead. Then the defending champion closed out the set, which lasted 1:08, the second longest in finals history to that point. Then Parker ripped off six straight games for a 6–1 win and never was in danger in the finale, a 6–2 verdict that gave him back-to-back titles. Talbert only managed 32 points in the last two sets.

Those victories proved to be the highlights of Parker's career. At age 52 in 1968, Parker returned to Forest Hills for his final pro tournament. He had a first-round bye and then lost to eventual champion Arthur Ashe in the second round, 6–3, 6–2, and 6–2. ★

A Couple of Royal Victories

Onalaska product Tim Gullikson made a name for himself on one of the biggest stages in tennis. On June 30, 1979, he ousted second-seeded John McEnroe to reach the quarterfinals at Wimbledon. Gullikson controlled the match, grabbing a 6–4, 6–2, 6–4 victory. However, his upset streak ended during his next match, a setback to Roscoe Tanner.

Another Wisconsinite pulled a major upset in London on June 12, 1984. Leif Shiras of Shorewood downed Ivan Lendl (7–5, 6–3) in the first round of the Steila Artois grass court tourney. Shiras advanced to the final five days later, dropping the match to McEnroe. ★

Knightly Distinction

Nicolet High School has produced the most state boys tennis tournament singles champions with 13 through 2003, while the Knights have claimed 23 team championships (one a tie), featuring eight straight in 1967–74. Cary Bachman's troops won titles during 19 of 24 seasons in 1967–90.

Individually, only two boys players have won crowns all four years: John Whitlinger of Neenah (1969–72) and Marc Eisen of Nicolet (1986–89). Bill Reed of Shawano was the first to win three championships, doing so in 1939–41. Charles Bleckinger of Oshkosh (1959–61) and Mark Loughrin of Greendale (1992, 1994–95) also did it. ★

The Girls Can Play Too

The Nicolet girls team has put up even more impressive numbers in the state tournament, dominating with 17 team championships, while Brookfield Central has won seven and Whitefish Bay 6.

Caitlin Burke of Cedarburg and Kaylan Caiati of Greendale, both from 1999 to 2002, joined Tami Whitlinger of Neenah (1983–86) as the only four-time singles champs. Burke fashioned a 108-0 mark, Whitlinger posted a 105–0 record, and Caiati won 104 of 107 matches. Lia Jackson of Nicolet was 93–2 while earning three consecutive Division 1 titles in 1995–97.

Teri Whitlinger of Neenah is the only girl to be a member of four state doubles title teams. Kara Metzger and Andrea Bukacek of The Prairie School won three Division 2 doubles events in a row (2000–02). The Wisconsin Interscholastic Athletic Association's girls tournament, which was established in 1971, has been a two-division event since 1994. ★

TRACK AND FIELD

Archie Hahn Sprints to Olympic Gold

Archie Hahn definitely earned the nickname Milwaukee Meteor during his heyday. The Dodgeville native was one of the world's top sprinters at the beginning of the twentieth century.

Hahn attended the University of Michigan in 1903–05, where he received his law degree but never practiced. He competed for the Milwaukee Athletic Club, winning the United States 100- and 220-yard titles in 1903 and claiming another National AAU 220 championship in '05. His best time of 21.6 for the 200 meters was a world record from 1904 until it was tied in 1921 and wasn't bettered until American Eddie Tolan did it in the 1932 Olympic Games. Hahn also was co-holder of the world 100-yard dash record with a 9.8 in 1901.

However, his brightest moment occurred during the 1904 Games in Saint Louis, where he blazed his way to a triple crown of gold medals, winning the 60-, 100-, and 200-meter events, making him the first man to complete the 100-200 double in Olympic competition.

That year's extravaganza was held Monday through Saturday, August 29–September 3, in conjunction with the Louisiana Purchase World Exposition, which drew 20 million visitors during its six-month run. Only 13 nations were represented, and of the 681 athletes, 525 came from the United States. Thus, Americans won 80 percent of the medals. Hahn was one of four triple winners, joining Jim Lightbody, Ray Ewry, and Harry Hillman.

Hahn grabbed his first gold by winning the 100 in 11.0, and then he added the 200 title with his world record of 21.6. He capped his performance with the 60-meter title in 7.0; this event is no longer held.

His daughter-in-law, Edwina, was married to Archie Hahn Jr. for 62 years and lives in Cape Coral, Florida. She kept records of Hahn's athletic and coaching accomplishments and talked to him extensively about his exploits on and off the track, keeping a journal of most of the interviews.

She related Hahn's recollections about earning that third gold medal. "Don't let anyone tell you I was calm for that race," he said. "My stomach was all tightened up. I lived an extra 14 years before that race got under way. In fact, that was the way with all of 'em. Anyone who says he isn't scared before a competitive event doesn't know what he's talkin' about. Believe me, I was always that way.

"I wanted to win this one. It was goin' to be all or nothin'," she recalled him saying. "Well, we were all lined up there for the start. They played a trick on me I didn't notice. In those days they used white tape as the marker for the finish line, but for this race they changed to red. This fellow on the left side of me, Hogenson, running for the Chicago A.C., saw the change but kept his mouth shut, not lettin' me in on the secret. I guess in that way he figured he might win. Anyway, we all got off to a good start, and before I knew it, I had crossed the finish line. I didn't even know it was there. I was goin' on an extra 20 when somebody waves me to slow down. I knew I was lucky in that one. In fact, everybody told me how close it was." Hahn repeated as the 100-meter champion at the intercalated Olympics in Athens, Greece, in 1906.

PEDAL POWER

A one-mile bicycle race was added to the boys state track meet lineup in 1896. Edward Comstock of Oshkosh won that initial event in a time of 3 minutes, 30 seconds, and defended his crown the next year in 3:02. The race was canceled in 1898 because of bad weather but resumed in 1899, when a three-mile race was added. However, both events were eliminated after the 1902 meet.

He was a football star for three years at Portage High after attending Dodgeville as a freshman, but neither school fielded a track team. So if not for his friend, "Red" Race, telling him about activities going on at the county fair in Baraboo as a junior, his love for sprinting might never have materialized, and his story and life might have been much different. "I never had the slightest thought this was going to take me to all of the places it did," Hahn told his daughter-in-law. "I beat all of my fellows at Portage in races prior to the county meet. We didn't have much of a place to run, just on the cow pasture away from the herd. Well, I'm feelin' pretty good about the race and report over to Baraboo the day it comes off.

"I didn't know any of the other guys. They looked somewhat older than I did, but I was determined to give them a good race. The winner's share I think was $25. Two of the fellows beat me in the 100 that day. I was timed in 11 seconds. I caught up with those sprinters the next year though. I had started practicing after my lickin' and I knew I could come back. The next spring I went over to Baraboo again. This time I won the 100 and was timed in 10.1."

Hahn continued that success during the next two decades. During his freshman year at the University of Michigan, he won every 100-yard dash, including the Big Ten finals. He competed in and won most of his professional races until retiring in 1918. He then continued in the coaching ranks, which he had done anyway since 1907. Later, Hahn coached at several universities across the country, including Princeton and Virginia (1929–51). His book *How to Sprint* was considered for years the classic text about the topic.

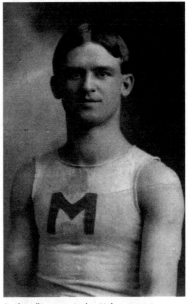

In his 1984 work *The Glory of Their Times*, Lawrence S. Ritter interviewed players from the early days of baseball, including Cambria, Wisconsin, native Davy Jones, who knew all about Hahn's speed. "Actually, track was my real specialty back then," Jones said. "I was always fast, fast enough to beat Archie Hahn several times before he won the Olympics in 1904. . . . [He] ranks right up there with Jim Thorpe and Jesse Owens as one of the greatest runners who ever lived. Odd isn't it, that Jim Thorpe and Jesse Owens are still very familiar names, but hardly anybody seems to remember Archie Hahn anymore."

Dodgeville native Archie Hahn was considered by many to be the fastest man in the world in the early twentieth century. (Photo courtesy of the Hahn family)

One person who can't forget Hahn is Jake Fitzsimons, 73. That's because Hahn was his great-uncle. Fitzsimons, a Dodgeville resident, saw Hahn periodically while growing up but recalled a holiday visit in 1951. "I was in the Navy in Bethesda, Maryland, which is only about 100 miles from Charlottesville, and I had four days off for Christmas," Fitzsimons said in a phone interview. "So I went down and spent a couple of days with him. He had a room, maybe 12-by-12, full of his medals and trophies. I had a really good time, and that was the last time I saw him."

However, it wasn't the last time he heard stories about his famous relative. For example, Hahn supposedly raced and defeated a horse in a 50-yard contest at a county fair in Burlington in 1910. "That's true. He got off to a better start than the horse and rider, but I'll bet your bottom dollar that if it would have been any longer than 100 yards that he wouldn't have won. But Archie was a short, stocky guy with really strong legs, and he had a tremendous kick at the end of most races."

Fitzsimons also said it's a shame more people don't know more about Hahn's significant role on and off the track in the early days of the sport.

"He's not a legend around here, which is kind of funny," Fitzsimons said. "If they're not my age or older, most folks don't know the name."

Well, the USA Track and Field Hall of Fame did, inducting Hahn into its ranks in 1983. ★

Larry Franklin Jumps to State Record

It was a gusty, humid day at Monona Grove High School. However, coaches and fans alike must have been wondering what the heck was in the water June 5, 1965—at least in the water that competitors in the broad jump (now called the long jump) were drinking during the 69th annual Wisconsin Interscholastic Athletic Association boys state track meet.

Larry Franklin, representing the old Madison Central High School, became the first state prep athlete to surpass 24 feet, accomplishing the feat during the preliminary round, bettering the standard of 23-7 that Ralph Welton of Shorewood had recorded in 1944.

But Franklin, who eventually won the gold medal, wasn't even the first one to reach that plateau in a legendary competition that produced four of the five best long jumps in WIAA history. Cal Mallory of Milwaukee Rufus King topped the previous mark with a 23-7 1/2 effort. Then Craig Ferris of Madison East jumped 23-9 1/4, and Pete Van Driest of Sheboygan North leaped 23-7 1/4.

Then late Central Coach Harold Rooney's star pupil took over. Franklin fouled on four of his seven attempts, but his good jumps proved to be more than good enough: 23-4, 24-2 1/4, and 25-3/4. The latter mark was less than four inches from the national record set in California earlier that season and remains the oldest Wisconsin state record on the books.

EARLY OLYMPIC SUCCESS

On August 31, 1904, La Crosse High School athlete George Poage earned a bronze medal in the 400-meter hurdles during the Summer Olympics in Saint Louis. According to *The Complete Book of the Olympics*, Poage became the first African American to win an Olympic medal. Wisconsin was well-represented in the event, as Menomonie's Frank Waller, also representing the United States, claimed the silver medal.

Almost four decades later, no one has come close to challenging Franklin's performance. The closest was Wauwatosa West's Dan Benson with his jump of 23-8 1/2 in 1977. On a much larger scale, Bob Beamon's record from the 1968 Olympic Games stood for 23 years before Mike Powell set the current world record of 29-4 1/2.

And to think that Franklin's actual distance could have been better. A *Milwaukee Journal* article the next day said that Franklin, because of his fouls, used caution during his approach on his record-setting leap, taking off about six inches behind the line. That meant he would have held the top spot nationally if he'd hit the board true.

Mallory returned to Milwaukee after attending Murray State University for a couple of years and serving in Vietnam. He said in a phone interview that he still cannot believe Franklin's showing that day. "I broke the city long jump record the week before and I had won the regional, so I was the one expected to win the title," Mallory said. "I was unbeaten until the state meet and was the first one to break the record. But then Larry came up and shattered all of that. I had the best jump of my career, and he beat me by a foot and a half. That was pretty demoralizing.

"I had never heard anything about him," Mallory added. "I'm not sure if he was in the top 10 or not, so I thought I was a shoo-in. But Larry came out of nowhere. I sure never expected 25 feet. I was also a high hurdler, and I think I was competing in the preliminaries of that event because I don't recall seeing Larry's jump. After that I concentrated on the hurdles and ran on one of our relays. We were trying to win as a team, but I think we got beat by half a point or something like that."

Kenosha Bradford won the Class A crown with 14 1/2 points, the lowest total ever in that level. But the team standings took a distant second place to what occurred in the long jump pit that weekend, and people still talk about and are amazed by Franklin's showing.

Former *Wisconsin State Journal* high school sports writer Don Lindstrom said the circumstances were hard to believe. "I think a lot of people were hoping Welton's record would go down, but 24 feet wasn't even considered," Lindstrom said in a 1995 *Milwaukee Journal Sentinel* article. "The remarkable thing about that day is that Welton's record stood for some 20 years, and then all of a sudden a group comes along and they all break it in one day."

Many have theorized why such a display occurred and why the marks have gone unchallenged for so long. They include the shortening of the track season and the addition of the triple jump event, which makes it less likely that an athlete will specialize in the long jump.

Franklin benefited from competing during an era when the season was two weeks longer, something the WIAA changed before 1989. Some coaches believe that hurts athletes because the event entails much more than running and jumping. Still, today's competitors are bigger, stronger, and faster, but nobody has come close to Franklin's feat.

"I was sitting at the broad jump take-off board with his coach [Harold Rooney]," Claude Hungerford, then the coach at Madison East, said in the 1995 story. "He had been having trouble with his steps and, on that try, he looked like he was going to foul again. He literally stopped, standing three steps from the board, and started again and hit it correctly. Coach Rooney saw him coming down with the wrong steps and thought he was going to foul again and looked away. He didn't even see the jump."

Others may not have seen Franklin's jumps either, but they sure have heard or read about them since. ★

Pat Matzdorf Shatters World High Jump Record

Pat Matzdorf admittedly had struggled for several weeks, but on July 3, 1971, he felt different for some reason. The Sheboygan native and high jumping extraordinaire had recently completed his junior year with the University of Wisconsin track and field team. He was in Berkeley, California, for the annual United States–Russia competition.

"I had been slumping a bit for about a month before that event," Matzdorf said via phone from his home in Chicago. "I only cleared 7-0 and finished in sixth place at the NCAA meet in Washington State. Then a couple weeks later at the national AAU meet I was off a bit."

Matzdorf's 7-2 effort at that Amateur Athletic Union gathering put him behind chief rival, Reynaldo Brown, who had made the 1968 Olympic Games in Mexico City as a high school senior. "He was probably the best U.S. high jumper during a six- to eight-year span," Matzdorf said of Brown. "He was a consistent, tough competitor."

But not even Brown proved to be a challenge for the Sheboygan North star who had won the Wisconsin Interscholastic Athletic Association title with a record leap of 6-11 as a senior.

MARQUETTE MEDALIST
Melvin Shimek of Marquette University became the school's first athlete to win an event in the NCAA Track and Field Championships. Nicknamed Buster, Shimek won the 2-mile run in a time of 9:34.4 at the competitions in Chicago's Soldier Field on June 11, 1927.

Recently, Matzdorf said the electricity surrounding the heated competition that day in California got his adrenaline flowing. "I remember reading through the program the night before about the history and highlights from past meets," he said. "It was a big deal at that time. The nostalgia and everything got me fired up. I didn't sleep much, but the morning of the meet I got ready early and went over to the track to take it all in.

"I was very focused and keyed up, and I couldn't wait for it to start," Matzdorf added about the festivities before an estimated crowd of 22,000. "I felt great during warm-ups."

Nobody, Matzdorf included, had an inkling of what was to come next.

However, the lanky Badger star, who stood six feet two inches and weighed 175 pounds, sensed something special in the works from the beginning. "My thought after the first jump of 6-8 3/4 was that I wonder if they had it at the right height because it felt so easy," he said. "I was anticipating it to be tougher. But my thinking wasn't about reaching my personal best [7-3], but rather doing well for the team and if that came, then great."

Each subsequent try usually went up five centimeters, or about two inches, and with each one, Matzdorf appeared to get stronger. He also cleared 6-10 3/4 and 7-3/4 before missing on his first attempt at 7-1 3/4, which he made on try two.

He then equaled his personal best of 7-3, which he had done at the Big Ten Conference indoor meet that spring, while bettering his outdoor best of 7-2. "At that point, my teammate Tim Heikkila said I should just go for the [American] record," Matzdorf said of the advice he received from the University of Minnesota athlete and Superior High School standout who had beaten Matzdorf for the prep gold medal when they were juniors.

He's glad he listened. Matzdorf got over 7-4 1/2 on his second try to pass Dick Fosbury's American standard by a quarter of an inch, an effort the latter had established during the 1968 Olympics. His effort knocked out Brown, and after more encouragement from Heikkila, Matzdorf shot for the stars.

His next target was Valery Brumel of Russia, whose 7-5 3/4 world mark had been set in the same meet in 1963. "Tim said, 'What have you got to lose?'" And the bar was set at 7-6 1/4.

"At that point I was ecstatic. I never thought about what would come next," Matzdorf recalled. "I was on autopilot. I tried to make it like any other meet and just hit my mark and make the jump. My first attempt felt very good, but I knocked it off. I was thinking, 'That was respectable, so just duplicate that effort, the same rhythm and explosiveness.' I did but barely grazed it and it came off again." One more chance.

"On the third attempt, I just wanted to be as consistent as on the first two," Matzdorf said. "And then right at takeoff, something didn't seem right, like I didn't have the same rhythm, like I had been kind of abrupt with it. But I carried it through and slid over. I was really shocked. I didn't think I had a prayer. I hit the pad and flopped, and when I saw it had stayed up I instantly jumped up and held my hands over my head. I couldn't believe it."

The crowd erupted in jubilation: Pat Matzdorf was a world record holder, a crowning achievement as the American men posted a 126–110 victory.

His Badger coach at the time, Bill Perrin, was optimistic that Matzdorf was close to just such stardom. "We've talked about the record," Perrin said upon getting the record-setting news. "Many of the drills we used in training were the drills the Russians used. Whether it be this year or next year, I felt that he had the ability, the potential and the technique to jump that high."

Not too bad for a basketball player who had to be talked into going out for track in high school. "My math teacher, who was the father of a friend of mine, had seen me playing and talked me into trying track," Matzdorf said. "By the end of that first year, my sophomore year, I had figured out what I was supposed to be doing and had made it over 6-0. Then I cleared 6-6 as a junior and got second in the state, and then I won state at 6-11 as a senior in the meet at Monona Grove."

Also not bad for an athlete who attained his fame using the traditional straddle technique in which the competitor is facing the bar while going over it. Most other high jumpers, including Fosbury, had switched to the flop form that is still used today. "Dick had enjoyed a lot of success with that technique and that's why so many people tried it," Matzdorf said. "One reason it became so popular was because of the rapid progress jumpers could make compared to the straddle, which was a lot harder to perfect. I switched to the flop later in my career because it put a lot less stress on my left knee and leg. I went as high as 7-4 1/4 that way."

Matzdorf competed through 1976 but never approached his record-setting height again, watching as American Dwight Stones shattered his mark in 1973. Now a computer software engineer and the father of three, Matzdorf said his

Pat Matzdorf, a member of the UW track team, gave his family and friends in Sheboygan something to celebrate during the July Fourth weekend in 1971, setting a world record in the high jump. (Photo courtesy of the University of Wisconsin)

biggest accomplishment in athletics isn't talked about much anymore around family and friends. But that day won't be forgotten. "It started sinking in during the days after because of all of the attention and publicity it got, all of the requests for interviews," he said. "I wasn't used to that before, except for in the Madison area, where we had a good track team.

"After that season, the increased attention at our meets and the expectations work on you psychologically, and then you put more pressure on yourself to reach another level," he added.

Before that July 4 weekend in 1971, nobody had gone higher. ★

Suzy Favor Wins Fourth State Crown

Suzy Favor Hamilton has never worked for the United States Postal Service. But the Stevens Point native sure knows how to deliver, and in all different kinds of weather conditions while making her rounds. That is, when it comes to delivering victories in track and cross-country events.

She has been one of the biggest names and stars in running circles since the late 1980s, when, as Suzy Favor, she dominated the Big Ten Conference and National Collegiate Athletic Association meets and, since then, has been one of the top runners in the world.

However, the former University of Wisconsin standout started her remarkable career with an unparalleled four-year high school run that saw her finish 40–2 in cross country races, including 35 consecutive victories to end her prep days.

MILE WAS HIS DISTANCE

In the 1940s, former Milwaukee Pulaski High School standout Don Gehrmann starred for the Wisconsin Badgers and became one of the nation's and world's best runners. His specialty was the mile, an event in which he won 39 consecutive major races starting with the 1948 Olympic Games and going to March 3, 1951. Gehrmann earned Big Ten outdoor titles all four years at UW and claimed National Collegiate Athletic Association crowns in 1948, 1949, and 1950.

She concluded that streak with a triumph in the Class A event November 9, 1985, which gave her an unprecedented fourth consecutive individual win. In the process, she became only the sixth girl in the country to accomplish the feat. Cathy Branta of Slinger had won three straight crowns from 1978 to 1980.

"High school was when I had the most pressure on me in my running career because I was so young and didn't know how to deal with all of that, and I'd be lying if I said that wasn't the case," she said from her home in New Glarus. "That's why after it was over it was more a sense of relief. But every title I won in high school was special, and getting the fourth straight was something I have cherished."

But in order to do that, Favor and her competitors had to win a battle with Mother Nature, who whipped up nasty, wintry conditions that postponed the event one week and played havoc with the competitions that day on the Yahara Hills golf course east of Madison. "There had been blizzardlike conditions, so it was really windy and cold," she said. "I wore a facemask that only my eyes and nose showed through. I remember thinking that I may look silly, but it was freezing and I wanted to be as warm as possible. So I was in tights and long sleeves and everything.

"The times were incredibly slow, but because it was on a golf course it was really even, so you didn't have to worry about any ruts or holes," she added. "It was mushy running in it, but mainly it was the wind and cold."

Favor hadn't experienced that kind of weather in posting a triumph at University of Wisconsin–Parkside her freshman year and back-to-back crowns at Christmas Mountain in Wisconsin Dells as a sophomore and junior.

Mike Olson, her coach at Stevens Point High School, had one goal in mind heading into the eventual record-setting performance, and it had to do with off-the-field factors. "Our biggest concern is keeping the pressure on Suzy to a minimum," he said at the time. "With her reputation, people expect a lot from her. She can't let the pressure affect her. She has to keep running the way she has."

AMERICA'S SECOND-FASTEST MILER

Running in the Jack-in-the-Box track meet in San Diego on February 22, 1980, former University of Wisconsin and McFarland High School star runner Steve Lacy recorded the second-fastest indoor mile by an American up to that time.

Lacy's 8:22.2 gave him second place to Henry Rono, a Kenyan running for Washington State, who won the event in 8:15.0. Lacy's effort was second fastest by a U.S. competitor after Steve Prefontaine's effort in 1975. In the meet, Lacy bettered his personal best of 8:31.9, which he had established in January 1977.

Then the event was postponed, but Olson remained confident in his number-one pupil. "It will affect a lot of teams, but I don't think it will affect Suzy because of the racing condition she's in," Olson said. "For other girls, it will be difficult to get psyched up all over again."

And the Pointers' star proved she had the tenacity and ability to overcome whatever roadblocks got in her way. "I remember it was really quite flat, and it was great for spectators, which typically isn't the case," Favor said. "You're usually out there by yourself except for at the beginning and the end. But you could hear all of the people cheering for you along the way.

"At that point in my career, I was very confident and knew that I could win the race, that God forbid I fell or suffered an injury, that I had a great shot at the title," she added. "My main competition was Mary Hartzheim of Lakeland, who became one of my best friends and was my roommate in college."

Favor, the daughter of Conrad and Rachel Favor, won in 11:58.5 over the 3,200-meter course. Hartzheim stayed behind Favor and Suzie Neas of Tomah, and then Favor and Hartzheim battled for the lead until the Pointer 17-year-old took control with three-fourths of a mile left, something that could have never happened had she not jumped over a fallen competitor early in the race. "I knew she was right behind me because I could hear people yelling on the sidelines," Favor said afterward. "I thought I was going to collapse on the last leg, but I held out."

Olson said it was the most impressive win for Favor, whose only two setbacks came to Jenny Hintz, a 1981 state champion, in her freshman season. "Her success hasn't gone to her head, and she doesn't make herself out to be above and beyond everyone else," Olson said after her high school finale. "Suzy is a normal person who happens to run faster than anyone else."

Favor, who watched the Pointer boys and the Stevens Point Pacelli boys and girls teams claim state championships, was looking forward to a bright future, which she has more than accomplished since. "I am pleased with the season because I ran my best times ever," she said afterward. "My goals are to choose a good college and improve. I just have to take one day at a time. My coach deserves a lot of credit because I couldn't have done it without him. It was a surprise to win my freshman year and the most exciting. However, each one became more rewarding. This one meant the most, and I'm never going to forget it."

She couldn't if she tried. "My school [Stevens Point] put up a life-size portrait of me, which was a really nice gesture," she said 18 years after the fact. "I had made history and I liked the attention, but I was more embarrassed at the time because I wanted to be like the

Suzy Favor enjoys the moment after winning her fourth consecutive state cross-country title for Stevens Point High School in the fall of 1985. (Photo courtesy of the Favor family)

other kids. I tried to be normal and not act any differently because of what I had accomplished."

In track and field, she won the 1,600-meter run four straight years. She also won the 800 in 1985, the 3,200 in 1984, and ran on a winning 1,600-meter relay in 1984. Those efforts were only the beginning for Favor, who, as Suzy Favor Hamilton, made the U.S. Olympic teams in 1992, 1996, and 2000. She won nine NCAA individual track titles, including four straight championships in the outdoor 1,500-meter run. She became a 14-time all-American in cross-country and track while earning 23 Big Ten titles (21 as an individual and two on relays).

Favor Hamilton established an American women's indoor record in the 800 meters (1:58.92) and set Wisconsin records in seven indoor and outdoor events. She was named Wisconsin's Female Athlete of the Year in 1987–1990. She became a three-time Big Ten Female Athlete of the Year, an award that was eventually named for her. Favor Hamilton was selected the Big Ten's Female Athlete of the Decade after winning 54 of 56 collegiate finals, including her last 40 races. ★

MORE RECORDS, STREAKS, AND AMAZING MOMENTS
COLLEGE TRACK AND FIELD
Not Quite Gold

In the 1930s, Ralph Metcalfe came up short in back-to-back quests for Olympic gold medals. The Marquette University star, one of the world's best sprinters in the first half of the twentieth century, settled for silver and bronze medals in the 1932 Games after winning the 100- and 200-meter dashes in the trials. U.S. teammate Eddie Tolan claimed the top spot in both races.

In the 100, they finished in a dead heat, and judges took several hours to declare Tolan the winner. In the 200, it was discovered afterward that Metcalfe had started three or four feet behind his competitors. Metcalfe turned down an offer to rerun the event so as not to jeopardize his team's sweep.

In the 1936 Olympics, Metcalfe earned a silver again in the 100, finishing behind Jesse Owens. Metcalfe won his only gold that year in the 400-meter relay. He won the 100 and 220 titles three straight years (1932–34) in the NCAA and AAU meets while at Marquette. ★

HIGH SCHOOL TRACK AND FIELD
Records That Still Stand

The Wisconsin high school state track and field meet for boys started in 1895, and while many of the records have given way in the past 10 or 15 years, several standards have endured the test of time.

And that starts with several field event marks that are the oldest on the books, dating back to the mid-1960s. The ultimate and oldest record is Larry Franklin's 25-3/4 effort in the 1965 Division 1 long jump competitions.

While the Madison Central star's accomplishment still staggers the mind, the leaders in other classes of the high jump have been around almost as long. Ken Peterson of Grafton set the Division 2 distance of 23-1 3/4 in 1966, while Iowa-Grant's Dag Birkeland leaped 23-6 1/2 in 1970 for the Division 3 mark.

Another record from 1966 still stands, and that is Stu Voigt's performance in the shot put. The Madison West, University of Wisconsin, and Minnesota Viking star heaved the shot 66-7 1/2.

The only double record holders are John Easker of Wittenberg–Birnamwood and Michael Bennett of Milwaukee Tech. Easker's number one spots in Division 2 are for the 1,600 (4:11.93) and 3,200 meters (9:08.08), both set in 1981. Bennett, a current halfback with the Minnesota Vikings, bolted to the top 100 (10.33 seconds) and 200 (20.68) times in the 1998 meet, both in the Division 1 preliminaries.

Only three competitors have won state crowns in the same event all four years. David Greenwood of Park Falls won the high jump in 1976–79, Kevin Bledsoe of Milwaukee South was on the 400-relay team that was tops in 1984–87, and Greg Bracey of Milwaukee Vincent did the same in 2000–03.

Darrell Jansen of Kimberly has the most state titles with eight, winning the 120 high hurdles and 180 low hurdles in 1958–60 and the high jump in 1959 and '60. In 2000, Stratford's Andrew Rock became the first boy to capture first-place finishes in four events at the same meet, winning the 100 and 300 hurdles, the 200 dash, and the long jump.

In the team standings, Milwaukee Riverside (then called East) won 11 titles by 1922 and all 16 of its trophies by 1938. Whitefish Bay has the most championships with 18, 16 of them coming consecutively from 1937 to 1952, all in Class B. Kohler has won 16 Class C titles, all from 1946 to 1979. ★

Five Medals in First Meet

Arguably the greatest track athlete Wisconsin has ever produced showed his talents in the first boys state high school meet in 1895. Alvin Kraenzlein of Milwaukee East (now Riverside High School) won the 100-yard dash, the 120 and 220 hurdles, the broad jump, and the shot put.

He attended Wisconsin but transferred to the University of Pennsylvania, where he became a world record holder in the 120- and 220-yard low hurdles. In 1900, Kraenzlein was one of the top performers for the United States Olympic team, which dominated action in Paris. Kraenzlein won the 60-meter dash in seven seconds, the 100 hurdles in 15.4, the 200 hurdles in 25.4 and the broad jump with an incredible effort of 23-6 7/8. ★

Dominating the Competition

Arlie Mucks Sr. of Oshkosh High School looked like a man among boys in the 1910 state track meet. He didn't just break the discus record; he surpassed the previous mark by more than 18 feet. An article in the *Milwaukee Sentinel* described Mucks's accomplishment: "The discus record received a bad jolt when Mucks, the Oshkosh weight heaver, hurled the Grecian platter out 130 feet 1 1/2 inches. Unsatisfied with his mark, Mucks then went out in earnest and in his third and final trial shot the discus out 132 feet 5 1/2 inches, breaking the previous best record by nearly 18 feet."

Despite the longer throw, Mucks's official record was listed at 130-1 1/2. Mucks's record stood for 21 years until Erv Rice of Milwaukee East broke it with a throw of 131-1 1/4 in the 1931 Class A meet.

Mucks's other record in 1910 came in the shot put, which he won with a heave of 47-4. His record wasn't bested until 1928 when Greg Kabat of Milwaukee Bay View won the Class A competition with a toss of 47-9 1/2. Mucks, who later played football and competed in track at Wisconsin, won both events the next year.

In 1912, he was the youngest athlete chosen for the United States Olympic team. Nineteen and just out of high school, he placed second in the discus with a heave of 145-11 1/2 in Stockholm, Sweden, where the United States dominated with 11 wins in 22 events. ★

Sweet Performances

In Oshkosh, the name Oaks means homemade candies, but in the spring of 1966, it meant pole vaulting.

That year, Bill Oaks of Oshkosh High School became the first prep athlete to reach the 14-foot plateau, winning the WIAA state meet title with an effort of 14 feet, 2 1/2 inches, in an event that lasted six hours.

Oaks and his older brother, Robert, honed their skills in a pit they had constructed in their backyard. Bill, who stood 5-5 and weighed only 128 pounds, always had trouble finding a pole that was the right fit. Finally as a senior, he settled on a fiberglass one made for a 140-pounder and broke the mark of 13 feet, 7 1/4 inches, which Brian Bergemann of Whitefish Bay had established in 1962.

Robert, competing for UW–Oshkosh that same year, won the pole vault in the Wisconsin State University Conference meet. ★

Sister Act

Mention the name Hyland in Wood County and the surrounding area, and people will immediately think of Nekoosa High School.

Jack Hyland was a long-time track coach for the Papermakers, and he raised a couple of state-caliber competitors named Heather and Hillary. Both were twice named Athlete of the Year by the Wisconsin Track Coaches Association: Heather in 1992–93 and Hillary in 1997–98.

Heather established a Division 2 state meet record with an effort of 18 feet, 11 inches in the long jump in 1993, a mark that still stands just one-half inch under the Division 1 and overall standard set by Brittany Rusch of Wausau East a year later.

Hillary wasn't to be outdone by her older sister, putting her name atop the Division 2 state charts with her 38-4 in the triple jump in 1997. ★

Four-Time Wonders

No fewer than 14 girls have earned state track championships in the same event four years in a row.

However, only three have been in the field events: Nekoosa's Heather Hyland in the long jump in 1990–93, Kate Juedes of Clear Lake in the Division 3 high jump in 1998–2001, and Amber Curtis of Monroe and Brodhead in the discus in 2000–03. Curtis won three in Division 2 and one in Division 1.

The other four-time winners include Sue Tallard of Madison Memorial in the 440 in 1971–74, Anne Mulrooney of Prairie du Chien in the mile in 1973–76, Carla Banks of Madison West as a member of the mile or 1,600 relay in 1979–82, Ann Kattreh of Kohler in the 400 in 1980–83, Suzy Favor of Stevens Point in the 1,600 and Catherine Jones of Milwaukee Riverside in the 300 hurdles, both from 1983 to 1986, Jessie Bushman of Rosholt in the 400 in 1989–92, Jenni Westphal of Marinette in the 800 in 1991–94, Jaclynn Kriegl of Florence in the 200 from 1995 to 1998, and Anna Monsen of Stoughton in the 100 in 2000–03.

Kriegl holds the record for most championships with 10, adding the long jump three times, the 100 twice, and the 800 relay once. Dana Collins of Milwaukee Marshall, Hyland, and Westphal are next with nine.

Meanwhile, Madison West has captured six team titles, including three in a row (1980–82), while Marathon has earned five. Prairie du Chien claimed its four titles in succession from 1975 to 1978 and shares four wins with Madison Memorial, Whitewater, and Rosholt. ★

COLLEGE CROSS-COUNTRY
Warrior Power

Sophomore Katie Webb from De Pere was a standout for the Marquette University women's cross-country squad, which hosted the Wisconsin Women's Intercollegiate Athletic Conference meet at Mitchell Park on October 30, 1982.

The Warriors won the event for a second straight season and qualified for the National Association of Intercollegiate Athletics championship. Coach Elliot Kramsky was named Coach of the Year in the conference, and Webb (second), Laurie Hottinger, Kara Hughes, and Mary Kay VanEss placed in the top 10 and earned all-league honors.

The NAIA meet was held November 20 at UW–Parkside, where Marquette placed seven runners in the top 40 of an event that featured 235 entrants. All-American Webb won the crown in 17:41. The other participants were senior Kathy Fynan, juniors Hottinger and Diane Held, sophomores Hughes and Mary Ann Ferguson, and freshman VanEss.

Marquette won with 48 points, outdistancing UW–Eau Claire by 61 points. ★

Katie Webb, front right, and the Marquette University women's cross-country team won a national championship in 1982. (Photo courtesy of Marquette University)

HIGH SCHOOL CROSS-COUNTRY
Quite a Run

Not many coaches have enjoyed as much success as Clinton High School's Bill Greer, who coached the Cougars' boys and girls teams for 25 years.

The boys program accumulated a dual winning streak that lasted from late in the 1976 season to the meet against Walworth-Big Foot in 1988, winning 11 straight Rock Valley Conference championships during that span.

At the state meet level, the Clinton boys were a title contender most seasons, grabbing the Class B trophy in 1983, '85, and '86 while finishing second in

1978–80. Kris Rogers won the individual title in 1985, but few have dominated the competitions like Paul Voss, who took top honors his final three seasons (1977–79), becoming the second of only four boys to accomplish that feat.

The girls turned in an even longer string of successes, winning 94 consecutive dual meets from late 1978 until the Orfordville Parkview outing in 1994. The Cougar girls won 15 league titles in a row. ★

Harriers in a Hurry

Four boys have earned three individual cross-country titles. Jim Brice of Wrightstown was the first from 1975 to 1977, and Clinton's Paul Voss soon followed in 1977–79. Then it wasn't until 1989–91 that Madison Memorial's Phil Downs accomplished the feat. Finally, Stevens Point standout Chris Solinsky did it in 2000–02.

In the team standings, Milwaukee Riverside won the first eight trophies starting in 1913 and earned six more from 1923 to 1928. It has won 16 championships, all before 1933. South Milwaukee is the only other double-digit winner with 10. ★

Paul Voss of Clinton High School races to one of his three WIAA cross country titles in the late 1970s. (Photo courtesy of Clinton High School)

Multiple Winners

The only other female runner to come close to Suzy Favor Hamilton's string of four state championships in girls cross-country is Slinger's Cathy Branta, who won the event three times (1978–80).

Ten runners have registered two state crowns: Susie Houston of Tomahawk (1975–76), Maryann Brunner of Waukesha North (1978–79), Jackie Anderson of Mount Horeb (1981 and '84), Clare Eichner of Wauwatosa East (1986–87), Amy Wickus of Baraboo (1988–89), Sue Daggett of Random Lake (1991–92), Avrie Walters of La Crosse Logan (1991–92), Kristina Betzold of Eau Claire North (1993–94), Rachel Earney of Cochrane-Fountain City (1995–96), and Liz Reusser of Middleton (1997–92).

Luxemburg-Casco and Waukesha West top the team standings with five championships, West having won four straight Division 1 titles in 1998–2001. La Crosse Central, Fennimore, Mount Horeb, and Albany have claimed four each. ★

EVEN MORE
RECORDS, STREAKS, AND AMAZING MOMENTS

BADMINTON
For the Birdies

As an athlete at the University of Wisconsin, Ann French earned all-America honors from the AIAW in badminton four times from 1979 to 1982 and finished among the top eight in singles competition every season. She captured the 1981 and 1982 AIAW national championships with her doubles partner, Claire Allison. Later, French was a member of the U.S. Badminton Association national team 12 times (1984–95) and became a three-time (1990, 1991, and 1996) USBA national doubles champion. ★

BOXING
Purveyors of Punch

In the early twentieth century, lightweight champions Oscar "Battling" Nelson and Ad Wolgast were two of the many fighters who made Milwaukee their home, often staying at Paddy Dorrell's, an Irish saloon and hostelry on Wells Street.

Nelson reigned as champ in 1905–06 and 1908–10. He fought in Milwaukee 12 times in 1901–04 and performed in Omro, Rhinelander, Fond du Lac, Oshkosh, Ashland, and Hurley. Wolgast held the title in 1910–12 while fighting in Milwaukee 18 times in 1907 and 1908. He also boxed in Oshkosh, Racine, and Fond du Lac. ★

Badgers' Ring of Champs

On April 1, 1939, the University of Wisconsin grabbed its first NCAA boxing trophy in front of a crowd of 15,000 at the UW Field House. Badgers Gene Rankin, Omar Crocker, Woody Swancutt, and Truman Torgerson claimed four of the eight individual crowns. Seven of UW's eight participants reached the semifinals. John Walsh was the coach during most of these glory years. He coached UW to eight NCAA team championships and 35 individual titles from 1934 to 1957.

Collegiate boxing was banned in 1960 after Wisconsin's Charlie Mohr died from injuries sustained during an NCAA tournament bout. Mohr, after losing in the 165-pound title match, lost consciousness on the way to the hospital and never regained it, dying eight days later. UW dropped the program less than a month later. ★

135 Pounds of Champion

University of Wisconsin standout Gene Rankin became the only boxer in NCAA history to win three national titles (1939, 1941, and 1942) at the same weight class, doing so at 135 pounds. He was also a key member of the Badgers' national championship squads of 1939 and 1942.

Rankin started boxing at age 12 or 13 and estimated that he competed in 65 amateur bouts before joining the Badger program. He fought out of Spike Dugan's stable in Superior; Dugan was a full-time truck driver and part-time trainer.

Rankin missed the 1940 campaign because he was academically ineligible but bounced back to claim his second championship the next year with a

Gene Rankin, a captain as a senior on the 1942 Wisconsin boxing team, became the first competitor to win three NCAA crowns at the same weight when he captured his final title at 135 pounds. (Photo courtesy of the University of Wisconsin)

decision over Washington State's Les Coffman. He then became a three-time winner with a victory over Johnny Joca of Florida in 1942. He honed many of his skills sparring with teammates Omar Crocker and Woody Swancutt.

Rankin only lost two matches during his collegiate career, the first being a decision to Coffman after grabbing the 1939 title while suffering from a shoulder injury that basically left him a one-handed fighter. ★

FENCING
Touché

Tim Gillham made his father proud—and that was important because his dad, Tony, was his coach for the University of Wisconsin fencing team.

Gillham won the Big Ten epee crown his first year and placed third at the NCAA championships. He repeated those titles at the 1984 and 1985 league meets, earning all-America honors while becoming the first fencer to claim more than two titles in 61 years of Big Ten competition. Gillham didn't get a chance to make it four in a row because the Big Ten discontinued the sport before the 1985–86 campaign. ★

GYMNASTICS
Ten Times on Top

Beth Weber of Whitefish Bay/ Shorewood has been the star when it comes to state action in girls gymnastics. She won 10 individual titles during her career and is one of only two competitors to have claimed the all-around crown three times.

She did it in 1995–97, matching Gabrielle Mahairas's feat for La Crosse Central in 1985–87. Weber and Danielle Longway of Onalaska have claimed the top spot in the vault three times, while Weber and Shanna Popp of Burlington/Badger/Wilmot are the only three-time champs in the uneven parallel bars.

Gina Piazza of Fall River, who has eight individual first places, Tricia Adkins of Sun Prairie, and Amber Rohde of Southwestern/Cuba

Beth Weber of Whitefish Bay/Shorewood earned 10 medals for gymnastics in Wisconsin Intercollegiate Athletic Association competitions, the most in the state's history. (Photo courtesy of the Weber family)

City are three-time winners in the floor exercise. No gymnasts have won three balance beam crowns.

In the team charts, Brookfield Central and De Pere have registered five championships, with De Pere's coming in succession (1986–90). Nicolet (1980–82), Waukesha West/North/South (1999–2001) and River Falls (2002-04) are the only other teams to win at least three in a row. ★

ROWING
A Big Part of the Crew

In the early 1940s, Carl Holtz was working out with the University of Wisconsin football team when the rowing coach spotted him. The rest is history, as Holtz earned varsity awards in 1942, 1946, and 1947 on the Badger crew

team. In 1941, he stroked the freshmen squad to second place at the Poughkeepsie Regatta and the Adams Cup. After a stint with the Army Air Corps in World War II, he returned to campus and stroked the 1946 varsity crew to the prestigious Eastern Sprint Regatta title, making it the first UW unit to win a national championship.

UW didn't enjoy that kind of success again until 2002, when its varsity eight won the grand final at the Eastern Sprints, beating Harvard by two seconds and Princeton by six, in a new shell named in Holtz's honor. He still maintains a farm near Mukwonago. ★

Carl Holtz was the stroke for the 1946 varsity crew, which won the Eastern Sprint Regatta title, making it the first UW team to claim a national title. (Photo courtesy of the University of Wisconsin)

SWIMMING AND DIVING
Diving Right In

D'Lynn Damron, a Madison native, became the University of Wisconsin's first women's national diving champion. A three-time national winner, Damron captured the one- and three-meter titles at the 1970 Division of Girls' and Women's Sports championships and the three-meter title at the 1973 AIAW national meet.

D'Lynn Damron became Wisconsin's first national diving champion in 1970. (Photo courtesy of the University of Wisconsin)

From Madison to Montreal

Madison native Jim Montgomery established a world record while capturing a gold medal in the 100-meter freestyle July 25, 1976, at the Olympic Games in Montreal.

A six-time state individual champion at Madison East High School, Montgomery also took home golds as a member of the 800-meter freestyle and 400-meter medley relay teams and earned a bronze in 200-meter freestyle. Montgomery became the first swimmer to shatter the 50-second mark in the 100 freestyle with his clocking of 49.99 seconds. ★

Owning the Event

Athletes have their specialties, but what about high schools? In the case of Germantown's girls swimming team, it has to be the 500-yard freestyle. The Warhawks have dominated the event, at least when it comes to the North Shore Conference. Germantown swimmers had won the 500 in 13 consecutive league meets through 2003.

Brandie Lauterbach earned top honors in 1990–93, Melissa Loehndorf was the champion in 1994–97, Megan Loehndorf won titles in 1998–2001, and Lisa Brendemuehl claimed first place in 2002. Lauterbach went on to win the Division 2 state title in 1992 and '93 and Melissa Loehndorf turned the trick in 1995 and '97, while Megan Loehndorf accomplished it in Division 1 in 2001. ★

Four Times Is a Charm

The WIAA girls state swimming and diving championships have delivered dozens of sparkling performances since its inception in 1970, but the competitions have witnessed only seven individuals win the same event four times in their prep careers, and five of them occurred since 1992.

They include Gina Kettlehohn of Brown Deer in diving (1992–95), Jane Evans of Madison Memorial in the 200 individual medley (1998–2001), Cortnee Adams of Appleton North in the 50 freestyle, Terri Jashinsky of Menomonee Falls/Hamilton in the 100 butterfly (1992–95), and Sarah Wanezek of Brookfield East in the 100 backstroke.

Kathy Treible of Brookfield Central became the first four-time winner when she dominated the 200 IM from 1976 to 1979. Connie Wright of Waukesha North joined her in 1978–81. However, Wright accomplished something nobody else has—she won four times in two events. She won the 100 backstroke and 100 butterfly.

Adams holds Division 1 records in the 50- and 100-yard freestyles, while Michelle Jesperson of Madison West set the 200-yard freestyle mark in 1992 and was a member of the Regents' 1990 400-yard freestyle relay team that established a state standard. Lindsey Highstrom of Cedarburg also holds two numbe-one spots in Division 2 in the 100 butterfly and 100 backstroke.

But the name listed most often in the record books is Jamie Belfor of Shorewood, also in Division 2. She tops the charts in the 100, 200, and 500 freestyles and swam a leg for the Greyhounds' 1996 400 freestyle relay unit.

The sister tandem of Katie and Emmy Heager of Whitnall had a stranglehold on the 50 freestyle state trophy in Division 2, with Katie winning from 1998 to 2000 and Emmy victorious in 2001–02.

In the team standings, Madison schools have dominated the competition. West (with 15) and Madison Memorial (with 14) have won titles all but three years through 2002. Shorewood has earned six crowns since Division 2 started in 1992. ★

Pool Partying

Several Wisconsin high school athletes have their names in the boys swimming record books in two different places.

In Division 1, Kyle Bubolz of Waukesha North/Kettle Moraine set the 50-yard freestyle mark of 20.76 seconds in 2002 and bettered it in 2004 (20.31). He took the top spot from Arrowhead's Ben Anderson with his 47.71

clocking in the 100 butterfly in 2003. Anderson's 1997 standard in the 200 individual medley (1:48.66) remains, and he and the Warhawks' 200 freestyle relay team are still atop the charts from 1997.

Nicolet's Garrett Weber-Gale equaled his 2002 mark of 49.73 in the 100 backstroke a year later and took over the number-one position in the 100 freestyle with a 43.49 in 2003, a record that Jay Mortenson of Madison West had held since 1984.

In Division 2, 1995 was and still is a good year. Brookfield East's Tom Wanezek set marks in the 50 (20.59) and 100 (45.18) freestyles while Hudson's John Cahoy established records in the 200 free (1:39.0) and 100 butterfly (49.99). Neil Walker of Verona's 1994 finishes in the 200 individual medley (1:50.8) and 100 backstroke (49.61) are still the times to beat.

Several swimmers have claimed titles in an event three straight years, but only three competitors have accomplished that feat in two events. Edward Garst of Wauwatosa did it first, winning the 50 and 100 freestyle races in 1945–47. Then came John Thuerer of Rhinelander from 1966 to 1968 in the 200 and 400 freestyles. And finally, Tom Shane of New Berlin Eisenhower (in Division 2) did it in 1996–98 in the 100 butterfly and 200 individual medley.

Waukesha won 15 state team titles before it split into North, South, and West. All but one came in 1958–74, including seven straight from 1964 to 1970. Madison West has claimed 13 crowns. ★

VOLLEYBALL
Hail to the Victors

The Wisconsin Volleyball Coaches Association lists 28 members as having led teams to more than 200 victories. Posting the most among those with Hall of Fame credentials have been four who've taken their schools to 500-plus triumphs. They include Steven Prahl of Lakeland Union, Dave Scher of Milwaukee Pius, the late Debbie Roesler of McDonell Central in Chippewa Falls, and Diane Harrod of Germantown. Three others have guided squads to more than 400 wins: Lynda Garbe of Oostburg, Mark Steiner of Wisconsin Lutheran, and Dawn Larson of Oconto Falls. ★

WRESTLING
One Tough Badger

Lee Kemp turned in the only undefeated season in the nation during 1975–76 to help Coach Duane Kleven's Badgers finish in fourth place at the NCAA tournament in Tucson, Arizona. Kemp compiled a 39–0 record that year and repeated as the 158-pound titlist the next two seasons in ending his UW career with a 143–6–1 mark. ★

Consistently Great

That describes the wrestling program at Luxemburg–Casco High School, which has enjoyed remarkably consistent excellence for over 75 years. And a great part of the success can be attributed to the head coaches.

George Gregor started the sport at Luxemburg in 1924 and coached for 25 years. Frank Chalupa directed the Spartans (the schools merged in 1967–68) for the next 25 seasons, and Emil Kuhn did the same before turning the reins over to Bob Berceau, who won three individual state titles himself, for 1999–2000.

Regardless of who has been at the helm, the success has continued. Before the 2003–04 season, LCHS had a 102–0–1 record since its last Packerland Conference setback in 1986 and won 97 consecutive league dual meets while winning the title 18 straight years. The Spartans won three Division 2 crowns in a row and seven of 12 since the team tourney was established in 1992.

Only Wisconsin Rapids had been as dominant in recent years, winning its eighth Division 1 team championship in nine years in 2003. Its only loss during that span was a 25-21 finals decision to Milton in 2002. ★

Real Mat Men

Only seven Wisconsin high school wrestlers have won four individual state titles: Matt Hanutke of Pittsville, Kraig Underwood of Athens, Brian Slater of New Lisbon, Scott Hady of North Crawford, Kevin Black of River Falls, Josh Miller of Arcadia, and Cole Wunnicke of Ithaca. All of them have accomplished the feat since 1987, when Hanutke started his run, and all of them competed from 98 to 135 pounds.

Thirty-five grapplers had claimed three championships prior to the 2004 state meet.

In the team standings, 47 schools have earned crowns. Wisconsin Rapids, under the leadership of Lewie Benitz, had won the most titles with 13. Mineral Point was second with eight, while Milwaukee South, Luxemburg–Casco, and Stoughton had seven apiece. Rapids won seven in a row from 1995 to 2001, Washington did it five times in succession from 1950–54 and Mineral Point was on top four straight times in 1980–83. ★

BIBLIOGRAPHY

BOOKS

Baker, William J. *Jesse Owens: An American Life.* New York: Collier Macmillan, 1986.

Beardsley, Cynthia. *Frank Parker: Champion in the Golden Age of Tennis.* Chicago: Havilah Press, 2002.

Browne, Lois. *Girls of Summer: In Their Own League.* Toronto: HarperCollins, 1992.

Butler, Tom. *The Badger Game: Mickey McGuire to Al Toon.* Madison, Wis.: William C. Robbins, 1991.

Cameron, Steve. *The Packers: Seventy-Five Seasons of Memories and Mystique in Green Bay.* Dallas: Taylor Publishing, 1993.

Cantwell, John Davis. *The Boys of Winter: Wisconsin's State Basketball Champions, 1956 and 1957.* Bloomington, Ind.: 1st Books, 2002.

Chaptman, Dennis. *Badgers Handbook: Stories, Stats and Stuff about UW Football.* Wichita, Kans.: Wichita Eagle and Beacon Publishing, 1996.

———. *On Wisconsin: The Road to the Roses.* Dallas: Taylor Publishing, 1994.

Chronicle of the Olympics: 1896–1996. New York: DK Publishing, 1996.

Danzig, Allison, and Peter Schwed (eds.). *The Fireside Book of Tennis.* New York: Simon & Schuster, 1972.

DuPre, Mike. *Century of Stories: A 100-Year Reflection of Janesville and Surrounding Communities.* Janesville, Wis.: Janesville Gazette, 2000.

Everson, Jeff. *This Date in Milwaukee Brewers History.* Appleton, Wis.: Everson House, 1987.

————, and Linda Everson. *Wisconsin Badgers Facts and Trivia.* Wautoma, Wis.: E. B. Hochin Company, 1994.

Goska, Eric. *Packer Legends in Facts.* Milwaukee: Tech/Data Publications, 1993.

Gregorich, Barbara. *Women at Play: The Story of Women in Baseball.* San Diego: Harcourt Brace Jovanovich, 1993.

Grimsley, Will. *101 Greatest Athletes of the Century.* New York: Bonanza Books, 1987.

Grubba, Rev. Dale. *The Golden Age of Wisconsin Auto Racing.* Oregon, Wis.: Badger Books, 2000.

Gruver, Ed. *Ice Bowl: The Cold Truth About Football's Most Unforgettable Game.* Ithaca, N.Y.: McBooks Press, 1998.

Hamilton, Raphael N. *The Story of Marquette University: An Object Lesson in the Development of Catholic Higher Education.* 1953.

Jansen, Dan, with Jack McCallum. *Full Circle: An Olympic Champion Shares His Breakthrough Story.* New York: Villard Books, 1994.

Kelly, Tom. *Birkie Fever: A 10-Year History of the American Birkebeiner.* Osceola, Wis.: Specialty Press, 1982.

Kopriva, Don, and Jim Mott. *On Wisconsin: The History of Badger Athletics.* Champaign, Ill.: Sports Publishing, Inc., 1998.

Kronenberg, Harold. *River City Sports: Seasons to Remember.* Eau Claire, Wis., 2002.

Kuechle, Oliver, with Jim Mott, *On Wisconsin: Badger Football.* Huntsville, Ala.: Strode Publishers, 1977.

Lazenby, Roland. *The Super Bowl.* New York: Gallery Books, 1988.

Lea, Bud. *Magnificent Seven: The Championship Games That Built the Lombardi Dynasty.* Chicago: Triumph Books, 2002.

Lucas, Mike. *Barry's Badgers: The Road to the Roses.* Madison, Wis.: Madison Capital Times, 1993.

McCann, Dennis. *The Wisconsin Story: 150 Stories/150 Years.* Milwaukee: Milwaukee Journal Sentinel, Inc., 2001.

Moran, Joseph Declan. *You Can Call Me Al: The Colorful Journey of College Basketball's Original Flower Child.* Madison, Wis.: Prairie Oak Press, 1999.

Names, Larry. *Green Bay Packers Facts and Trivia.* South Bend, Ind.: E. B. Houchin Company, 1994.

North, Andy, with Burton Rocks. *The Long and the Short of It.* New York: St. Martin's, 2002.

O'Brien, Michael. *Vince: A Personal Biography of Vince Lombardi.* New York: William Morrow & Company, 1987.

Peterson, Robert W. *Cages to Jump Shots: Pro Basketball's Early Years.* New York: Oxford University Press, 1990.

Schaap, Dick. *An Illustrated History of the Olympics.* New York: Knopf, 1963.

Sowers, Richard. *The Complete Statistical History of Stock-Car Racing: Records, Streaks, Oddities and Trivia.* Phoenix: David Bull Publishing, 2000.

Westcott, Rich. Winningest Pitchers: Baseball's 300-Game Winners. Philadelphia: Temple University Press, 2002.

NEWSPAPERS
Appleton Post-Crescent
Beloit Daily News and its "Legends of Sports" series
Charlotte Observer
Dallas Morning News
De Pere Journal-Democrat
Dodgeville Chronicle
Dubuque Telegraph Herald
Eau Claire Leader and *Leader-Telegram*
Forest County Republican
Green Bay Press-Gazette
Iron Mountain Daily News
Janesville Gazette
Kenosha News
Las Vegas Review-Journal
Los Angeles Times
Madison Capital Times
Marinette Eagle-Star
Marquette Tribune
Milwaukee Journal
Milwaukee Journal Sentinel and *Packer Plus*
Milwaukee Sentinel
Orange County Register
Oshkosh Daily Northwestern

Peshtigo Times
Pittsburgh Post-Gazette
Portage County Gazette
Portage Daily Register
Racine Journal-Times
Raleigh News and Observer
Rocky Mountain News
Saint Louis Post-Dispatch
San Francisco Chronicle
Sheboygan Press
Tri-County Press
Wausau-Merrill Daily Herald
Wisconsin State Journal

MAGAZINES AND OTHER SOURCES

International Tennis Hall of Fame and *American Lawn Tennis* magazine.
Marquette University's yearbook, *The Hilltop.*
Sports Illustrated Presents, 1997.
Team media guides and/or Web sites of the Green Bay Packers, Milwaukee
    Brewers, University of Wisconsin, Marquette University, UW–Platteville,
    Wisconsin Intercollegiate Athletic Conference, Wisconsin Interscholastic
    Athletic Association, and the Milwaukee Bucks. ★

INDEX

INDEX